PLAYGROUNDS OF THE GODS

MAINSTREAM SPORT

PLAYGROUNDS OF THE GODS

THE FULFILMENT OF A SPORTING FANTASY

IAN STAFFORD

MAINSTREAM
PUBLISHING

EDINBURGH AND LONDON

First published in Great Britain in 1999 by
MAINSTREAM PUBLISHING COMPANY (EDINBURGH) LTD
7 Albany Street
Edinburgh EH1 3UG

ISBN 1 84018 371 3

This edition 2000

A catalogue record for this book is available from the British Library

Typeset in Berkeley Book
Printed and bound in Great Britain by Cox and Wyman Ltd

CONTENTS

To Karen, Charlotte and Harry
– the best team in the world

ACKNOWLEDGEMENTS

One of the truly gratifying elements of writing *Playgrounds of the Gods* has been the friendly and overwhelming support I have obtained from a wide range of characters connected to sport all over the world. At any stage during 1998 one of my sporting adventures, if not the whole book, could have collapsed without the benevolence of a large number of people that makes the cast list from the film *Gandhi* look small in comparison. These benefactors range from those lending me equipment or facilities to some of the greatest names playing sport today. All played their part in this book, the end product of my experiences. If you can bear with me, I would like to name those most deserving of a credit.

Football: To the players and management of Flamengo FC, I thank you for your patience, time and willingness to share with me your secrets and pleasures. Jimmy Frew and his family housed this total stranger for a couple of days, while his son, Duncan, and their friend, Frederico Pinheiro, both acted as willing chauffeurs. The Sheraton Hotel, Rio de Janeiro, also volunteered to accommodate me for half a week. Without Jader de Oliveira, the BBC World Service's Brazil man, my time in Brazil might never have happened.

Squash: A special thank you to Jansher Khan, who not only had the decency to put up with me for a week, but also ensured that my time in Pakistan would be unforgettable. Similarly, the whole Khan family, of which there are many, treated me like a friend, if not a brother. I appreciate Satinder Bajwa's help in arranging the project, and BBC Radio 4 for helping to fund my time in the North-West Frontier in return for a documentary.

Athletics: Again, the key players in this chapter were, of course, the athletes themselves. I am forever in debt to all at the Nyahururu training camp, especially Moses Kiptanui and that jack of all trades Jimmy Beauttah. I will also always appreciate the help from David Okeyo and Ibrahim Hussein at the Kenyan Amateur Athletics Association. Kim McDonald and Duncan Gaskell in Teddington proved to be invaluable in arranging my whole trip, and William Tanui helped enormously at both the beginning and the end of my high-altitude stay. Kenyan Airways made my journey to and from Africa both comfortable and cheap. Finally, my gratitude goes to Kip Keino for his support and great encouragement.

Rugby Union: I would not even have kicked off without fulsome support from the Springboks' enlightened coach Nick Mallett and his inspirational captain Gary Teichmann. Thanks, guys, for taking the risk. To a man the players, management and support team from the magnificent South African rugby squad bent over backwards to accommodate me and my questionable methods. I appreciate the honour bestowed on me, especially during the Kontiki session and on the day of the big match. John Dobson, *South Africa Rugby* magazine's editor, also played an instrumental part early on in preparation, whilst South African Airways eased the burden on my wallet.

Rowing: I will probably never know how big a distraction I was at a time of crucial importance, but to the boys at the Leander Club and the Great Britain coxless fours, I thank you for a week of high achievement, self-examination and pain. Steve Redgrave, Matthew Pinsent, Tim Foster and James Cracknell, together with their coach, Jürgen Grobler, gave me a tough, eye-opening but strangely enjoyable ride. Thanks also to Peter Haining, not only for the ergometer he provided me with for general and specific training, but also for the hours on the River Thames spent trying to turn a landlubber into a water man.

Cricket: This event would have been a non-starter without the initial green light from the Australian Cricket Board, Test captain Mark Taylor and vice-captain Steve Waugh. In Queensland a Pom was integrated into the full Australian cricket squad with welcome arms and, once again, every single member of the Australian playing and management team gave me their full support. Thanks for the many wonderful chances you arranged for me on the field, and also for the après-cricket, even if you tested my alcoholic intake. Maybe we can all sing 'Khe Sanh' the next time we meet? I'd also like to mention Bickley Park, Bromley Common and Old Suttonians cricket clubs, for providing me with some badly needed practice. British Airways ensured that my long, long journey across the world and back became a pleasant and comfortable ride.

Boxing: Just three weeks before he was due to defend his world title, Roy Jones junior allowed me to join him in training for a week in Florida. It was not easy for any of us, but I am grateful for his invitation, and for an experience which will forever be lodged in my memory. Thanks must also be expressed to the Peacock Gym in Canning Town, and to the Bowers family, who gave up much of their time and patience in attempting to transform me into a boxer. Frank Bruno offered invaluable advice, whilst Reuben Shohet at the Lonsdale Sports Shop in Beak Street was generous with the provision of boxing sportswear and equipment.

In general, a special thanks must go to Sarah Connors, Kevin Lidlow and everyone at the Oakfield Physiotherapy Clinic in Thurrock. Sarah, in particular, would find herself working on various parts of my body for the best part of a year. She deserves a medal merely for listening to so much rubbish for so long. The David Lloyd Leisure Club in Sidcup also kindly lent me their facilities for training. This, in particular, came in useful for the early part of the book, especially when I needed some squash coaching and a health and fitness check-up.

Finally, and most deserving of all, I must mention Karen, Charlotte and Harry, the best team of all. I'm sorry I went away so often and for so long. Each time I left for the airport it became harder to leave my wife, my daughter and my son. Karen was a rock throughout 1998, manning the fort whilst I went off to fair and distant lands on my personal crusades. She also had to endure me at home, training, writing or just thinking of matters elsewhere, and even found time, as a journalist herself, to read and sub-edit my words with objectivity. Perhaps, most of all, she was as aware as I of the potential and very real dangers that could have reared up in my face during most of my adventures. To her credit, she kept most of her concerns to herself. Without Karen's help and support, this book would never have been written.

THE BEGINNING

I don't know about you, but I've just about achieved everything there is to achieve in the world of sport. I'm not too modest to admit that I have been there, seen it and done it all, in front of the largest audiences, throughout the planet and when it mattered the most. When my team, or my country, needed someone to produce something spectacular, something extraordinary, to win the day, I was their man. I have always been their man.

You don't believe me, do you? Well, it was me who came on as a second-half substitute in the FA Cup final with my team two goals in arrears to score a devastating hat-trick (a diving header, a left-foot shot and a right-foot volley) and win the match. It was me who crashed over the All Blacks' line at Twickenham to notch up England's winning try in the World Cup final. And yes, it was still me who smacked a straight six into the Lord's pavilion to win the Ashes.

As if all this is not enough, I've also won the Wimbledon men's singles title, sunk a ten-foot putt to claim the British Open and beaten Michael Johnson with a lunge to the tape to snatch an Olympic gold medal. All in time for tea.

Pretty impressive, hey? And you know the best part of it all? I've managed all this without any training, or any sacrifice, or any pain. No, all it has taken is a nice, warm bed and an active imagination coaxing me into a deep sleep.

There. I've come clean. I actually do this. Not every single night, of course. There are other things men think about in bed. But pretty often, and especially after watching a major sporting event. It is the child inside me, and I don't have a problem with it, even if I am supposed to be a sports writer who should be above all this. The point is, I'm a sports fanatic as well.

But you know what I'm talking about. Well, at least some of you do. You are the same as me. You've been at Wembley too, scoring the cup-winning goal, although it was probably for your team, not mine. Your drop-kick won the World Cup for Wales, for South Africa or for Australia. Wasn't it you who clean bowled three West Indian batsmen to claim a Test hat-trick? I don't recall seeing you there, but you were, weren't you?

Let's face it, most of us are sports fans. I don't just mean football supporters, or race-goers, or athletics buffs. I mean sports nuts. We love the football world cup. We adore the rugby world cup. The cricket world cup is an absolute must. So too is the Grand National, Wimbledon, the British Open, Formula One Grand Prix racing, the Olympics, probably even custard-pie throwing from Madagascar. We don't play any of these sports, at least not at a world-class standard, but we can at least dream about playing them. There's no harm in that, is there?

There's another admission to make as well. I still don't know why, specifically, my 34th birthday hit me like a thunderbolt. I mean, why not my 35th, or my 33rd? Up until 16 September 1997, I had always seen myself as a bit of a youngster. I looked young, so I continued to delude myself. I dressed young. Hey, I even acted young – man. And I had always been made to feel the young buck throughout my working career in the national media as a sports writer and bit-part broadcaster. As far as I was concerned, 34 should, by rights, still be classed in the 'early thirties' bracket, and that, in my language, meant both young and experienced. I had the best of both worlds.

Yet something was evidently changing in my life. It was bad enough feeling this at home. My nine-year-old daughter, having just discovered the merits of make-up, the Spice Girls and Leonardo di Caprio, started to point out that I was too old and embarrassing to be seen dancing at her birthday party. I had rather hoped that when she was 18 and I a mere 43, we and her friends would still be enjoying each other's social company down some bar or club, but already, nine years prematurely, this dream had evaporated.

Yet witnessing the ageing process at work was even harder to bear. In media terms I was still, of course, comparatively youthful, although I had noticed, seemingly overnight, how younger people were beginning to rise up to my level and beyond in journalism. It was more in the field of sport that the unwelcome home truths were thrust into my face. For the past 12 years I had prided myself on talking, eye to eye, with a sportsman or sportswoman about topics of mutual interest, like music and fashion, women (always worked well in a male dressing-room) or fitness. I wasn't some old, fat-faced, fat-arsed hack. No, I was a fellow youngster. They, in theory, could relate to me.

Now, suddenly, these same interviewees were ten years younger than me. They couldn't give a damn about my kids and suburban lifestyle, nor my feeble jokes about growing old, comments which were supposed to generate wholesale denials but rarely did. They were too busy eyeing each other up or dreaming of sporting glory to pay as much attention, or to give off as much, if any, respect, as they used to.

The only situation worse than this was talking to sportsmen of a similar age. In their world they were now classed as 'veterans', men (and sometimes women) who had enjoyed a glorious and successful career and were now seeing out their days in the twilight of their chosen fields. They talked of how their sports had changed so much, why their creaking bodies could not take too much more and what they would be saying in their autobiographies. Against my will, I was surrounded by people who were making me feel old.

In the 12 years up to my 34th birthday that I had been covering sports, I had been tremendously fortunate to have witnessed many of the greatest sporting events on the planet and, indeed, interviewed most of the biggest names worldwide. I can hardly complain. I know, because people tell me, that many would like to be in my shoes.

My time writing about sport has been incredibly exciting, interesting and, at times, challenging. But it has also been frustrating. The truth of the matter is that I am a frustrated sportsman, probably just like you. I suppose I always have been. In public terms I am a good all-round sportsman. I played in all my school first teams, made a few junior county and university appearances and still play a whole range of sports when given half a chance. I also happen to possess a hugely competitive nature, especially when it comes to sport. I like competition and I don't like losing, especially if I have not done myself justice. I'm not revealing anything new here to those who know me. My friends and family formed an opinion long ago that taking pleasure out of winning penalty competitions in my garden against my five-year-old son bordered on pathetic.

Occasionally, and especially when I have been watching top-class sport, I have wondered whether I could have been good enough to have become a professional sportsman. It has never quite reached the stage of envy, but I have certainly wanted to swap places many a time with the man who had just scored that wonderful goal, that breathtaking try or that effortless century. He could come and sit in the press box and I would happily take his place out in the middle of the sporting arena. Deep down, for all my confidence and so-called sporting qualities, I suspected I probably did not quite possess all the attributes required to succeed at the highest level. Of course, I had no real way of knowing, short of winding back the clock 17 years and setting out again as a promising and single-minded young sportsman who had no intention of ending up in Fleet Street.

As I opened up my 34th birthday cards, most of which offered side-splitting jokes about my 'old age', I came to the conclusion that if I did not at least try to do something now to erase my yearning to play sport at the highest level, I would never have the chance, nor the ability, to do so again.

This is how *Playgrounds of the Gods* was born. It represents, quite simply, my last chance to become a 'proper sportsman' and to taste a morsel of mixing it with the very best. It also allowed me to enter into the surreal world of my dreams, where fantasy and reality could merge for a short time. Some may interpret all this as my first, and somewhat early, mid-life crisis. I see it as a fond farewell. *Playgrounds of the Gods* is both my youth going out with a bang and my chance to live out my sporting fantasies.

The idea, in theory, was simple. I would spend around a week in the company of the very finest sportsmen and sports teams throughout the world in an attempt to match them in all they do. There would be no dispensations and, therefore, no chance of me actually succeeding in becoming a belated sporting success story, but it would be interesting to see how far I could go and how much I could take.

I was determined not to cut any corners. What would be the point of it if the project turned out to be a mere stunt? I had to become a professional sportsman, not only during the weeks I would be sharing with the best in the world, but also in preparation. I would go to wherever these people are, to witness them in their own environment, and attempt to stride that massive gulf between writer and sportsman. In short, I would try and become one of them.

Even persuading the world's greatest sportsmen and teams seemed a tall order on the face of it in the late autumn of 1997. I had interviewed some of the people I had in mind, but fixing up a 45-minute conversation is one matter; arranging a week with them at home in their own countries, living with them as much as possible and then playing with or against them to boot, appeared a trifle far-fetched.

Then I took a more positive outlook. Nobody had ever really written such a book before. True, Paul Gallico's 1930s epic *Farewell to Sport* includes a chapter in which the author steps into the ring to face the then world heavyweight boxing champion Jack Dempsey. In the late 1960s and early 1970s George Plimpton, that fine American writer and participatory journalist, wrote a series of memorable books relating to his experiences playing baseball, American football, golf and, to a lesser extent, boxing.

But all this was a long time ago now. Sport, in the past 25 years, has in many ways changed beyond recognition. Now we have television in abundance, and sponsorship. We have agents and corporate hospitality. Perhaps we have pressure now that was never felt before. Those who play sport have become huge household names and, as a result, less accessible to the public and, indeed, to the media. The taking-part element of sport somehow does not appear to be as important as it used to be. The winning of it has become all-consuming. 'Whoever said the taking part is what counts in sport should be shot,' an Olympic champion athlete told me a couple of years ago. He thought such an attitude made him a better sportsman. It did not. But I suppose it made him a winner. Sport has become big business and money dictates just about everything to do with it.

Yet those who actually participate must, despite all this, possess the same qualities as their predecessors. The sportsmen of today still have to train until it hurts, digging deep until close to their physical and mental capacities, to achieve their goals. They experience the tremendous highs and lows that those in sport have always had to deal with, the winning and the losing, the joy and the pain. It would be to these people that I would appeal. They would play a part in my sporting record of the late 1990s that would, at least in my mind, remain as much a testament to them and their achievements as it would to my own fantasies.

Above all else, I hoped to make this a global book. I wanted to see these amazing sportsmen at home and in their own environment, where they remain true to themselves. There would be no sound-bites, no press conferences and no sponsor-orientated events. There would just be the greatest sportsmen in the world doing what they are best at doing. And there would be me, allowed into their inner sanctum. Maybe, just maybe, there would be a link too, all the names featured in this book possessing, despite their different backgrounds and cultures, beliefs and standards, one common thread that makes them all winners amongst winners.

Gaining permission from some of the greatest names in world sport and the subsequent organisation of my sporting adventures is detailed in the book. Suffice to say it took a lot of time, effort and luck to persuade people who, in their own countries, are considered near deity to face up to the questionable challenge of training and playing with me.

Then there was the small matter of my physical fitness. I had to ensure that I was in the right shape to carry out what would become an enormous test of my stamina and ability. Having spent so much time in the company of sportsmen, I appreciated that my idea would only work if I could be seen to be, at the very least, competent, fit and trying my hardest. If I stood any chance of surviving each sporting challenge, let alone being accepted by my new-found colleagues, I knew it was imperative to be fully prepared.

The fitness preparations began on New Year's Day 1998. For once I was determined to meet the requirements of a New Year's resolution. The hitherto demands of fatherhood, marriage and, in particular, journalism meant that I had plenty of physical work to do before I could step into any kind of sporting arena. After the initial pain, the regular dosage of exercise became an integral part of my life. Slowly, my weight began to fall and muscles began to appear, like small animals emerging from a long and deep hibernation.

I chose seven contrasting but popular sports, some I had played many times before, others representing new challenges. The people and the teams who invited me into their lives can be found dotted all over the world, from Asia to South America, Europe to Africa, and North America to the Antipodes. In my mind there is little debate that the individuals and teams you will be reading about in the following pages were, at least at the time of writing, the very best in the world. They would come to play a monumental part in providing me with moments, regardless of this written outcome, that I am never likely to forget.

What follows is an autobiographical account of my sometimes successful, sometimes hapless, adventures in the company of the sporting gods as I lurch from one unlikely scenario to another, around the world in the space of nine months. I discover what makes these people function, how their social and cultural environments have played such a crucial part in their success, and what it is really like to be, at least for a while, a part of their professional set-up.

Above all else, I learn much about myself, live out many of my fantasies and play sport at the highest level. It all may amount to a mere flicker in the fire for the sportsmen and teams I encounter, but the experiences will keep me warm long into the winter of my life.

FLAMENGO

The Best Sound in the World . . .

Sometimes I convince myself that I remember the day when England won the World Cup. Those images – a dancing, toothless Nobby Stiles, the third England goal which never was, Geoff Hurst hitting the top corner of the net as 'some' people were on the pitch, and the late, great Bobby Moore lifting the Jules Rimet trophy in just the one hand – are as clear as yesterday. Then I come to terms with reality. I was not even three years old in the summer of 1966. I don't remember that sunny Saturday afternoon at all. I have merely seen the television pictures, over and over again, year after year, decade after decade, until they have become etched into my psyche.

I do recall the World Cup of 1970, though. Very clearly. I can tell you most of the results, if you like, especially the England ones. I dined with Bobby Charlton a few years ago and he still could not understand why Alf Ramsey substituted him against the then West Germans in the quarter-finals, sparking a revival that saw the English lose a two-goal lead and the match. Yet even Charlton had to concede that the best team won the 1970 World Cup, and that team was Brazil.

The South Americans had already helped themselves to the World Cup in 1958 and 1962, when the likes of Mane Garrincha and a young Pelé turned defences inside-out with their extraordinary skills, but it was that team of 1970 which many argue was the greatest ever. Magnificent players, with magnificent names, they played the game of football as beautifully and as creatively as an artist at work at the easel or a concert violinist midway through a symphony.

In the ensuing 28 years they have often flattered to deceive, winning the World Cup only once, in 1994, but, more often than not, producing the best football and the best team. Still, no other country has won the World Cup as often as Brazil, no other country has provided so many of the world's all-time great players and no other country can guarantee a captive global audience whenever they play. The English proudly claim that they are the founders of the great game of football. Maybe, but the greatest football nation is undoubtedly Brazil.

My own football 'career' was never given the opportunity to flourish. I went to a school in Lincolnshire which believed that football was a game for 'yobs'. So I played field hockey in the spring term, on cold, wet February afternoons, when the ball would hit a bump on the muddy pitch and leap up to crack my unprotected shins and knees. We would then all disappear after school and kick a football around on the rugby and hockey pitches, as if we were having a secret cigarette behind the bike sheds.

Many footballers I know can list most of their goals. So, rather sadly, can I. There was my first ever 'official' goal, when the ball cannoned off my shoulder and into the net. I was playing for my primary school team at the time and insisted that the strike was wholly intentional. Then there were the various long-range efforts during my teenage years, goals that have become increasingly spectacular as the years have passed and my memory has become more selective.

In 1988 I found myself playing in a British journalists' XI against our Dutch counterparts. We were in Germany, where I was covering the European Football Championships for a national newspaper. Rather dubiously, we managed to include Bobby Charlton, together with other former England players such as Trevor Brooking and Steve Coppell, in our side. Midway through the first half, 'England' took a corner kick, the ball sailed over everyone's heads and fell at my feet at the far post. Instinctively, I smacked the ball on the half-volley and watched as it crashed against the underside of the bar before a Dutch defender hooked it away. Rather proud of my effort, I turned round to face my illustrious colleagues, only to receive the most fearful rollicking from Brian Talbot, the former Ipswich and Arsenal player, for missing what he termed 'an open goal'. Since then my appearances have been restricted to the odd game of park football and, as I entered my thirties, ill-tempered parents' matches at my daughter's and son's schools, where respectable dads turned into competitive animals.

It would not be hard to argue that, in the light of my own playing curriculum vitae, what I had in mind would be a leap of Neil Armstrong proportions. My first port of call on my sporting fantasy trip was going to be Brazil. Despite all my travels as a sports writer, I had never been to South America, but I knew that Flamengo, the Rio de Janeiro-based side, were the biggest and best-known club in Brazil. As I sat in my study in Bickley, a neat, tidy Kent suburb of London, and looked out over my back garden, carpeted by a thick layer of November frost, I wondered how I could possibly end up as a footballer, albeit for a week, in a place as magical as Rio.

I telephoned the Brazilian Embassy in London and explained what I proposed to do. They told me that I needed to contact Jader de Oliveira, the BBC World Service's Brazil office man in Bush House. I wrote a long fax, stating who I was, what I intended to do and with whom, and sent it off to Jader. The next day we spoke. 'I'm going to Brazil next week,' he told me. 'The man I need to speak to on your behalf is Rodrigo Paiva. He's the General Manager at Flamengo. I'll be back in ten days' time.' He seemed to think there would not be a problem. A week before Christmas I contacted Jader again. 'Yes, you can come to Flamengo,' he said. 'Get in touch with Rodrigo and he will arrange the dates.'

'What, is that it?' I asked Jader in disbelief.

'Yes, that's it,' he replied, laughing down the phone. 'I must admit, I'm a little surprised myself. But you are English, so maybe they're not too worried about being shown up.'

I put the receiver down, sat back in my chair and tried to picture myself playing football with the pick of Brazil's players. It seemed a ludicrous but wonderfully exciting notion.

It took a little more time to tie up the loose ends. Rodrigo Paiva's English, at least on a mobile phone six thousand miles away, was patchy, whilst my Portuguese is appalling. Jader told me not to concern myself with this but, when in Brazil, just to use my arms in a wild fashion and to pull a series of facial expressions. I discovered this to be a useful tip, but not when it came to long-distance telephone calls. At the end of one detailed telephone conversation, just when I felt we had covered a great deal of ground concerning dates, Rodrigo announced: 'So, we will see you tomorrow morning, then, at training!' He thought I was already in Rio. Eventually a date was set. The fact that my time with Flamengo would coincide with Carnival at the end of February was entirely coincidental and purely down to the club's schedule, but few believed me. I mentioned this to Jader on the phone. 'Oh my God,' he spluttered back, in between great guffaws of laughter. 'Does your wife know about the Carnival? And is she happy about this? Let me tell you something, my friend. The Brazilian Government are distributing ten million free condoms for the public in Rio during the four days of Carnival. And you know what? In my view, that's not enough.'

Actually, my wife had already discovered the delights of Carnival. Ever helpful, she had taken out a few books on Brazil from the library for my interest. One of them opened up on the table rather too naturally to reveal a beautiful woman dancing in the streets of Rio. She, like many of her colleagues, was baring her breasts for all to see.

We gleaned similar information from the Internet, courtesy of Plinio's 'RioWithLove' web site. According to Plinio, Barraca do Pepe beach boasted the best-looking girls, a particular show in Rio included samba-dancing girls wearing bikinis so small that the locals referred to their costumes as dental floss, and the clubs were definitely where the city's most beautiful girls entertained themselves in the evenings. 'Well, as far as I'm concerned, I'm going there to work,' I told my wife adamantly, as I opened up my suitcase on the bed. Her eyes lowered suspiciously to the case and to the swimming trunks and sun cream already placed inside.

Three days before departing, having convinced myself that I was in excellent physical shape after several weeks of running, swimming and general exercise, I decided to put this to the test. The David Lloyd Leisure Club in Sidcup offered me a physical induction course. 'Don't be afraid to tell me the truth,' I told Donna Ramm, my young instructor, with absolute confidence. She produced a pair of tongs and promptly enacted a body-fat test, squeezing dollops of flesh on my arms, back and waist. A chart was pinned to the wall stating body-fat percentages and a less-than-subtle verdict. I felt the wording could have been a little kinder. According to the chart, 14% to 19% was considered 'acceptable', 20% to 29% 'over-fat', and 30% onwards 'obese'. The chart designers are probably annoyed with themselves now that they had forgotten to incorporate the word 'slob'.

Donna tapped away on her computer for a few seconds and then revealed her ego-shattering conclusion. 'You have 20.58% body fat,' she said, failing to disguise a little smirk on her face.

'Surely you're not saying I'm over-fat, are you?' I implored.

''Fraid so,' she confirmed.

The results proved that of my 83kg in weight, an amazing 17kg was nothing more than fat. Imagine if all that was found on just one part of your body, like your right thigh, or your arse!

Thankfully the test went better from that point, and whilst my blood pressure and body flexibility proved to be 'normal' or 'average', my lung function and cardiovascular fitness were both deemed 'good'. Two hours later I left, convincing myself that you can be slightly out of shape but still very fit. Besides, I was only half a per cent 'over-fat'. But as I drove home I came to one, happy conclusion. Thank goodness I had not been tested a few weeks earlier, before I had started training. Donna might have needed a scoop.

Flamengo is probably the biggest football club in the world. Rio boasts other major clubs, like Fluminense, Botafogo and Vasco, but none of these can lay claim to the staggering fact that Flamengo enjoys the support of 35 million Brazilians. They say in Brazil that, even in the deepest, darkest corners of the Amazonian jungle, you will always find someone with a red-and-black stripy scarf, the colours of the team I was about to join. Consequently, every away game seemed like a home appointment, such is the extent of their popularity. Flamengo, like the other Rio clubs, play their home games in the Maracana Stadium, a sporting citadel that has been known to cram 200,000 spectators into its confines, making it by far the largest sports stadium in the world. As I was reminded of all these facts, I made a mental note to make sure to see the Maracana for myself. To a sports fanatic like me, the Maracana would be as important a landmark as Sugar Loaf Mountain.

That night I took Jader to the BBC Club at Bush House for a thank-you drink. The third Test match between the West Indies and England was being shown on a large screen and Jader was taking particular interest in the battle between the big, brooding Caribbean fast bowlers and the rather concerned-looking English batsmen. I found it faintly bizarre that a Brazilian was not only watching a game of cricket with such interest, but was also telling me the tactical manoeuvres the West Indian captain, Brian Lara, should have been making. A small, bespectacled, middle-aged man, wearing a tank-top jumper and with a soft, welcoming expression, Jader was still laughing at the thought of me arriving in Rio right in the middle of Carnival. He told me how the Brazilians, and especially the Cariocas (those who live in Rio), did not understand the meaning of sleep, or work, during Carnival. He talked of the great football players of the past, of Pelé and Garrincha, Tostao and Zico, many of whom he had met. And he gave me a jovial, but disturbing, last piece of advice.

'If anyone tries to mug you, and he turns out to be a Flamengo fan, tell him that you are training with the team,' he said. 'Then, I promise you, he will treat you like a king.'

'What if he turns out to be a Fluminense supporter?' I asked.

'Oh well,' Jader replied, with a friendly slap on my back. 'Then he will probably kill you.'

I suppose landing at Rio airport has to be one of the great arrivals in the world. The Manhattan skyline comes to mind too, as does Sydney's harbour. Perhaps, to anyone other than a blasé Englishman, the long run in to London's Heathrow Airport, over many of the famous landmarks, is pretty special too. But to me, seeing this sprawling city, around and often up a series of enormous granite peaks, with its huge bays, white, sweeping beaches and Sugar Loaf keeping a watchful eye over all proceedings, confirmed that a dream was about to become a reality. The drowsiness of the overnight flight was immediately replaced by exhilaration. I, if everything went to plan, was about to play football. With some of the best Brazilian footballers. In Brazil!

Jimmy Frew was there to meet me at the airport. Jimmy, the Scottish representative in the British Chamber of Commerce and the President of the St Andrew's Society, had been based in Rio for the past 15 years, building up his business interests. A contact of mine at the Ayrton Senna Foundation had suggested I should get in touch with him if I needed a friendly face and a helping hand. His red, Scottish face grew even friendlier when I presented him with a bottle of Laphroaig, fresh from the Rio duty free, and two large plastic bottles of HP Sauce from England, which he had specifically asked me to bring. Having failed to find a hotel room, due to the worldwide popularity of Carnival, I was to stay with Jimmy and his family for a couple of days, until the Sheraton Hotel, who helped to support my trip, could provide accommodation.

We telephoned Rodrigo Paiva at home. It was midday and his wife explained that he had been at Carnival the night before and was still asleep. We telephoned again two hours later. This time his wife told us to turn up at the Fla Barra training ground that evening. Killing a couple of hours in the afternoon, I pored over my Portuguese phrase book, trying desperately to master a few extra words. I remembered my first holiday in Greece as a 20-year-old, when I spent the best part of the first week smiling at the locals and saying 'Calamari', which I mistakenly believed meant 'Good morning'. I then discovered that I should have been saying 'Kalimera', and that 'Calamari', as I have later been reminded in various restaurants, meant 'squid'. I did not particularly want to make the same kind of mistake with Romario, the best-known player at Flamengo, if not in Brazil.

The Fla Barra training ground can be found just south of the city, near the affluent area of Barra, where all the players tend to live. This is where Plinio, my Internet contact, informed me the best beach, and therefore the best girls in Rio, was situated. Surrounded by mountains, the training ground is so new that the paths leading to it have not yet been treated, which means that even the wealthiest footballers in Brazil have to steer their sports cars and four-wheel drives around, and often through, potholes, craters and muddy puddles.

By the time Jimmy and I arrived, the players were already on one of the four pitches, limbering up, stretching and chatting animatedly to each other. They, like a beaming Rodrigo, who appeared from the dressing-room, had been at Carnival the night before and had every intention of doing so again that night. I could not quite see a British football manager giving his men permission to dance the night away with a host of semi-naked women. The tabloid newspapers would have a field day. But down here in Rio, Carnival is seen to be an immensely important date in the calendar, and to be invited to join a competing samba school is indeed a great honour.

Rodrigo, a happy, active man in his mid-thirties whose mobile telephone seemed to ring every minute, led me closer to the pitch. The horde of fans, press and camera crews, who assembled each morning and night at training, looked on quizzically. There, before me, were some of the finest footballers in Brazil today, men like the brilliant defender Junior Baiano, the effortless Ze Roberto and their international colleague Romario.

I felt it was correct merely to make contact and observe on my first day. Some of the players were taking long-range shots at the goal. I was encouraged by the fact that a few of these efforts sailed high or wide. Maybe, I reckoned, I won't stand out too much when I get my chance. Worryingly, Rodrigo explained that he was going to have a quick chat with Paolo Autuori, Flamengo's esteemed new coach. It turned out that, despite inviting me to make the minor trip from the northern hemisphere, he had not yet managed to put my idea to the one man who would say either yes or no. This man was famous all over Brazil after winning the South American Libertadores Cup with the São Paulo-based Cruzeiro and the Brazilian championship with Botafogo. But he was also under pressure. Flamengo, a team that is expected by its huge support to win every game, had fared badly recently and Autuori, a fairly intense man by all accounts, was more serious than usual.

It felt like the aftermath of a job interview. 'Mr Stafford, would you kindly leave the room for ten minutes whilst we discuss your application?' I was standing no more than 20 feet away, straining to hear what Rodrigo was saying into Autuori's ear, yet trying to look completely unconcerned. I had managed to swipe a ball for myself and was attempting to impress anyone who cared to watch. If this sounds ridiculous, it is because it most probably was. I had managed to juggle the ball with my right foot for ten kicks or more on a number of occasions – incredible by my standards, but a walk in the park to the Brazilians – but just when I became aware that Autuori was looking across at me, the ball rebounded off my toe and rolled away.

I had managed just one kick, or one and a half, if you counted the effort with my toe. Autuori walked away with a frown all over his face, and Rodrigo returned.

'Come with me,' he ordered. He led me through the dressing-room, beyond the showers and into the kit room, where Luis Carlos, the club's kit man, could be found. 'Luis, can you prepare some training kit for this gentleman?' he said. 'He's going to play for Flamengo tomorrow.' This is what I had been led to believe was always going to be the case, but after the strain of my 'job interview', I felt a sudden surge of excitement. 'Thank you, thank you, obrigada, obrigada,' I said to a bunch of bemused players and officials, rather pleased with one of the few Portuguese words I could say with confidence. Later, I double-checked the word in my phrase book, just to make sure I had not been running through the Flamengo dressing-room shouting out 'jelly fish'.

That night Jimmy gave me a guided tour of Rio, a city of breath-taking splendour and contradiction. Vibrant, loud and colourful, it is a huge conurbation of some 12 million Cariocas, where wealth sits next to poverty in equal and ordered measures. Up on the slopes of the peaks, the slums, or *favelas*, can be found, some of them cities within a city. The largest of them, Rocinha, somehow houses 60,000 people in tiny shacks that are regularly engulfed in mud slides. This was largely no-go territory, where drugs and guns are handled with great effect by a small but powerful minority. Recently, according to Jimmy, a police helicopter had been shot down from one of the houses in the *favela*. Somebody up there had employed a bazooka. Down by the beaches, however, the beautiful people roamed, up and down the streets next to Copacabana and Ipanema, seemingly without a care in the world and always with the samba beat not far away. A *banda*, a marching band with drums, would arrive from nowhere and people would surge out of the beachside bars and on to the street to dance until dawn.

There was no point attempting anything the following morning. Rio was closed. The Cariocas, in their millions, were asleep, and if I had bothered to venture into the city, I would have felt like the sole survivor after the bomb had been dropped. Besides, it was hot and I was training that evening. I had to act like a professional Brazilian footballer, so I went back to bed.

I was the first to arrive at Fla Barra later that day, however, a little over-eager to get started. The 'other' players turned up slowly, one after another, in their flashy cars, many in just a pair of loose-fitting shorts and no shirt. Most sported medallions hanging from chains around their necks, had beautiful, muscular bodies and amazing names. There was Romario, of course, Palinha and Renato Gaucho, but my personal favourite was Fabiano. If I turned out to be the brilliant new signing for Flamengo, I decided I would change my name to something like 'Superbo', or 'Fantastico', and give Fabiano a run for his money.

Most of the players looked at me in the dressing-room as I changed into the Flamengo training kit. One or two said hello, but the majority just wondered what on earth this Englishman was doing. As I compared my improved but still inferior body to the magnificent brown torsos around me, I felt a little insecure, as if they, too, had reached the conclusion that I was 'over-fat'.

Bounding on to the pitch's grass, as springy as a trampoline, I joined the rest of the team and lined up for some shooting practice. Rodrigo Paiva moved amongst the players explaining who I was and what I was trying to do. Occasionally I heard a few words, like 'Inglese' and 'Michael Schumacher', 'Jornaliste' and 'Tiger Woods', followed by an 'Ahh', uttered by a footballer. Jamir, a defender and one of the characters of the team, was in goal. This should have been the domain of Clemer, the team's first-choice goalkeeper, but Clemer was a frustrated centre-forward, who always liked to show off his shooting prowess before training became too serious, as if to prove that the world of Brazilian football had made a big mistake. Jamir, in the meantime, liked nothing better than to spring, like a demented lamb, from one corner of the goal to the other. It was almost as if he needed grass all over his sweaty face before he could play in the outfield.

Eventually, someone passed me the ball. This was it. This was the moment when I was going to take my first pot shot as a Flamengo player, in front of all the team. Out of the corner of my eye I noticed that Romario, always the last to turn up for training and the first to leave, had ambled on to the pitch, casting a questioning glance over towards me. I took an unnecessarily long run-up and struck the ball well, but high. As I watched it soar over the crossbar, Jamir stuck his tongue out in ridicule and blew a raspberry. The next few shots were all cleanly hit but went wide, high or straight at Jamir. Then something wonderful happened. As far as I could work out, I did not do anything differently to any of my previous attempts, but this time the ball swerved dramatically and, despite Jamir's spectacular upward dive, hurtled into the top corner of the net. I turned round and shouted out 'Rivelino', the name of the famous Brazilian player of the 1970 World Cup-winning team renowned for his powerful shot. The players laughed, including Jamir, who had picked himself up off the floor, and we enacted a series of high fives. This was the moment when the ice was broken. The goal had not just meant my acceptance by Flamengo, but had also shot straight to the top of my personal all-time greatest scores.

When the players got down to the serious stuff, I was asked to stand aside. Grateful for the rest in the humid Rio evening, I sat next to little Patrick Baiano, Junior's four-year-old son, who was also decked out in full Flamengo colours. For the next 30 minutes we smiled at each other and watched some of the finest footballers on the planet go to work, two children together, just happy to be allowed into the inner sanctum of the world's largest football club.

As training ended, a strange thing happened. Paolo Autuori had not said a word to me in two days. In fact, he had not even acknowledged my presence. But there he was, showered and changed, looking younger and fitter than his 41 years of age might have suggested, making a beeline for me. 'Welcome,' he said, smiling, as he shook my hand vigorously. 'I hope you have a good time here and you learn about football in Brazil. See you tomorrow.'

Later that evening I sat in Copacabana with a warm glow inside me. Not only had I scored a goal that, within a few hours, had grown measurably in terms of the distance from the net, but the main man at Flamengo had finally given me the seal of approval. Jimmy's son, Duncan, was keen to celebrate with a number of beers, but after a couple I called it a night. After all, I was a Flamengo player now!

Rio slowly came back to life around Wednesday lunchtime. That morning I had been invited to train alongside the rest of the squad. From then on I would be at Fla Barra every day, save for Saturday, when the players enjoyed a rest. As I ran out to join the players for our usual shooting practice, Rodrigo collared me for an instant and advised me not to get changed back into my casual clothes afterwards. 'We have something special for you,' he said, with a laugh, just as his mobile phone let out a shrill ring.

I might have stood on the side of the pitch wondering what he meant for some time had Jamir, clapping his gloves impatiently in goal, not shouted out: 'Hey, Rivelino, c'mon, baby.' I happily obliged, secretly pleased to be referred to as 'Rivelino', queuing up with the rest of the players and firing the ball in from the edge of the penalty area. Like the night before, most efforts ended up high, wide or too close to the makeshift goalkeeper, but my customary one 'rocket' found the other top corner of the net, this time staying straight and true and leaving Jamir sprawling. Some of the players whooped with delight, partly at the shot and partly at the sight of Jamir beaten by an English journalist, whilst others looked on disdainfully, regarding it as nothing more than a feat they could produce with their eyes closed.

I ran into the dressing-room, where a chilled orange energy drink was always on tap, and bumped into Romario, who had arrived for treatment on his troublesome knee. We had not actually spoken before, but Rodrigo Paiva had informed him of my project. 'But why have you come to Flamengo?' he asked. 'Because you are the best in the world,' I answered. He seemed to be pleased with that and promised that we would have a good chat before I left for England. It was a promise he would repeat every day.

As the other players trooped off the pitch after morning training, drenched in sweat and clearly thankful that they had finished, Paolo Sosa, the team's assistant trainer, wagged his finger towards me. 'You can come with me,' he said. 'Your work's about to begin.' Like a schoolboy on detention, I followed him back out on to the training pitch. Sosa threw a bag of balls down on to the grass and gestured towards a jug of iced water. 'Take a drink. You're going to need it.'

He was right. Under the watchful eye of the assistant trainer, I headed, dribbled, volleyed, shot and sprinted for nearly two hours. Some of the other players walked past on their way to their cars, shouting out and laughing at what they saw as my ordeal, but I was enjoying myself. 'You must learn that here, in Brazil, we form a special bond with the ball,' Sosa explained, in between exercises. 'We see it not as a toy, but as something that is alive and a part of us. If we do not have the ball at our feet, then we learn to always find a place on the pitch where the ball will come back to us.'

One particular moment summed up Sosa's philosophy. I was darting in and out of a series of poles, like a skier on a slalom course, before thumping the ball, supplied by Sosa, into the net. After three or four attempts, he stopped me in my tracks. 'Listen to that. Did you hear that noise?' he asked. I looked around, somewhat stupidly, wondering what the man was talking about.

'Shoot again,' he said. As the ball burst into the back of the net, forcing it to bulge outwards, Sosa put his finger to his ear. 'There, that was it again. That very special sound when the ball hits the net. Do you know, in Brazil, that is the most beautiful sound in the world. Nothing is better for a Brazilian than to hear that noise.'

'Nothing?' I repeated. He grinned. 'No, nothing, not even making love. Though that comes a close second.'

The session ended and Sosa, who had been at Flamengo for ten years, advancing from the youth team in the process, fixed his eyes on the exhausted man in front of him, who looked like he had just had a shower but in fact desperately needed one. 'Not bad, not bad at all,' he said, with a pleasant smile. 'A lot of the things you did today were as good as some of our players when they first came. Even Romario. You played this game much before?' That was nice of him. If he had been Pinocchio his nose would have poked me in the eye at that point, but it still felt good to hear such words.

I ran into an increasingly friendly Autuori, who was still hanging around the training ground. He told me how a nasty injury, obtained as a 14-year-old when he was playing *futebol de salão* (indoor football, a major craze in Brazil), had scuppered his chances of ever becoming a professional footballer. He had gone on, however, to enjoy great success as a trainer, both in Brazil and in Portugal, most notably with the Lisbon giants Benfica. One day, he said, he wanted the national team's job.

You might have thought a man with his coaching pedigree would have a series of logical reasons for Brazil's consistent brilliance over the decades. He did not. Instead, he was passionate and emotive. 'It's in our blood,' he said, with a beaming smile. 'In England you learn how to play football, don't you? Here, in Brazil, we are born with it. A bird will always fly. Swimming comes naturally to a fish. And a Brazilian will always be able to play football. Of course, we don't just accept it. We work hard to improve our game, but the natural talent is already there.'

I asked him what he tried to do with his players during training. His words echoed Sosa's. 'Everything we do is connected to the ball,' Autuori explained. 'We practise and practise so that, in the end, the ball almost becomes another part of our anatomy. A Brazilian player only feels uncomfortable when he does not have the ball and then, because he understands the movement of the game, he will always make himself available to receive it again. Our success is no accident. Skill and technique always beat tactics, systems and the physical game.'

Frederico Pinheiro, a Carioca who had been recommended to me by Duncan Frew, was waiting by his van for me. He would be transporting me around for the week, and although his English was as bad as my Portuguese, we had struck up a good rapport, using mainly the universal language of football. He also happened to be a die-hard Botafogo fan. To be hanging around the Flamengo training ground was, to a man like Frederico, akin to a vegetarian working in an abattoir. But he gave me the thumbs-up sign when he saw me waving goodbye to Autuori. 'Botafogo,' Frederico said, pointing at the Flamengo coach. 'He was at Botafogo.'

I rested for a couple of hours back at the hotel, exhausted by my exertions in the heat of the midday sun, before Frederico picked me up and we returned, once more, to Fla Barra. Arriving early, we sat in the training-ground bar, where the waiter, who always gave me a friendly nod, supplied us with the same drinks we had ordered the day before. He looked rather pleased with himself that he had remembered our order without even asking, so I decided against telling him that I fancied something different this time.

He returned a few moments later, waving a small piece of paper in his hand. It turned out to be an old bill. The waiter explained that it belonged to Ronaldo, the famous Brazilian centre-forward who, in joining the Italian giants Inter Milan, had broken the world record transfer fee. 'He ordered a cheese and ham sandwich, and an iced tea,' the waiter explained, in great detail. 'And he never paid for it. You would think he could afford to pay for it. But no, he ate his sandwich, he drank his drink, and he left!'

I asked him why he had kept hold of the bill. Was he hoping that one day, on seeing Ronaldo, he would march up to him and, as if it were a court subpoena, present him with the slip of paper? 'Oh no,' the waiter replied. 'The bill's worth much more to me than the charge of the food and drink. I'm just going to keep it.'

That evening the press, who had been mysteriously missing for a day, returned in their droves. Cameramen poured out of television vans, reporters appeared from their cars and a larger than usual throng gathered by the side of the pitch. Rodrigo, having managed to extract the mobile from his ear for a split second, came over.

'I'm going to have to talk to them about you,' he said, with a worried expression. 'You see, we don't want them to get the wrong idea. If we play badly next week, then they will blame the fact that we let you play with us. It won't be your fault, of course. It will be ours. They expect so much from us, all the time.'

He strolled over to them, with a friendly smile and a few slaps on backs, and began to talk in earnest. It felt like the Autuori 'interview' all over again. Out of earshot, I can only guess what was said, but there was one moment when all of the assembled media turned and looked in unison at this English guy kitted out in full Flamengo training kit. One of them, who could speak a little English, told me later that they had all assumed I was a new player, just signed from Europe. They were about to interview me about my past career and why I had joined Flamengo. This made me feel rather pleased with myself. They actually thought I looked like a footballer!

Before we all began shooting practice, the rest of the players gathered in the centre of the pitch with a large red-and-black

Flamengo flag and started to sing and dance. The camera crews rushed forward, desperate to catch this moment on film. Rodrigo, seeing my blank face, explained that the night before, the last night of Carnival, the team had been invited to join up with two samba schools, Mangueira and Beija-Flor, as they shook and shimmied themselves along the Sambadrome, Rio's very own samba avenue, flanked by stands that accommodate 80,000 spectators. The two schools ended up as joint winners of the 1998 Carnival, which meant a double celebration for the team.

After my usual mixed bag of shots, the players broke up into departments, with the defenders heading off into one corner of the pitch whilst the attackers moved over to another. The three goalkeepers, always in a club of their own, began to dive from left to right in the goalmouth, first on the floor and then high into the corners. To my great surprise, the television crews gathered round in order to interview me about my project. They all wanted to know how I had managed to persuade Flamengo, particularly at a pressurised time like this, to let me join them for a week. One after another, from O Globo TV to Sports TV, national and regional television, they lined up, and for the next 20 minutes I stood on the touchline talking about football, the other sports I hoped to play, and Romario. Every interviewer wanted to know my thoughts on Romario. What is it like to play with him? Is he famous in England too? Can Romario win Brazil the World Cup? I somehow stumbled my way through, talking about a man who kept promising to chat with me but, as yet, had not.

Rodrigo found the whole affair hilarious. 'Now you are famous,' he said, with a broad grin on his youthful face. 'But that is how it is in Brazil. Even religion and politics do not compare. Nothing is more important than football. Nothing.'

This was the day when the penny finally dropped for me. Up until then I had just accepted the situation I found myself in. In 13 years of sports writing I had grown used to being in the company of some very famous international sporting figures. From England, setting up a week's training with Flamengo was, naturally, exciting, but I had no real idea what such an experience would mean until I was in Brazil. There was a moment, during a general kick-about, when someone passed me the ball. To my left was Junior Baiano, to my right was Ze Roberto, and in front of me, with imploring eyes, stood Romario. His eyes, and his standing, won the day and I hastily despatched the ball on to him. He skipped away, like a small child in a meadow. It suddenly dawned on me how bizarre, how ridiculous and how dreamlike my situation was. To the vast majority of the Brazilian public, the gates of heaven had been opened to me. I was in the playground of the gods.

In the dressing-room, I changed next to Romario, who always used the same peg to hang his vest and shorts, right at the end of the bench. When he played for PSV Eindhoven in Holland, he used to be coached by Bobby Robson, the former England manager. I told Romario I used to know Robson quite well. 'He is a good man,' he replied, as he jangled his car keys and made to head off. 'Can we talk some time?' I asked. Romario shook my hand. 'Yes, of course,' he said, and left.

Junior Baiano was fussing over Patrick, his boy, who had once again turned up in his Flamengo kit. 'You know what was the very first thing given to me, when I was a new-born baby,' he said, by way of explaining the Brazilian love affair with the game. 'It was a football, of course. It's the same with every child in Brazil, boy or girl. A football is the most important thing anyone can have in Brazil, and because we are a poor country it is also one of the few things most of us can still afford to have.'

I pictured Rocinha and the other slums dotted all over Rio. What happens when a family cannot even afford a football? 'Then they kick a tin can around,' Junior answered. 'Or a rag. Or anything.'

I asked him why he always seemed so happy. 'I'm a very happy guy. I am doing what I love and I am playing for a team I always dreamed about. I want to play for Flamengo for the rest of my career.' He placed a large, comforting arm around Patrick. 'Maybe his dreams will come true also,' he added, as he too made his way home.

A boy approached me with a Flamengo shirt and a pen. He wanted my autograph, mistakenly believing that I was a player. I suppose it made sense. I had just emerged from the dressing-room with the rest of the players, showered and changed, in conversation with Junior and playing around with Jamir, for whom I had 'promised' to fix up a transfer to a big city club in England. The boy presented me with a moral dilemma. I reasoned I could not possibly sign his shirt. I would feel like a fraud. I shook my head, saw his disappointed face as he walked away and immediately felt bad.

For some reason the biggest, baddest and thirstiest mosquitoes hit Fla Barra that evening. They probably could not believe their luck when they discovered that a new prey had come to their patch, a white, fleshy Englishman with gallons of top-quality blood. They led a well-orchestrated attack and found their target with consummate ease. Whilst I was talking to Junior, he must have wondered why I was acting like a thigh-slapping Bavarian dancer.

I mentioned this to Frederico as we drove away from Fla Barra. He shook his head and pulled a face. 'You don't get mosquitoes at Botafogo,' he said.

It was quite a shock when I looked at myself in the hotel mirror the following morning. My legs looked as if I had contracted smallpox overnight. They were covered in big, red, ugly blotches. But my face looked even worse. Amid the excitement of my technical session the previous day, it had escaped my attention that a red-haired, fair-skinned Englishman and the Rio midday sun did not exactly mix well. Even if I had given it some thought, I probably would have been too embarrassed to have broken off my training in order to slap high-factor protection cream all over me. The end result was that my head now looked like a ripe tomato.

I was acutely aware of this as I arrived at Fla Barra. The other players – the Fabianos of the world – all stripped off in the dressing-room, their perfectly formed bodies toned and tanned by their lifestyles. In contrast, I revealed a body that was white, where the training kit of shirt, shorts and socks had covered my flesh, and red everywhere else. My legs must have looked particularly attractive. A ten-inch patch of red between the top of my socks and the bottom of my shorts divided up a larger area of white, dappled with blotches. My arms, too, from where the shirt sleeves ended, glowed. From afar, my naked body probably resembled the colours of a football team, like Arsenal, in reverse. Some of the players could not take their eyes off my legs. Renato Gaucho, the old man of the team, said something to Romario in Portuguese. Here was a man I had been trying to talk to for the past four days. Now he initiated the conversation, although it was not quite what I had in mind.

'Some of the players want to know what is wrong with your legs?' asked Romario.

'Mosquitoes,' I replied, trying to appear unconcerned about the problem.

'They must like English blood,' he said.

'That's because they know that we will win the World Cup,' I said, in jest.

Romario repeated my comment to those around him. Some of the other players crowded round, as if the stakes had just been raised in a poker game. 'You like Brazil?' he asked.

'Yes, it's fantastic,' I said. 'An amazing country.'

'You like the girls here?' he added, apropos to nothing.

'Well, yes, they are beautiful,' I answered.

I was half expecting the next question to be along the lines of:

'Whilst we're on the subject, what's happened to your face?' But Romario didn't say anything after that. He just looked down at my legs again.

When morning training ended I was invited to join Iranildo, the free-kick specialist, in some extra-curricular practice. I had often noticed the little man heading off with one of the many trainers at the training ground, a bag of balls over his shoulder. He always struck me as a solitary figure, especially in the evenings, when the gloom of the night would start to descend on Fla Barra. But his was a very important role.

The Brazilians are known for many tricks in football. One of them has to be their free-kicks. When a Brazilian team is awarded a free-kick anywhere near the goal, you sit up and take notice. The chances are that the ball will end up in the net, usually after a swerve of such outrageous proportions that the hapless goalkeeper has already decided not to bother moving. The responsibility of Flamengo's free-kicks nearly always fell on Iranildo, who took his role very seriously. He had no problem with the fact that his team-mates would be in the showers, laughing and joking and throwing the soap around, whilst he was still out there on the pitch. He was practising his trademark.

Each morning and evening he would studiously take one hundred free-kicks, approaching each attempt with the concentration of a seamstress threading cotton through a needle, first from the left- and then from the right-hand side of the penalty area. Ten yards in front of him, blocking a natural route to the goal, stood a four-man and rather comical-looking wall of metal defenders. It was Iranildo's job to lift the ball over the expressionless defence and to find the top corner of the net. More often than not he did.

'I want at least 40 of my free-kicks out of 50 on each side to be probable goals,' he admitted midway through his impressive session. 'By that I mean that if there was a goalkeeper standing there, he would struggle to save my shot. Usually, this is the case.'

I stood and watched as, over and over again, he curled the ball over the defenders and into the net, as if he possessed a remote control that directed the flight of the ball. When the coach ran off to retrieve some of the balls, I took over as the chief provider for Iranildo. This meant simply that I would tap a fresh ball to the man from a few yards away after each free-kick, but such was the intensity of the occasion that I felt rather important.

Paolo Sosa then turned up, and when Iranildo finished his first 50, Sosa turned to me and said: 'Right, now it's your turn. You can take 20.' Iranildo and I swapped positions, and on each blast of Sosa's whistle I would loft the ball over the wall and into the net. Most found their target, prompting Iranildo to laugh and tell Sosa that maybe I should take over the free-kick role at Flamengo. Eventually, he made a valid point. 'Perhaps you could put a little more power into your shots.' He was right. Although I was evading the wall and finding the goal, the ball was plopping into the net. Any goalkeeper facing my free-kicks would have had time to have read *War and Peace* before turning his attention to saving my effort.

As we trudged back to the dressing-room, Iranildo told me that his hero was Zico, the little midfielder who played for Flamengo and his country during the early- and mid-1980s. He was still well known and revered in Brazil, especially in Rio, where, as well as many other commitments, he had established a boys' football club, partly to discover new talent and partly to give them a chance to escape the streets of the *favelas*. He had a penchant for spectacular goals, especially from free-kicks.

'If I can take free-kicks like Zico, then I am happy,' Iranildo told me. 'For me, he was the greatest. He could do anything he wanted with the ball.'

That afternoon I visited Iranildo's hero. Zico is held in such esteem in Brazil that the week after we met he was appointed as the technical co-ordinator to the Brazilian World Cup squad for France 1998, working in tandem with the much-maligned national coach Mario Zagallo. But that afternoon he could be found at his boys' club, a truly first-class establishment, just a mile away from Fla Barra.

I wanted to know his explanation for both the importance of football in Brazil and his country's success. We stood by his sports car, me in my Sheraton 'Carnival' T-shirt and him in his own 'Zico' designer-label vest, looking out over the pristine pitch he had built for the boys.

'Don't be fooled by some of the wealth you may see in Rio,' he began. 'Brazil is very much a Third World country. Not much goes right here, which is why football has become so important to the people. When we do well in football, the whole country is happy and forgets about its troubles.

'The good thing about football is that it is a cheap game. Ayrton Senna was also a hero in Brazil, for sure. But he drove a multi-million-dollar car and he achieved something that was beyond the possible means of ordinary people. In football, all you need is one ball, 22 players and four large stones, or maybe shirts, to make the goalposts. It's something that the street kids play. It's not like it is in Europe, or in America. Our kids don't have computer games and videos to go home to. So they play football, develop their skills and dream that, one day, they can escape the poverty and become a famous footballer. It is like the boxer from the inner-city American ghetto. For many Brazilians, it is just about the only way out.'

Zico had to hurry off for a meeting he should have begun three hours earlier, but he left me with one piece of advice. 'You should get yourself down to Copacabana Beach,' he said. 'Not at night time, but in the late afternoon and early evening. You will see what I am talking about.'

I had just enough time to make it back to evening training at Fla Barra. A right commotion was taking place. Neguinho, the Beija-Flor samba school singer, had arrived to thank the Flamengo players for their support. Every other minute he would suddenly burst into an impromptu rendition of samba song, and some of the players on the training pitch would noticeably move to the beat as they collected and then delivered the ball. I found myself surrounded by a moving, throbbing mass of footballers, with me, as ever, the odd man out, with my fading blotches and flaky nose.

Rodrigo Paiva suggested I should be involved in a penalty competition against Clemer. He, like goalkeepers at every football club, was a complete individual. Despite the stifling heat, which resulted in the outfield players grabbing every opportunity they could to rip off their shirts and shower themselves with ice-cold water produced from a hosepipe by the side of the pitch, Clemer would insist on wearing a thick goalkeeper's jersey and black tracksuit bottoms. 'It's not that hot,' he would insist, as the gauge recorded 38 degrees.

Although he kept asking me my Christian name, he always forgot within moments and resorted to calling me 'Gringo'. I had always imagined that the only people who used such a term were Pancho Villa-type figures, galloping across the Mexican plains with their bullet-studded belts criss-crossed across their torsos and their sombreros flapping behind on their backs. A number of the players began to shout out 'Gringo', a term that merely translates as 'foreigner', when they wanted me to pass to them. Jamir, however, stuck to either Ian or Rivelino. He had been to London on a couple of occasions and told me how much he liked it. Then he frowned. 'But the girls are difficult there,' he said.

'How do you mean?' I asked.

'Well, they are not friendly with you at once,' he replied. 'You have to spend time talking to them before they do what you want. It's not like it is here in Rio.' I sympathised with his problem. Always a nuisance, having to talk to someone first before you achieve your sexual goal, I reasoned with him. Women, of course, were always a major topic in the dressing-room. Romario's enquiry about my verdict on Rio's girls was often repeated to me by others. Some of the questioning became quite specific, and I was approached by the players with some seriousness. Was I more into breasts or bums? Which physical department were English girls noted for? My answers – delivered rather off the top of my head to satisfy their thirst for detail – were then digested by the rest of the players as they continued to change into training kit.

Clemer had been feeling rather sick the day before. He did not know why, but I felt it might have had something to do with what looked like a cheese sandwich he insisted on consuming moments before running out to start training each morning. This day, however, he was more in the mood and his eyes lit up when the penalty competition was suggested to him. I was to take five penalties against, reputedly, one of the best goalkeepers in Brazil.

'How many you score against me, Gringo?' he asked as we jogged our way to the goal. Buoyed by my reasonable showing each day during shooting practice – reasonable, I hasten to add, compared to my pre-Brazil visions – I told him three.

'Three?' he said, stopping in his tracks for a moment in genuine surprise. 'Three?' He stretched his gloved hand towards me, licked his lips and said: 'Okay, five thousand dollars.'

This made me think again. 'Okay, two penalties, then,' I replied. His hand shot back to his side and he positioned himself in the centre of the goal, eyes looking straight at me. He stretched out his arms in front of him, his palms facing out as if he were Marcel Marceau feeling an imaginary window. 'Let's go,' he shouted.

I lined up the first ball, aware that a small group of players had gathered behind me and were whispering to each other. Taking an absurdly long run-up, I scuffed my first attempt so badly that it trickled past the left-hand post. Clemer let out a loud, confident chuckle.

Take two. This time I hit the ball much better. In fact, I would go as far as to say that it was very nearly the perfect penalty. Clemer was so badly beaten that he gave up on the job and watched. The ball proceeded to cannon off the inside of the right-hand post and back towards me. Clemer laughed again. I wagged my finger at him, telling him that he had been extremely lucky.

My third attempt was reasonable. As I ran up to kick the ball, Clemer had crouched his body low down and was swaying from side to side, pointing his finger out to his left by way of daring me to place the ball in that direction. This was a game of bluffs and double bluffs. Should I call his bluff and place the ball exactly where he was pointing? The only problem with that decision, however, was that this was where my previous penalty had been directed. Instead, I chose the other way. Clemer leapt to his right almost before I had kicked the ball, and sprung on his prey like a cat pouncing on a scared mouse. A decent penalty, but a good save and an effective slice of psychology.

Three down, two to go, and still no goal. This was turning into a humiliation. Clemer was now clapping his hands together loudly, moving his body confidently and shouting out: 'C'mon, c'mon.' The crowd of players had grown and Clemer was enjoying playing to the gallery.

I sent my fourth penalty the same way, but this time the ball sped closer to the far left-hand post and away from Clemer. I knew the moment I hit the ball that it would be a goal, providing Clemer did not produce something special. This time he was beaten. His first movement was to dive the other way, and by the time he had checked himself, the ball was past him and into the back of the net. A small cheer emerged from behind and I punched the air with delight. It actually meant quite a lot to me to score a goal past the number-one goalkeeper. Clemer collected the ball from the corner of the net and lobbed it back to me, a wry smile on his face.

I had one, final penalty, and if I could convert this chance I would have achieved my revised aim of two goals. This became a challenge to both of us. Clemer stopped clowning around. He prepared himself fully for the kick, crouching low in order to spring in either direction and staring at me, straight ahead. I hit the ball well, in the same direction as the previous two penalties, and watched in horror as it scraped the outside of the left-hand post, with Clemer rooted to the spot. The goalkeeper would have stood no chance with that one, if only the ball had been six inches closer. Instead, he let out a huge roar of delight and I hung my head. I had scored just one penalty out of five, a figure I regarded as pretty measly, even if it was against Flamengo's first-choice custodian of the net.

As we made our way back to the dressing-room – Clemer with a broad smile all over his face and me with a rather glum expression – I asked him why he had decided to become a goalkeeper. In England, some of our greatest players have been keepers, but Brazil was not a country known for footballers who wore the number-one shirt. Surely he had wanted to be the next Pelé, or Zico, when he was a youngster?

'Sure, of course I did,' he acknowledged. 'And I really tried. I used to be a centre-forward. I thought I was quite good, but it was clear that there were many more players better than me. So then I thought about it. Why not become a goalkeeper? The competition would be a lot less, because hardly anyone wants to be one.' He laughed. 'So, here I am.' And there he was, a reluctant goalkeeper, but a good one nevertheless, who certainly saw me off that day.

I had talked with Junior Baiano about all this earlier. He had made his fame and fortune as a big, strapping defender, both in Germany, where he used to play for Werder Bremen, and in São Paulo. Now he was at Flamengo, a team expected to score for fun. His role was to stop the opposition from finding the net, but wouldn't he rather be up in the front line bagging goals for himself?

'Whenever we play in a training game which is not too serious, I play in attack,' he said. 'I love to score goals. Everybody does in Brazil. If I was in England I would be expected to kick the ball from defence, but here I am encouraged to run with the ball. Sometimes I score for Flamengo and that makes me very happy. But what makes me happiest is just to play football here.'

I had asked Paolo Autuori whether he would prefer his team to win 2–0 or 5–3. It took him a split second to consider this question. '5–3,' he said. 'Every time.'

I mentioned this later to Junior. 'It's true,' he said.

'But doesn't Paolo mind about the three goals his defence has conceded?' I said.

'No, as long as we score more goals than the other team,' said Junior.

As I left to find Frederico, a boy approached me. Like the youngster the other night, he had a felt-tip pen and a Flamengo shirt in his hand. Now he wanted the prize possession of my autograph. I looked down at the shirt. I recognised Romario's signature, and Cleisson's, the speedy striker. I then looked at the boy again, who held his pen out towards me. I decided to sign the shirt. I did not want to turn away another disappointed but clearly misinformed young supporter, but as soon as I had returned the pen and watched him skip away, I regretted my actions. That boy will, no doubt, show off his shirt to his friends and schoolmates. Amid a whole host of other autographs, you could see, quite clearly, three names bunched together – Romario, Cleisson and Ian Stafford. In years to come, Cariocas will look at that shirt and say: 'Who the hell was that?'

I took Zico's advice that afternoon and went down to Copacabana Beach. I saw what has to be one of the most amazing sporting sights in the world. The name 'Copacabana' conjures up images of glamour and wealth, beautiful people and Barry Manilow crooning away to swooning, blue-rinsed ladies. Yet, in reality, Copacabana means football. From its beginning, under the shadow of the Sugar Loaf, to its end, four miles on, where Ipanema Beach takes over beyond the headland, Copacabana boasts hundreds of football pitches. Each day, but particularly from around five o'clock onwards, 80, 90, maybe as many as a hundred organised football matches take place. Elsewhere, impromptu games spring up. Occasionally, I would come across a beach volleyball court. 'So they don't just play football here,' I thought. But no, on closer examination I realised that the locals play a version of football where the ball, through a series of headers and volleys, always remains in the air.

On one of the football pitches you will see a match involving four- and five-year-old boys and girls. On another, middle-aged men will battle it out in the sand. As far as the eye can see, football goes on. The most staggering thing about all of this is the skill and technique involved in these games on the beach. Carpenters and plumbers, estate agents and accountants, ordinary artisans, they all flock to Copacabana at the end of a day's work to reveal ball skills that you might just see at an English professional club but never, ever on the various parks in England on a Sunday morning. What became abundantly clear is that while the gulf between the national teams of Brazil and England may not be vast these days, at public level, a game between a random Brazilian beach XI and their English counterparts would make the Alamo seem like a closely fought contest.

Various writers, notably from Britain, insist that the notion of finding talent on the beaches is a misconception and a cliché. The reality, they argue, is that the clubs incorporate young talent into their academies. This is true, but where do they think these children first worked on their skills and technique? The clubs select those who they believe possess the most talent, just as they do anywhere else in the world, but whilst the kids hope and pray for the call-up, they play on the beaches and in the streets.

The other point about Copacabana is simply that the vast majority of the thousands of evening players will obviously not make the grade in professional football in Brazil. But their skills are still vastly superior to those of their counterparts elsewhere in the world.

I found this out for myself. Deciding it was high time Copacabana Beach bore witness to my questionable skills, I removed my trainers and managed to persuade some lads on one of the pitches to include me in their game. I may as well have not bothered. While the rest of the players moved around the beach like figure skaters on ice, my heavy feet seemed to be stuck to the sand. The best I could do was clump the ball forward, in a very English way, and let my superiors get on with dribbling and juggling the ball mesmerically towards the goal. The game just seemed to pass me by. After a while, having decided I was a better player with boots on my feet, I decided to retire and do what most Cariocas like to do on Copacabana when not playing football.

Buying myself a cold Chopp, the popular local beer, I turned my chair around so that my back faced the beach and I could look out towards the pavement and the street. This in itself provides great entertainment. Serious-looking runners would jog by, decked out in all the right designer gear, followed by speed walkers, identified only by the way they would jerk their arms upwards in sudden and dramatic fashion. Beautiful women would saunter by, sporting nothing more than those dental-floss bikinis Plinio described and in some contrast to the elderly men who would follow, strolling leisurely, mostly in twos and always wearing either white or khaki socks that would be pulled up to just below their knees.

Men would arrive to sample the mini fitness centres found all along the edge of the beach, honing their biceps on the metal pull-up bars and improving their washboard stomachs on the benches. A Bolivian panpipe band would suddenly appear from nowhere, set themselves up on the pavement and produce the most wonderful music. And every so often a transvestite would swagger past, some more obvious than others. Rio, certainly one of the more liberally minded cities in the world, is home to thousands of transvestites. Robert, a Fla Barra security guard, had been talking to me about this one day. I told him that I was married and he decided that this was probably a good thing. 'You never know what you're getting into bed with in this city,' he said, with a hearty laugh. 'You could end up with the shock of your life.'

Saturday proved to be the only day off for Flamengo. 'One-day vacation,' is how Jamir put it. I asked Frederico if he could take me to the Maracana Stadium. On the way we passed a tiny, weed-filled football pitch, surrounded by flyovers and concrete. 'São Cristovo,' said Frederico, pointing out of his window. 'That is where Ronaldo started.' It truly was a world away from where the Brazilian striker was plying his trade now, in the San Siro stadium in Milan. A clutch of small boys were playing on the bumpy, São Cristovo pitch, home to a poor side in the Rio league's second division. Each one of them would have had their dreams. After all, if Ronaldo had escaped, why not them?

The Maracana may not have the history and tradition of Wembley

Stadium, nor the architecture of the San Siro or the Nou Camp, but in terms of sheer size, it remains awesome. A huge bowl of a stadium, it has concrete steps circumnavigating the pitch and rows of seating rising so high into the sky that the players down below are merely dots on the pitch. Whenever Flamengo play there, the stadium is full of wild-eyed, screaming fans, with their red-and-black scarves and banners and their flares, which burn constantly into the night sky.

Inside the stadium, beyond the dressing-rooms and the warm-up areas, photographs of Pelé, Garrincha, Zico and other great players from Brazil's wonderful past adorn the walls. I pointed Zico out to Frederico, who shrugged his shoulders. 'He used to play for Flamengo,' he said, looking singularly unimpressed. 'And he missed that penalty against France.' Frederico was referring to the World Cup quarter-final game in 1986, when Brazil drew 1–1 with the French after Zico had, indeed, failed to convert his spot-kick. Brazil went on to lose the penalty shoot-out after extra time and were knocked out of the competition.

Next stop was Gavea, where Flamengo's offices could be found, along with a pitch on which the football club used to play minor matches. All the Rio clubs have similar set-ups, with grandiose offices dotted all over the city. Before we arrived at Gavea, Frederico made a detour. I was unaware of this until we drove up to a large wall and a gate, from where one could see a small stadium. 'Botafogo,' Frederico announced. He looked like a pilgrim outside Canterbury Cathedral. This is where his particular Pearly Gates could be found.

The trophy room at Gavea made the Crown Jewels in the Tower of London look like nothing more than a second-rate collection of junk jewellery. Trophies and trinkets, shields and cups all glistened and sparkled in their glass cases. Not all had been obtained through the achievements of the Flamengo football team. Clube Regatas do Flamengo also boasted a whole host of other sports teams, ranging from handball and gymnastics to judo, swimming, tennis and rowing, the last being the reason why the club was first founded in 1895. It was only later, in 1911, that some of the players from Fluminense left to introduce football at Flamengo. By doing so, they created the biggest football club in the world.

The following morning was to be my last training session with the biggest football club in the world. The team would later be flying north to Salvador, in preparation for their Brazilian Cup match against lowly Vitória, and I was to return home to England. My blotches had just about disappeared and the red in my face had changed into a preferable light tan. Before I left, though, I was determined to talk to

Romario, the one player who had kept his distance for much of my time at Fla Barra.

I had taken a special interest in Romario de Souza Faria. It was not just because he was such a sporting superstar, a man voted player of the 1994 World Cup tournament. It was more his whole manner. I wondered which car he would turn up in, his blue family Porsche or his red sporty Porsche. Whatever the case, he would always leave it in exactly the same position, right next to the dressing-room entrance, just a few paces away from the kerb. He would often be dressed in just a loose-fitting pair of shorts, but sometimes deigned to wear a vest as well.

While the other players would begin their training on the pitch, Romario would undergo a series of individual stretching exercises on a mat, before transferring to an exercise bike in order to work on his troublesome knee. He was always accompanied by at least one of the trainers, who seemed to be specially assigned to him. Often, ten minutes before Romario would leave, one of them would run out to his car and switch on the cool blowers, so that the temperature inside his Porsche was just right for when the football star departed. At the age of 32, he had developed a small bald patch at the back of his head, and I wondered whether a man who seemed to possess so much pride was bothered by this.

On the pitch he possessed all the time in the world. Whilst others ran around him at lightning speed, he would stand in the middle, organising proceedings, with a subtle flick of his boot here and a stab of his toe there. A short but powerful man (one of his nicknames was 'Shorty', but I decided I stood a better chance of him talking to me if I stuck to Romario), he only really moved when he sniffed a goal. Then, like a lizard snatching a fly with his tongue, Romario struck. In the blink of an eye his shot found the back of the net, leaving Clemer to retrieve the ball with a shrug of his shoulders and a moan at his defenders.

I had grown almost used to the surreal lifestyle I had been leading for the past week, but I realised that this would be the last time I would ever train in Brazil with some of the best footballers in the world. Much had happened in the past week. Paolo Autuori greeted me each day with a smile and a thumbs up, a far cry from the rather cool reception of the first couple of days, and the players had grown to regard me as just one of them each morning and evening when I arrived with my newly washed kit in hand. The back-up staff – men like Luis, the kit man, and Deni, the masseur, who used to joke that the whole of Flamengo would be nothing without him – had eyed me suspiciously at first, but were now greeting me with high fives.

Even the press had stopped looking at me as if I were a fairground attraction and joined in the general banter of the occasion. 'Has Paolo picked you yet?' one of them would ask me each time he saw me limbering up. 'No, not yet,' I would answer, with monotonous regularity. 'But he will.' The same conversation was repeated day after day, as if we were two spies delivering passwords to each other.

On the pitch I had noticed that the players had become a little more tense. They, by Flamengo's standards, had endured a poor run of results and, after a short break enforced by early elimination from the Rio–São Paulo Cup, they were about to play a crucial cup match in Salvador. My services were not welcomed so much on this last day. Matters had become more serious, and although I was allowed my customary shooting practice, crosses, headers and general kick-about, when it came to specific moves and a practice match, I had to sit it out on the touchline. None of this bothered me. I had already fulfilled my football fantasy.

Towards the end of practice Romario jogged off the pitch and sat down outside the dressing-room, a bottle of water in his hand. There was an empty seat next to him. I moved quickly, but I hope not too obviously, to make sure it was mine. To my surprise, Romario smiled and offered me a swig from his bottle.

'Which teams do you think could win the World Cup?' he asked me. I gave him my considered verdict, as if he really cared. 'I think maybe six can win, Romario. Brazil, of course, Germany, Italy, the French, because the World Cup is being held in France, maybe Argentina and . . . well, possibly England.'

Romario swirled the water around his bottle and replied. 'I think only Brazil, Argentina and Germany can win. You English have a good team, though. Maybe you can make it to the semi-final.'

His English was of a good standard and certainly better than most of his team-mates'. Feeling as if he had finally opened his door to me, I asked if he minded the constant attention from the public and from the likes of me.

'At first, yes, I did,' he said. 'It wasn't too bad when I played in Europe, but in Rio I couldn't go anywhere or do anything. Now I am used to it and I don't mind it so much. I am a Carioca, you see, and I understand how important football is to the people.'

Another pause followed. Romario suddenly seemed interested in me. 'Who else will you be seeing for your book, then?' he asked. I went through a list of hopefuls and he nodded his head approvingly. 'Not bad,' he said. 'Do you now understand why football is so important in Brazil?'

I said I did. I told him about the couple of hours I had spent wandering around Copacabana Beach. Romario shifted round more in his chair, took his eyes off the training match still being played out on the pitch and looked at me. 'What does Rio have above all else?' he asked.

I wasn't sure whether he expected an answer from me or not, but, if he did, he gave me no time to reply. 'The beach, of course,' he said. 'We hardly have any parks or football pitches, so we make do with either the street or the beach. The good thing about the beach is that it doesn't make any judgements. You can be the wealthiest man in Rio, or the poorest boy. But we can all go down to the beach to play football.'

Is this what the young Romario used to do? 'Of course,' he answered. 'I am like everyone else in this city. I learnt to play football on the streets and on the beach. The uncertainty of the sand means that you have to learn quickly how to control the ball, both in the air and on the ground. It is the best way to develop skills.'

Yet the burden of public expectation in Brazil can make life difficult as well for a footballer. In 1994 Brazil won the World Cup in the United States. The team came home to a less-than-enthusiastic welcome. 'It was the way we won,' Romario explained. 'As far as the people were concerned – and the players, for that matter – drawing 0–0 with Italy in the final and winning the penalty competition that followed was no way to win a World Cup. We were happy to win, of course, but not that happy.'

I thought about the reaction back home in England. Not that happy to win the World Cup? The English would settle for a goalless draw in the World Cup final anytime! So what were Brazil expected to do in the summer, then?

'Oh, we have to win the Cup,' Romario said matter-of-factly. 'Nothing else will do. To come second, even in the World Cup, is to come last.' I pulled a face, and he smiled. 'Hey, that's okay. We should win. We are Brazil. We play football.'

Training finished. I ran on to the pitch for my last kick of the ball, a shot that Clemer tipped somewhat dramatically over the bar, and then joined the others in changing back into my polo shirt and shorts.

My time had come to an end. Paolo Sosa and Jamir swapped addresses with me, some of the other players shook my hand whilst others waved, and I thanked Rodrigo Paiva and Paolo Autuori for their patience and kindness over the past week. 'Any chance of playing for Flamengo?' I asked Autuori. 'If you pay me enough I might consider the offer.' He punched me playfully on my shoulder and walked off. I took that as a 'no'.

Frederico was driving me to the airport. We had an hour to kill, so he took me on the cable car up to the top of Sugar Loaf, from where the whole topsy-turvy sculpture of the magnificent city of Rio de Janeiro can be experienced. From up there you can see Copacabana and the statue of Christ the Redeemer, his sweeping arms outstretched in a reassuring way. Frederico shifted my attention elsewhere. 'Look,' he said, 'Botafogo.' And, sure enough, beneath the murky haze of the late summer sunshine, you could just make out a small stadium and club offices.

He had never really revealed much about himself, but as we arrived at Galeao International Airport, Frederico suddenly announced that he and his wife were expecting a baby in September. I told him how pleased I was for him. I asked him a question, knowing his probable answer.

'What's the first thing you will buy the baby?'

Frederico held his hands out wide, as if I had just said one of the daftest things imaginable. 'A football,' he said.

Of course he will. I thought of Romario's last comment as I said farewell and headed off for departures. This, after all, was Brazil.

In Brazil, they play football.

JANSHER KHAN

It Must Be an Act of God

It proved to be a hellish flight back from Brazil. After being delayed half the night in São Paulo due to engine trouble, we eventually set off across the Atlantic only to be informed in mid-air that the London- and Copenhagen-bound plane would fly direct to Denmark in order to catch up on lost time. Those bound for England would be dropped off on the return journey back from Copenhagen to Rio a few hours later.

A mini-riot broke out on board. Some of the English stormed the cockpit to remonstrate with the captain, whilst the Scandinavian passengers argued it was for the best. 'I am a personal friend of Richard Branson,' somebody told the singularly unimpressed purser. 'You can't do this.'

Well, they did. And so it came to pass that I found myself wandering through Copenhagen Airport's terminal the next day, when I should have been tucked up in my own bed countering jet lag, a process thus delayed by some 14 hours. With nothing better to do, I sat down in the bar and observed people going about their daily business. I wondered if any of them had ever played football with Romario. I doubted it, somehow, assuming they cared. Then I turned my attention to my next sporting dream. It would involve another long flight to another strange and distant land and, once again, I had absolutely no idea what would happen to me.

I have never quite worked out how a sport such as squash can be so popular as a participatory activity and yet create relatively minor public interest when it comes to the professional game. It boils down, I suppose, to the difficulty in selling squash to television, always the first necessary ingredient for any high-profile game, but it remains, nevertheless, a huge and keenly contested activity.

Any leisure and squash centre I have ever visited in Britain has always been packed full of superfit executives clinching sets in the same aggressive, competitive manner that they use to secure deals, pot-bellied, middle-aged men who possess the technique but, worryingly, not always the fitness, housewives who turn to the game as an alternative to their step classes, and people like me, who enjoy a long, hard game and spend the rest of the day shattered, especially if they lose. Occasionally, you stumble over someone who can really play. Then you wonder just how they can control the ball, the racquet and consequently the game with such nonchalance.

A game like squash finds me out. On reflection, it always has done. I played for my school team on a few occasions, winning one important match by stamping my feet on the wooden floor each time my opponent attempted to hit the ball. Not very sporting, I grant you, but I was genuinely unaware that such tactics were illegal. Fortunately, so was everyone else present that day. In my first year at London University a squash court was conveniently situated within the grounds of my halls of residence. As a less-than-hardworking history student, I managed to squeeze three or four games of squash a week into my packed social diary. I became, I think, quite good. I was certainly better than almost anyone else who challenged me. Yet whenever I played either of the two serious squash players living in the halls, it was a totally different and one-sided story. I tried to steer clear of them. It was much better fun seeing off the others.

In the ensuing 17 years I have continued to play the game, but only sporadically. The problem with squash is that it takes a long time to gain the fitness necessary to be able to run in short, sharp bursts around a court. The first, hard game after a lengthy absence away from squash will leave your lungs bursting for air during the session and your thighs and buttocks so stiff and sore afterwards that even the simple process of getting in and out of a car can be painful.

Nevertheless, I felt confident that I would be able to put up a decent show, if given the chance, against a man who, until very recently, was arguably the most dominant sportsman in the world. There may well be more famous sportspeople plying their trade, and there may well be wealthier ones, but no individual has controlled his or her sport in recent times in the manner in which Jansher Khan has held squash in his firm grip.

The idea interested me immensely. Jansher Khan, having burst on to the scene in 1987 when he became world champion at just 17 years of age, had been collecting World and British Open titles, the two major tournaments in the squash calendar, for fun ever since. At the time of writing Khan had assembled 14 of them. Perhaps even more impressive was the stunning fact that the man had been world number one for ten years. Ten years, in a sport as gruelling as squash!

What made all this more appealing was that Jansher was the latest in a long, long line of Khans from the North-West Frontier Province of Pakistan who had all reached the very top of their sport. Since Hashim Khan left the village of Nawakille in 1952 and returned with the British Open under his belt, the Khans, a prominent family in the Pathan tribe, have been producing champions. Nearly all have stemmed from this small, poor village one mile outside the frontier town of Peshawar. It is an extraordinary story, about an extraordinary family, and one that I wanted to witness at first hand.

But how? I had interviewed Jansher on a couple of occasions when he had been over in England, so at least some contact had been made in the past. One person most influential outside his family is Satinder Bajwa, a man I had known for a number of years through ventures we had both worked on with Advantage, the sports client and management company that advised the makers of the Tom Cruise film *Jerry Maguire*, where he is the Director of Squash.

'Baj', as everyone calls him, is a Sikh of Indian origin who decided to swap life as an aeronautical engineer for playing and coaching squash at West Point, America's famous military academy, before becoming a players' agent. He has been a personal friend and mentor of Jansher for the past ten years and whenever I have wanted to interview the Pakistani I have always gone through Baj. He appreciated the notion of me playing Jansher on his home court in Peshawar, suggested that I should get into training and claimed that the only problem would be in finding a slot in the diary.

That was good enough for me. My first instinct was to see Peter Nicol. The 24-year-old Scot, who was based in the north-east of London, had just replaced Jansher as the world number one, ending an almost unbroken run of ten years at the top. This, as Nicol readily acknowledged, was partly down to the fact that Jansher's knees had been playing up, an occupational hazard for any long-term squash player, and he fully expected an onslaught from the 29-year-old Khan once full fitness had returned. Besides, as he modestly accepted, he had been number one for five minutes. Khan had topped the field for ten years and was a legend in his sport.

Still, Nicol was, and is, some player. Rather stupidly, I thought a match against him would give me some indication of where exactly I stood. It wasn't the brightest idea at the best of times, but especially after having not picked up a racquet in six months, let alone darted around a squash court. We played five sets. I failed to trouble the scorers. Nicol demolished me 9–0, 9–0, 9–0, 9–0, 9–0. Within ten minutes I was sweating like David Attenborough in the jungles of Borneo and panting like a dog on a hot summer day. Nicol rather enjoyed himself. Refusing to let up for one second, he revealed the ruthlessness that any sporting champion must possess to reach the top. I doubt he would have given one of his grandparents a point that morning, let alone me. Once, I dived full-length across the court in a vain attempt to retrieve the ball. As I picked myself up, Nicol looked incredulously at my cut knee. 'I can't remember the last time someone did that against me,' he said.

Afterwards, as I lay prostrate with a towel over my face and he sat with his sweat-free face beaming at my discomfort, he told me about the stark reality of my forthcoming engagement with the legend of squash. 'Whatever you do, whatever shot you play, everything will be up to Jansher,' Nicol said, leaning over towards me to gain maximum effect. 'At any time he can finish the rally. No matter what you do, he can decide when and how to end the rally with a winner.'

Did he have any tips at all? I mean, I only wanted one point off the man. Nicol watched the rivulets of sweat race against each other down my cheeks and considered the options. 'Try and break up the game,' he said. 'Talk to him in between points. And do what you did against me. Dive around on court a bit. That will show a bit of endeavour. It won't win you the point, but he will be smiling so much you just might catch him off guard on the next point.'

As I drove back home I felt in a particularly foul mood. I obtain absolutely nil enjoyment out of being thrashed out of sight, and my natural, if unrealistic, competitive streak meant that I could derive no consolation out of the fact that it had been against the world number one. What on earth had made me play against Nicol without even having one practice match under my belt first? Next time, I promised, it would be different. I would return from Pakistan and challenge the man again.

I mentioned all this to the sports editor of the *Independent* newspaper later that afternoon.

'So let me get this straight,' he said. 'You are annoyed because you have just lost to the world number one?' There was a pause on the other end of the telephone before he delivered his verdict. 'I think you're mad!'

Baj contacted me the following week. He wanted me to see Jansher, who was making a flying visit to London, and put the idea personally to him. We arranged to meet at Heathrow's Terminal 3 at 4 p.m. This involved a two-hour return drive around the M25 motorway for what turned out to be a ten-minute conversation. But it was worth it. Jansher's flight for Karachi was about to leave, and when I turned up, Baj, Jansher and his coach, Mehboob Khan, were waiting to hear my piece. I spoke passionately about the Khans, Pakistan and, especially, about Jansher himself. I talked about the other great sporting names who would play a part in my project, even if most had not yet quite committed themselves, and I threw in the line George Plimpton tended to use in America about it all being in the cause of literature.

The Terminal 3 tannoy system announced the final call for the Karachi flight. Jansher nodded his head, then looked at a smiling Mehboob, then Baj, before gazing back at me. 'Okay,' he said. 'I'll do it. You can come to Peshawar, and you can play me.' And with that he was gone, through customs with a flash of his passport and a sports bag full of squash racquets wrapped around his back.

I had four weeks to prepare myself for this unlikely encounter. The plan was that I would return to Pakistan with Jansher and Baj straight after the British Open had finished, a tournament I assumed the great Khan would add to his awesome collection. In those four weeks I had to gain the lung capacity and the strength in my legs to be able to give Jansher some kind of a game. Despite having just returned from spending a week playing football in Brazil, I now required a totally different level of fitness.

At the David Lloyd Leisure Club in Sidcup I found two willing practice partners. Steve Kemp lives locally to me and is a training partner for the World and Olympic javelin silver medallist Steve Backley. He, Backley and I had enjoyed many a game of squash in the past couple of years and I knew that Kemp, with his excellent fitness, younger age and never-say-die attitude, would always give me a good run around. The previous year we had more or less matched each other, but I found it harder to gain squash fitness this time, hence Kemp's run of victories. Backley reckoned it was down to the fact that I was shielding my ligament-damaged left foot, but I found, as each game passed, that my fitness and technique were improving.

My other partner was Derek Thompson, the David Lloyd Leisure Club's squash coach and a man who in his time had trained the Egyptian professional Gamal Awad. I always believed that my problem in squash was a lack of necessary fitness. Once I had gained this, I thought, then my shots would naturally improve. Thompson, on one look at me on court, tore my game apart. I ran far too much, instead of stretching. I employed tennis shots, instead of adopting a squash style of play, and I always ended up far too close to the ball. Apart from that, everything was fine. I was left with next to no time to change the squash-playing habits of a lifetime.

Injury struck ten days before departing for Pakistan. Steve Kemp and I became involved in a marathon match which went the full distance. Both of us were playing, by our club standard, good squash and both were determined to win. Kemp emerged the victor, after clinching the fifth and final set 10–9. That was hard enough to take, but what proved to be a bigger problem was the fact that my right calf muscle had begun to seize up midway through the last set. Later that evening, I could barely walk.

Sarah Connors, my long-suffering physio, shared a practice in Thurrock with her fellow British Athletics team physiotherapist Kevin Lidlow. Steve Backley had recommended her to me when, during the summer months, I had chipped a bone and torn ligaments in my left ankle and foot after a freak volleyball accident in Greece. Sarah did her best the next day to alleviate the longevity of the injury, kneading my leg with her hands as if she was making pastry, slapping jelly and then an ultra-sound machine on to the damaged area and even adopting laser treatment, but I could not get away from the fact that the muscle needed total rest if I hoped to get through a match against Jansher Khan. Great! Having finally gone close to rediscovering my best fitness and my best game, I was now medically required to do nothing for ten days before playing arguably the greatest player in the history of squash.

That afternoon, more pain was inflicted on me, courtesy of a series of inoculations required before visiting Pakistan. I do not know of anyone who actually enjoys such an experience, even less so when, like me, you are required to have yellow fever, typhoid and gamma globulin inserted into both arms and, rather awkwardly, into your right buttock, a buttock already sore from the previous evening's squash. I am not that used to pulling my underpants down and sticking my backside into the air in front of a woman I have never met before, hence my nervous joke about the nurse probably seeing more bums in a day than most see in a lifetime. The silence from the nurse at the British Airways medical centre in London in response to my feeble offering was as numbing as the effect the vaccinations had on my rear end.

Jansher arrived in London the day before the first round of the British Open. He had nearly withdrawn because of his knees, and was far from sure how well he would fare in a tough tournament with such a handicap. I came to watch him struggle through his first-round match against a good opponent from Belgium. Jansher scraped it, but he needed all five sets to do so, leaving me feeling reassured that perhaps, after all, I might steal a few points off him back in Peshawar.

Later, Jansher, coach Mehboob, Baj and I lunched together at the Lambs Club in the City of London. Jansher was happy just to have come through the game in one piece and was telling the rest of the entourage, whilst looking at me, how he would be facing a much tougher opponent in Peshawar the following week. I asked Mehboob if he had been at all worried watching Jansher nearly lose. He threw his eyes up to the heavens and replied: 'He's been putting me through this sort of thing for over ten years now, so I'm used to it.'

In a sudden spurt of friendliness, Mehboob, both Jansher's cousin and his brother-in-law, then placed his hand on my arm and made a promise. 'You will enjoy yourself in Peshawar,' he told me. 'And you will have no reason to worry about your safety.' My safety had not crossed my mind, at least not until Mehboob's final offering. 'You must remember, my friend, I have a Kalashnikov.'

A producer at the BBC, whose family lives in Peshawar, proved as helpful in the reassurance department as Mehboob. 'They are friendly people, but don't cross them,' he advised me. 'Spit on a man's shoe and he will kill you.' He looked at my clean-shaven chin and added: 'Maybe you should grow a beard, or at least a moustache. That way they will see you as a man.' I looked at myself in the mirror that night and at my freckled face, dotted with small shoots of stubble that seemed to take an eternity to burst out of my skin, like crocuses after a long, cold winter. I wondered if the Pathans would accept me as a man, or as a smooth-faced boy.

Jansher went on to lose in the final of the British Open to Peter Nicol. It was Nicol's first major triumph in such a tournament and I was pleased for him. He dedicated his victory to his late mother, who had died from a rare disorder a few months after he had left Scotland for London as a determined teenager. Despite the loss, Jansher was also happy to have done so well. 'If I can make it to the final with two injured knees,' he reasoned, 'then what will I do when I'm back to full fitness?' It was a fair point.

Two days before I was due to depart I had good cause to be concerned. Pakistan International Airways finally decided to tell me that they could not help me out with a ticket. I then discovered that I would be arriving in Pakistan right in the middle of Eid, one of the most important religious festivals of the year. It meant that everyone was trying to fly back home. The best I could come up with was a ticket to Karachi. I would be on the waiting list to fly on to Peshawar and, on my return, home to London. Baj was in a similar position and decided to pull out of the trip altogether. He had important meetings in London and without any guarantee of getting home in time could not afford to take the risk.

I was driving in the middle of London, trying frantically to finalise all my arrangements, when my mobile telephone rang. It was Jansher. I pulled over and listened to what he had to say. 'Ian. Everything will be okay. I will look after you. I have a guest house where you can stay and I will make sure you catch your planes. It's no problem.'

It was nice of him to call me, but as I turned up at Heathrow Airport's Terminal 3 the following afternoon, where Mehboob and Muhammad Shafi, Jansher's physiotherapist, were waiting for me, I was still anxious. I would be flying to a part of the world I had never visited before, to stay in a guest house I knew nothing about, without any guarantee, save Jansher's rather vague promise, that I would be coming home again on time.

Jansher, in typical fashion, arrived as the last call for Karachi shrilled out of the speaker system. With him were his wife Naseem, his five-year-old son Ayaz, his six-year-old daughter Sidra and their three-year-old sister Sana. Little Rabia, Jansher's 18-month-old daughter, was waiting back home in Peshawar. A couple of hours into the flight I was summoned to come and join the Khan family. I showed them photographs of my children and played games with theirs. 'You are a guest of mine in Peshawar and that means you will be looked after,' Jansher told me. 'If you want anything, just ask. What do you like to eat? Chinese?'

I told him anything he liked, although I wanted to live like a Pathan for the week. 'I don't want you to wake up in the morning feeling like shit,' he said. 'You must not have any excuses when you play me.' He tapped both his knees with his hand. 'Me, I have two bad knees.'

'That's nothing,' I replied. 'I have torn ligaments in my left foot, a sprained calf muscle in my right leg, a damaged left thumb, a sprained right wrist and I'm five years older than you, so don't tell me you have an excuse. You should win easily. I will try my hardest, but you should not allow me to win one point.'

Jansher laughed and then proceeded down another line of attack that remained a running joke throughout my stay in Pakistan. 'When your book makes you famous, you will forget me,' he said. 'When I turn up at your door, you will close it in my face.' Not, I answered, if he pointed his Kalashnikov at me.

Meanwhile, Mehboob was singing a Pathan song. 'I am the best singer in the family,' he said happily. Sidra and Sana were playing one potato, two potato with me, and Ayaz, full of energy, was delving into my bag and swiping my pen and some chewing gum. I figured a clip on the ear at this moment in time would not be the smartest move to make, especially on my first day, so I just smiled at the boy and gritted my teeth. The PIA air hostesses, one by one, filed up to obtain Jansher's autograph as we flew over Turkey and onwards to Pakistan.

On arriving in Karachi I witnessed further evidence of Jansher Khan's standing. In Britain and elsewhere in the sporting world he is known, of course, but in Pakistan the man is exceedingly famous. There were PIA officials waiting to greet the Khans in the arrivals hall. Despite the long queue of foreigners waiting to have their passports and visas stamped, Jansher simply handed my passport over to a waiting official and I walked straight through, feeling rather important. Photographers were waiting for him and as we all walked past they snapped away feverishly. A minibus took us to the Midway House Hotel, where we would spend half the day until our afternoon connection to Peshawar was ready. It may have been seven o'clock in the morning in Karachi, but it was four hours earlier for the rest of us used to British time.

While Jansher and his family headed off for one room, Mehboob and I had to share a double bedroom, albeit with two single beds, which caused great mirth and merriment to everyone else. 'Mehboob is your girlfriend for today,' Jansher announced. 'You can sleep with him, but don't tell Sultana.' Sultana, Jansher's sister and Mehboob's wife, was back in the village of Nawakille, waiting for her husband's return. It was a little awkward for both of us in the bedroom, waiting politely for each to finish in the bathroom before stripping down to our underwear, but we were so tired we soon fell asleep. Later, we talked in our beds, like children enjoying an overnight stay at a friend's house.

Mehboob had been a very fine squash player in his own right, yet a family trauma had changed his life, and the life of Jansher Khan. Jansher's elder brother, Mohibullah, had been one of the very best players in the world in the late 1970s and early 1980s. He played in the inaugural World Open final, losing to Australia's Geoff Hunt, but ended up winning a whole host of other tournaments. In 1982, however, his career came to an abrupt and controversial end. Mohibullah was arrested at Heathrow after drugs were found smuggled in his suitcase. Despite his protestations of innocence, later proved to be true when a former friend admitted placing the heroin in his luggage, Mohibullah Khan spent the next six years inside Dartmoor Prison.

This devastated Jansher, who had already shown a great deal of promise on the squash court. Mohibullah rightly saw a future champion in his younger brother and, from his prison cell, asked Mehboob to take over coaching duties. 'Jansher was always a more natural player than I was,' he explained from his side of the bedroom. 'I had to work harder.' Mehboob readily agreed, forsook his own playing career and has been coaching Jansher ever since. This, I put to him, must have been a very big decision to make. After all, who knows what Mehboob might have achieved himself as a player? 'Maybe to you,' he replied. 'But not to a Pathan. We are family.'

So it was an easy choice to make?

'Of course, no problem.'

I stared at Mehboob's content face, betraying not a shred of bitterness. Did he ever think about what he might have achieved as a player?

'No, but I think about my son, Farhan. I want him to be world champion one day.'

The room's bell rang, ending the conversation. Muhammad Shafi, who had returned briefly to his Karachi home, entered and proceeded to work on my injured left foot and right calf muscle. I had been granted the use of Jansher's physiotherapist, and Muhammad's hands certainly helped to lessen the nagging pain. 'You will be okay against Jansher,' he told me. 'As long as the rallies are not too long.' His expression suggested this was an unlikely scenario.

That night we finally arrived at Peshawar Airport. Mohibullah was there to greet us, giving his brother a huge hug, picking up and kissing his nephew and nieces, and then shaking my hand. 'Welcome, welcome,' he said. 'Come, follow me.' We all traipsed off into the car park, where Mohibullah's car was waiting to take us first to Jansher's guest house. As we passed by a huge poster of Jansher in his squash kit, bearing menacingly down on the street directly outside the airport entrance, I was wondering just what they meant by a guest house. I rather envisaged some kind of bed and breakfast hotel owned by the Khans, the sort you find in any English seaside resort, although I could not quite imagine Jansher standing at the door waiting for me to get home by 11 o'clock and then making a full English breakfast the following morning. It emerged that Jansher owned a house for guests, and some house it turned out to be.

Many of his trophies adorned the cabinets and tables of his lavishly furnished, six-bedroomed property. Photos of Jansher the squash player and Jansher the father were dotted around, and as he showed me upstairs I noticed that the banister was made out of wood shaped like squash racquets. We paused next to a large picture of Jansher in a suit. 'Handsome man,' Jansher said to me, looking up at the picture. I wasn't entirely sure whether he was joking or not, so I agreed, rather lamely.

I was taken aback by the luxury of the house, which I seemed to have all for myself. Aulia and Quddus, a couple of Jansher's employees, would be ever-present in and around the house, acting as both helpers and bodyguards, and Jansher would be 50 yards up the road, where he and his family lived.

As I unpacked in my bedroom, the biggest and best in the house, Aulia and Quddus sat and watched. I asked them both what their surnames were. 'Khan,' they replied. Stupid question, really.

The fact that Jansher was being so accommodating was due to two reasons: first, he and his family were being genuinely helpful. Yet, as a Pathan, he also had a long-held tradition to uphold. The Khans, like other families in Peshawar and surrounding districts, have a code of honour known as 'Pukhtunwali', which includes exacting vengeance on any injury done to themselves and extending protection to anyone who approached them. Another element of Pukhtunwali is 'Melmastia', which means 'hospitality'. Melmastia, in the form of food, accommodation and entertainment, is offered to every guest of the Pathans and it is often well beyond the means of those who provide it. Although this was patently not the case with Jansher, a millionaire through his tournament wins and contracts, he nevertheless took Melmastia as seriously as anyone else in Peshawar. I was a guest of Jansher Khan and it was therefore his duty to look after me.

Dinner was brought to my room, served up on a silver tray. A variety of curry dishes plus the regulation nan bread was on offer. I eyed it suspiciously. For someone who prides himself on being adventurous, this characteristic does not extend to Asian food. When I have a curry in England, I stick, with monotonous regularity, to a chicken tikka starter, followed by a chicken korma. Occasionally, if I am feeling dangerous, I just might go for a meat korma. The prospect of eating in Peshawar had been a minor concern of mine, together with what I thought would be an inevitable stomach bug. To my surprise, the food that evening, and every subsequent day, was delicious. I had fully expected to lose weight during the week. By the time I returned to England, I had piled on three pounds. That first night, Aulia and Quddus told me about the mass slaughter of goats during the Eid festival as sacrifices to Allah. As I demolished my plateful of food, I asked them what kind of meat I was eating. 'Oh, don't you know?' they said. 'It's goat.'

I was woken by a strange and mournful noise. I looked at my watch. It was five o'clock in the morning. Blaring out of the loud-speakers attached to the nearby mosque came the voice of the muezzin, the first indication during my stay in Peshawar of the importance of Islam to my hosts and neighbours. All Muslims, and 97 per cent of Pakistan, follow the Islamic faith and have to pray five times a day, starting early in the morning. Religion, as I was later to discover, played an important part in the story of Jansher Khan and his family.

I managed to grab a few more hours in bed before rising late in the morning. Emerging from the shower, I was confronted by two boys, who had arrived with my breakfast. The younger one turned out to be Waqar Mehboob Khan, Mehboob's seven-year-old son. The other was Imran Mohib Khan, Mohibullah's 14-year-old son, who just happened to be Pakistan's Under-14 national squash champion. I showed Imran my squash racquet, as one fellow player to another. 'Very good, very nice,' he said, but I noticed he still rearranged the strings before telling me that he preferred a different make of racquet. I asked him what he hoped for in life. It was an easy question to answer. 'I want to be like Jansher,' he replied. 'I want to be world champion.' He paused, and then added: 'Inshallah.' It was a word which would be repeated often over the next few days. In English, this Urdu word means simply 'God willing'.

That afternoon I was summoned to the Khan house. Jansher lived a few yards down a street which was filled with neat, clean apartment blocks all owned by the squash champion. I had to bang on the metal doors to his garden before Jahangir, one of Jansher's two personal policemen provided free of charge by the Pakistani Government in a mark of respect, opened up. The first thing I saw was Jahangir's Kalashnikov, so I held my arms up high in mock surrender. Over the course of the following few days Jahangir would accompany me frequently, always with his rifle by his side. This was supposed to comfort me, but it had the reverse effect. I've never had the use of a bodyguard before. You don't, do you, at least not in leafy Kent? I spent the whole time standing away from the direction the gun, was pointing. Just in case.

In front of me, seated out on the lawn, were most of the Khan family. I noticed that Jansher had exchanged the polo shirt and slacks he had worn the day before for a more traditional *kameez* and *shalwar*. With him were his brother Mohibullah, Mehboob and their various children, all playing on the large lawn.

Tea was served to us. It was the main social drink in the absence, of course, of alcohol in a Muslim society. It is taken in Peshawar with hot milk and poured out of a steaming jug with the tea, milk and sugar already mixed together. Almost always a selection of cakes was also served up. As we sipped our tea, another of Jansher's brothers, Atlas, arrived. He, like Jansher and Mohibullah, had been no mean squash player either. A former world amateur champion and four-times winner of the Singapore Open, Atlas had also worked for the united Khan cause of creating a professional world champion out of Jansher. To this day, he works as Jansher's conditioning coach whenever his brother is back home in Peshawar. He also has four sons, one of whom is the national Under-16 champion.

Atlas had a certain way of introducing himself. 'Hello, hello,' he would say. 'Atlas Khan, the world's strongest man.' He would then flex his biceps, hidden underneath his *kameez*, before adding: 'I hold up the world, you know.' He would repeat all this every time I saw him. After a few days, I would stop him short and say: 'I know, I know, you are the world's strongest man.'

An old man wearing a waistcoat and a hat came over. This was Bahadar Khan, the father of the three brothers, who enjoyed their total respect. I said hello to him in Urdu – at least I hope I said hello to him – and he smiled back. Bahadar had never played squash in his life. With 11 children to feed, he worked for the Pakistan Air Force. But when Mohibullah, his eldest son, had first begun to make ground as a squash player, Bahadar Khan had been quick to encourage him. He understood how squash provided just about the only way for many Pathans to make a good living.

Jansher was holding court. His nephews turned up, one by one, to greet the returning hero and all were met with the customary hug and handshake. I noticed how all of us present had to shake each other's hands, a friendly custom which, coming from a less demonstrative country such as England, I appreciated. Jansher's children sat on our laps, more tea was produced and the two policemen laid down their rifles, a little too close to me for my comfort, and joined us. Mohibullah said that young Imran wanted to play me after I'd played Jansher. I said that would be fine. No 14-year-old was going to get the better of me. Mohibullah just shook his head. 'There's no way you will beat Imran,' he said, in a manner which begged for no debate.

This sparked Jansher off. 'We will play on Sunday morning, then. I hope you will be ready for me, because I'm ready for you.' I decided to take the offensive line. 'No problem, Jansher, but do you think your knees will be able to take it? I mean, I can last for hours out on the court. Can you?' Gentle laughter was heard amongst the small gathering, and as I looked at Mohibullah and Atlas, both had expressions of gleeful anticipation on their faces.

Jansher asked me if I had liked the food. I said that it was wonderful, but too much. The Khans were being too kind to me. I then suggested that Jansher was fattening me up on purpose, so that I would be easy work on the squash court. 'We shall see,' came back the reply. 'We shall see.'

The sound of the mosque's loudspeakers changed the subject. 'You know,' Jansher said, as his voice turned serious, 'my talent is God-given. I thank God and give him credit all the time. For if you are kind to God, he is kind to you. It is the same for all the Khans. It helps, being a Muslim, if you want to be a champion. You can't drink alcohol. You can't fuck other women. And you must work very hard. You need the same discipline for your religion and your sport.'

I asked him if he feared his career might be drawing to an end. Jansher shook his head. 'No, I will recover from my injuries and I will win the World Open next December, no problem.' But what about Peter Nicol? 'He's a good player,' Jansher conceded. 'He can beat me when I am 80 per cent. But when I am 100 per cent, I win easily.'

The sun dipped beyond the horizon and the mosquitoes began to appear in force. Jansher yawned, a sign for everyone to stand up abruptly and bid each other good night. 'Tomorrow, I will take you to Nawakille,' Jansher promised. 'Then you will see for yourself how our success has come from God.'

That night I lay in bed, mulling over what had taken place that day. I decided I liked many aspects of a society I had never come across before. Primarily, the friendliness of the people was overwhelming. At times it was almost embarrassing for me. I noticed how the elderly and the children also deserved special attention, something that is sorely lacking in England.

Driving around this colourful town had proved to be some experience. There were no traffic lights, and so the assorted collection of cars, colourful buses with people hanging off the sides, three-wheel motorised rickshaws and mules and carts would all nudge forward simultaneously and negotiate, through force and pipping horns. It looked like utter chaos to me, but organised chaos. In a whole week I saw no accidents, although I will never know why. The drivers used their horns interminably. They would appear right behind someone in front and pip away until access was given. This practice is totally acceptable in Peshawar, all carried out in a friendly manner, but there is no way it would work in London or, I would think, most other cities. Road rage, it seems, has not yet reached North-West Frontier Province.

There was one final aspect I considered before falling into a deep sleep. The men used the term 'fucking bastard' frequently when describing someone who had irritated them. Now, this is strong language in any walk of life, but the Khans, bizarrely, translated this as nothing stronger than, perhaps, 'idiot'. Often I would hear them rabbiting on in either Urdu or Pushtu, long, rambling sentences intersected suddenly by the words 'fucking bastard'. Heaven knows what they say when they are really angry with someone.

On Saturday morning Jansher took me to Nawakille in one of his five cars. Mehboob came too, together with Jahangir and his friend, Mr Kalashnikov. Turning away from the main street, where a colourful bazaar was in full, commercial flow, we trundled across a bumpy, dusty track surrounded by houses made, primarily, out of mud. On stepping out of Jansher's jeep, a handful of children ran up to us. Within a few minutes this number had increased to as many as 40. Mehboob explained that it was a big moment for the villagers. Not only had the greatest squash champion returned home, but he was being accompanied by a red-haired, red-faced Englishman. Since Partition between India and Pakistan and the removal of the British in 1947, not too many Westerners walked the pothole-ridden roads of Nawakille.

Mehboob took us to his house, where he produced his own collection of Kalashnikovs. The house, as he readily admitted, was in a poor state. Made of mud, it had three rooms and so many family members living there that, when asked, Mehboob was unsure of the exact number. It was in some contrast to Jansher's abode in nearby Peshawar, but Mehboob and his family were happy. Within moments the house and its small yard became crammed with inquisitive children. The conditions were undoubtedly poor and dirty, yet everyone remained absurdly friendly. 'Come and take tea with me,' said one villager. 'No, come and have lunch with us,' said another.

Jansher seemed pleased to be showing me his roots. He explained that, as a boy, he had lived in the house we were now standing in. Far from being reluctant to reveal his former poverty and the current conditions of the vast majority of people living in Nawakille, Jansher was keen to reveal all. 'Now you can see,' he said, with a broad smile on his face. 'Eight world champions have come from Nawakille in 50 years. We have no squash courts here, no proper roads, we have nothing. It's impossible to imagine, isn't it? It must be an act of God.'

Looking around at the scene in front of me, it seemed like as good an explanation as any other. As I wrote down some notes, I noticed that the pen I was using had the Sheraton Hotel, Rio, stamped all over it. It had obviously returned with me from my stay in Brazil. One night in the Sheraton, so I discovered, cost the same amount of money that most residents of Nawakille earned in a year. Yet I was in a village of champions.

Most of the boys seemed to possess a squash racquet. All had dreams of becoming the next Jansher. Squash represented just about the only way of making money in this part of the world. Each day the boys would take the two-mile walk to the squash courts in Peshawar. Out of the 500 boys who practised daily, 450 would come from this village, play two to three hours of squash and then return to the poverty. One day, they all think, life will be different for them and for their families. Just like Jansher.

Nawakille had become a squash production line, but this was no accident. From the moment Hashim Khan returned to the village with the British Open title in 1952, life in Nawakille would be changed irrevocably. Here was a man who had proved that anything was possible. Haji Umra Khan, an old man who, in his time, used to play squash against Hashim despite being a tennis professional, recalled those days to me.

'When Hashim came back, the elders of the village all decided to use him as an example to others. They realised that if the village made a united effort, we could produce more champions who could help to make a living for everyone. It was the only way we could gain honour, money and glory. So, from that day until now, we have been throwing all our efforts behind the youngsters, in the hope that some may become champions themselves.'

Hashim went on to win the British Open seven times, before his younger brother, Azam, took over the mantle. Cousin Roshan followed, then nephew Mohibullah senior. Azam's son, Wasal, became world amateur champion, as did Atlas Khan. Mohibullah junior also includes this prestigious title amongst all his others, Nasrullah Khan coached Britain's Jonah Barrington to world-title glory and the great Jahangir Khan, the winner of 16 World and British Opens, also stems from this tiny village. Hashim's son, Sharif, became the king of the North American circuit and a whole host of other Khans also secured a number of other titles around the world. And then, of course, we have Jansher Khan.

Jansher, on listening to all this, joined in the conversation. 'People say that, after me, there is nobody else in Pakistan to follow. This might be true for a year or two, but I am convinced that we will have many more world champions from Nawakille.' I looked around at the horde of expectant young faces. Maybe one day, one of them would be the next Jansher Khan. It was very possible.

Haji Umra Khan was also the man who told a young Mohibullah, a promising tennis player, to switch to squash. Without this advice, Mohibullah might well have stuck to tennis and his younger brother Jansher might never have become a squash player, let alone world champion. It was initially down to the old man, then, that I was facing a sound and potentially humiliating beating from Jansher the following morning.

We eventually left Nawakille for the day and headed off to the Peshawar Club. I say eventually, because it took 20 minutes to say farewell to what seemed like the whole street, who, to a man, woman and boy, queued up to shake hands and have their photograph taken with either Jansher or, oddly enough, me. I found the two-hour visit strangely moving, not only because of the inspirational story amidst the poverty, but also for the genuine kindness from people who, on the face of it, are disadvantaged. They, however, do not see it this way. They are happy with their lot and happy in the knowledge that, Inshallah, Nawakille will remain the centre of world squash.

On the drive to the Club, Jansher and Mehboob talked of the impending game against their English guest. 'I am playing for the honour of my people,' Jansher said to his brother-in-law, in a loud and purposeful voice. 'I cannot be seen to play badly. I must make sure that the Englishman returns to his country as a beaten man.' He was only joking – at least, I presumed he was only joking – but even this made uncomfortable listening. Jahangir was in the back of the jeep next to me and, as he gripped his rifle, he looked at me and laughed, as if to say that I should enjoy the day, because tomorrow I would die.

Built in 1862, the Club in Peshawar was the social centre of the British army. It was here, at the turn of the century, that squash courts were constructed and it was here that a young Hashim Khan first fell under the spell of the game. He would watch British officers play from above and then return the ball whenever it was hit out of the court. After a while the officers paid Hashim to do this, money that came in useful back home in Nawakille. As he watched, so Hashim learned all about the flight and bounce of the ball. When the officers retired, Hashim used to jump down and play squash by himself. Within a few months he had become unbeatable. 'Even back in the village, Hashim used to find a bare space of wall and hit a ball, or a rolled-up piece of cloth, against it with his hand,' Haji Umra Khan had told me.

I took my shoes and socks off and walked on to the stone floor of the old court. It now had a roof, but in Hashim's day, when he used to play bare-footed and in the heat of the midday sun, there had been no protection. It must have been incredibly tough to play in such conditions, but this is the very reason why Hashim would prove to be unbeatable as a squash professional around the world. His stamina and strength were, so everyone told me, unsurpassed by anyone.

Rahimullah Yusefzai had joined me from his office in Peshawar. I was interviewing one or two of the main characters for a BBC Radio 4 documentary that would be aired in December 1998, and Rahimullah was helping out as a producer and general guide. We decided to interview Mehboob in the middle of Hashim's old court. Earlier I had related what Paolo Autuori, the coach at Flamengo, had told me when he was asked why Brazilians are such naturally gifted footballers. 'A bird will always fly. Swimming comes naturally to a fish. And a Brazilian will always be able to play football,' he said. As I thrust the microphone in front of Mehboob's face, I asked him a similar question. 'What is it about the Pathans that makes them so dominant in squash?'

Mehboob cleared his throat, stuck his mouth down towards the microphone and answered: 'Well, you know, Ian, birds know how to swim, fish know how to fly and Pathans know how to play squash.'

Jansher came up with a more understandable offering later. 'We are Pathans,' he explained. 'We are born fighters and we do not like to lose in anything we do, whether it is war or squash. We never give up, you see. We also firmly believe that our talent has been given to us by God. You saw Nawakille for yourself. But Hashim also provided inspiration for everyone else to follow. If he could do it, then why not others?'

And so they followed, one after another. Some of these champions were present that night back at Jansher's house, where he was holding a function for his neighbours, who were celebrating the first birthday of their child on his vast lawn. It had nothing to do with Jansher, who pretty much kept himself away from the proceedings. It was purely an act of neighbourly help, another typical aspect of life in Peshawar. But most of the Khans were there in any case, just to talk, sip tea and enjoy the balmy evening.

'Hello, hello,' said a familiar voice. 'Atlas Khan, strongest man in the world.' And with that, Atlas shook my hand vigorously and introduced me to Flt. Lt. Gaulam Ali, who, a few years back, had been the physical trainer for Mohibullah junior and Jansher, as well as Qamar Zaman (Khan), the world's number-one player back in the late 1970s.

'Jansher used to train for 16 hours every day as a teenage boy,' Gaulam told me, as festivities began inside the large marquee in the garden. 'He used to run along the Bara river, where the sand on his bare feet helped to prevent him from becoming a flat-footed player. His willpower and dedication were truly incredible. This is what makes him different from all the other champions, even Jahangir and Qamar. He never gave up, even when he seemed close to death. When he finished training with me, he was too weak to tear a piece of bread in half.'

Jansher heard the latter part of the conversation. 'I had many reasons,' he said, rather quietly. Was he referring to his brother, Mohibullah? 'Yes, of course. When Mohibullah went to prison I was so upset I thought about giving up squash completely. But he asked me to become champion and so I did, for me, for my family's name, and especially for Mohibullah. It helped to take some of the pain away.'

Some of the children queued up for Jansher's autograph. Then, to my surprise, they asked for mine too. As I signed their books, scraps of paper and even hands, I remembered the boys in Rio de Janeiro. At this rate children from all over the world would possess my signature, without ever knowing who I really was.

A journalist from the *Daily Jang*, one of Pakistan's national newspapers, turned up to speak to Jansher and then, so I discovered, to me. 'There is much interest in your game tomorrow,' he said. 'I will be there to cover it. Do you think you will win?'

He obviously had not quite grasped what I was trying to do. Adopting a serious tone, I explained that it would be difficult for me, because I was injured and I was playing away from home on Jansher's favoured court. He held all the cards and it would be an upset if he lost. But we would just have to wait and see. The reporter left with his notebook, leaving me to reconsider my verdict. An upset? It would be a bloody miracle!

As Jansher's neighbours piled kebabs, chicken and nan breads on to my plate, I realised that Jansher had been missing for some time. Suddenly I heard my name being shouted. Looking up towards his house, I saw Jansher waving from his opened bathroom window, brushing his teeth and preparing for bed. 'Ian, I am going to sleep now. I have an important game of squash in the morning. A very important game of squash. So I must be ready. Goodnight.'

I looked at my watch and then down at my plateful of food. Jansher was taking this too seriously for my liking. Far too seriously. I decided I ought to be professional about this and also retire to my bed. The time was 10.30. I would be playing the greatest squash player ever in 12 hours' time. I, too, would need a good night's sleep.

I did not get one. At first my state of mind kept me awake. Just what would be the outcome of tomorrow's game? Would Jansher humiliate me? Could my various injuries withstand the onslaught? I pictured Jansher's forehand. I imagined his backhand. I thought about his volleys, shots that all produced the cracking sound of a whip each time the ball rebounded off the wall. I saw myself, huffing and puffing, gasping and sweating, chasing the ball in vain from corner to corner, whilst Jansher stood serenely in the centre of the court, in total control of the proceedings. Then I caught sight of Jansher's piercing eyes, fixed so firmly on me that I felt as if he was boring a hole into my body with them. These eyes reveal everything, and then nothing. They are the eyes of a proud, ruthless and arrogant man. They are the eyes that do not accept a blundering English buffoon on court. Most of all, they are the eyes that will not accept defeat. They are, when Jansher chooses them to be so, the most haunting pair of eyes I have ever seen.

I must have been in the last throes of consciousness when one of the worst noises imaginable reverberated around my left ear, the high, whining buzz of a mosquito. We have all been here before, haven't we? One tiny insect has the power to wreck a sane human being's night and his state of mind. I had not heard or seen one in my room since I had arrived in Peshawar, but tonight, of all nights, a mosquito came to wreak havoc.

Mosquitoes are clever insects. Not only do they have the teasing habit of flying right up to your ear in the dark, so that you can hear them but not see them, they also have the admirable ability of escaping from tight spots, even when you are convinced you have caught them with an uppercut from your training shoe. Apart from my various inoculations back in London, I was also required to take malaria tablets, especially now that a new and deadlier strain of the disease had broken out in parts of the world. There was therefore no way I could sleep with such a killer in my room.

The lights went on, full consciousness was instantly regained and I began to hunt, moving stealthily like a cheetah in the African plains before launching an attack on an unsuspecting gazelle. I saw the mosquito once, hovering below the ceiling before settling. My training shoe was set for a direct hit until the mosquito's radar system warned him and he disappeared from view, leaving the shoe to rebound back down harmlessly on to the carpet.

I know this sounds ridiculous, but the longer this went on, the more I turned into a psychopath. I was playing Jansher Khan, for God's sake, in the morning, and I was being kept awake by a flaming mosquito. I saw what I thought was a mosquito on the bathroom door handle and squashed it with a right jab of my training shoe. But as I went to bed I had my doubts. It did not look exactly like a mosquito to me, and it failed to move an inch when my shoe bore down on it. Very unlike the blood-sucker I had been chasing.

He waited until I was almost asleep and struck again, just above my ear. I was out of my bed in a split second, shoe in hand and lights on. This mosquito was a clever one all right. But I was clever too. The bedroom was not big enough for the two of us and, as the good guy in this battle, I knew my time would eventually come. He settled once more on the ceiling. I positioned myself immediately below him, took a couple of practice aims and then launched my training shoe upwards. This time my Nike Air was straight, true and very fast. Both shoe and mosquito fell to the ground before I finished off the job with aplomb. I retired for a final time. It was 2.30 in the morning by now. Eight hours later I would be facing Jansher Khan.

Quddus woke me up in the morning with a cup of tea. 'Today you play Jansher, yes?' he asked. I nodded, as I scraped the grit out of my eyes and told him about my battle with the mosquito. Quddus left the room, laughing aloud. When I emerged from the shower, Mohibullah had appeared. As I changed and performed a variety of stretching exercises, as much for effect in front of Jansher's brother as for my well-being, we talked.

For a man who had seen not only his squash career taken away from him when he was still challenging strongly for all titles but also six years of his life in a strange prison in a strange country, Mohibullah seemed a remarkably content man. Now 42 years old, he appeared anything but plagued by the memories of an ordeal which had begun when drugs were planted in his suitcase. How bad had it been for him?

'At first, it was terrible,' he replied. 'I had brought shame to my family and to my people, and I knew my career was over. I could speak very little English and I could not understand what had happened to me.'

But surely his family knew Mohibullah was innocent? 'Yes, but others only had my word for it. Even though the people involved have since admitted putting the drugs in my case back in Pakistan, I think I am still remembered more for going to prison than for being a squash champion.'

What saved Mohibullah's sanity inside Dartmoor was Jansher. 'I knew he could be world champion and, now that my chance had gone, I was determined to make sure that Jansher succeeded. He came to me and was very upset. I told him not to be. He must be strong; he must study Jahangir Khan's game and learn how to beat him. He must become world champion, for me and for our family. When he won his first world title in 1987, I cried with happiness. After that, nothing upset me in prison. My brother had become the champion of the world.'

I felt sorry for Mohibullah, although he did not seek my sympathy. He was happy with his lot, despite the injustice of six years' imprisonment. Like Mehboob, Jansher's success had fulfilled him. Now, as he led me over from the guest house to his own house, I felt like the convict on death row, making his last walk to the gallows. 'Just try your best,' was all Mohibullah could come up with as Jansher appeared, dressed in squash shirt, shorts and trainers.

I sensed a seriousness about the man as he barely acknowledged me on his way to the car. His manner had suddenly become urgent and intense. The friendliness of the night before had temporarily gone. A ruthless executioner had appeared before me. On arriving at the Pakistan Air Force Squash Complex, I noticed a crowd of people milling outside the entrance, including a few photographers. This, I thought to myself as I signed a number of autographs for a group of children, was getting out of hand. Just who did these people think I was? Rahimullah Yusefzai, who was also present to witness the execution, told me that there were many there who genuinely did not know the reasons for this game. 'Word has got round that you are the British champion and you have come to Peshawar to challenge Jansher,' he said. In which case, I thought, they would be in for quite a shock.

Emerging on to the court, where Jansher was already smacking the ball against the wall with consummate ease, I turned round and looked upwards towards the gallery of spectators. There before me sat many members of the Khan family, including Mohibullah, Mehboob, Atlas Khan, aka the strongest man in the world, and Qamar Zaman. There too were all the champion children, like Imran and Shazad Khan, Mohibullah's national Under-19 champion, and even Wasal Khan, Azam's London-based son, the British Under-19 champion, who was in Peshawar for the week with his wife and daughter Carla. Right up in the corner of the gallery sat the *Daily Jang* man with a couple of other sports writers, poised to record the proceedings.

Jansher and I decided to play American rules, which meant that each set would be played up to 15 points, with a point awarded to the winner of each rally, regardless of who was serving. That way, I reckoned, I stood more chance of gaining a point. We shook hands.

Mehboob announced that he would be the match referee and scorer. A hushed, expectant silence fell from upstairs in the gallery, and then we began.

It did not start well for the English challenger. I served as fiercely as I could and, within a few seconds, found myself slamming my body against the back wall in a vain attempt to return Jansher's shot. 0–1. Jansher served, somehow sending his ball so close to the wall that I wondered whether he had a remote-control system under his shirt. I missed the ball with my attempted volley and cracked the wall instead. 0–2. And so this went on. Occasionally I would force Jansher to the back of the court, taking position in the centre in the mistaken belief that I now had control of the rally. Instead Jansher's return shot would pass by me like a bullet. Sometimes I managed to get these returns back, only to set Jansher up for the kill. Other times I reacquainted myself with the wall.

In the gallery the silence had been replaced by a quiet but constant murmur. I could see, out of the corner of my eye, people leaning over and whispering to each other. Maybe they had reached the conclusion that if this was the British champion, heaven help British squash. Enough was enough. The comeback would start, and it would start right now.

The 0–10 score quickly became 2–10. First, I stunned Jansher with a drop shot so perfect that not even a legend of the game could make a telling reply. Okay, so it happened to be a lucky shot and a total mishit of the wooden part of the racquet that resulted in the ball falling on to the only part of the wall beyond Jansher's reach, but I was not going to own up to it. A round of applause echoed around the court, and even Jansher acknowledged the shot. 'Beautiful,' he said. 'Beautiful.' I gave him a nonchalant look. Plenty more where that came from, Mr Jansher Khan.

I served again, Jansher returned, I hit a forehand that sent the ball into the champion's backhand corner, and his reply forced the ball out of play. Ha! Now I was rolling, and he was rocking. Jansher gave me a look, positioned himself ready for the next shot and then returned my serve with such force that, by the time I saw the ball, it had bounced twice in the far corner of the court. 2–11. Suddenly I felt tired. Whilst Jansher remained calm and serene, I was sweating profusely. Within a couple of minutes he had taken the first set 15–2, despatching the ball with such thoroughness that I wondered how anyone on this earth could live with the man on a squash court, let alone me.

At the end of the first set I was aware that while Jansher stood on the court patiently, without a drop of sweat in evidence, I towelled my face, arms and legs and swallowed large mouthfuls of water. A visiting spectator, unaware of the scores and the gulf in class, would have had no difficulty in telling which of the two players was leading. One was tall, lean and athletic. The other was fuller in figure, red in the face and completely out of breath.

The second set began like the first. Jansher leapt to a 7–0 lead. During one point I tried to hit him, albeit gently, with the ball in order to win a point. This may not appear to be in the spirit of the game, but I was desperate to avoid a total whitewash. In any case, I missed him by a couple of inches and Jansher took the point.

Then I managed to win a further two successive points, first with a legitimate drop shot from the back of the court, then with a second, disguised one from the front. Both shots prompted loud applause from the audience and acknowledgements from my sporting opponent. That is one of the beauties of playing sport. If you can play any game at a half-decent level, you can produce something that even the world's best might be happy with. In my case, this may happen once in a whole game. In Jansher's case, this can occur at will. The 7–2 scoreline soon became 10–2, at which point Jansher suddenly stopped, held his knee and announced that he had played long enough. He was planning to have both knees operated on in a fortnight's time and did not want to take any more risks.

We shook hands, had further photographs taken and then chatted to members of the Khan family who emerged beside the court. Now, I am not sure whether this constitutes a win for me by default. After all, if a player retires hurt during a game, does this not mean the opponent is the winner? Besides, maybe Jansher was growing tired and sensed that I was on the verge of launching a dramatic and telling comeback. Maybe not. It was an argument I decided not to pursue, however, certainly not when surrounded by the Khans in the middle of a squash complex in Peshawar.

The Khan boys were queuing up to play me. They must have liked what they had just seen. Despite now being drenched in sweat, I agreed to give first Farhan, Mehboob's Under-11 champion son, a set, followed by Imran, Mohibullah's son, the national Under-14 champion. I approached the set with Farhan as if it was nothing more than a practice session. Before I knew it, my 11–8 lead had been transformed into a 12–15 defeat. Even if I had tried, I am sure Farhan, at the ripe old age of 11, would have given me a very hard game. Imran was a different story altogether. You could see his determination to claim a prized English scalp and he started our set like a young man possessed. It did not help that every last ounce of energy had left my body, so I was quite pleased just to get the ordeal over with, even if I lost 15–8.

As I left the squash complex I was not quite sure how to sum up my performance against Jansher. The other sets were unimportant, but the match against my host meant a great deal to me. It was clear that, in Pakistan, to play against a man like Jansher was a great honour. A 15–2, 10–2 scoreline seemed pretty conclusive, but the Khans, and even the *Daily Jang* man, were all very positive about my efforts. 'You are a good player,' Mohibullah said, more out of kindness than truth. 'You run too much, but you have some nice shots,' said Atlas. Even Jansher, a great deal friendlier now that the match was over, joined in. 'You did well,' he said. 'You won four points off me.'

Perhaps I did, I thought, as I was dropped off at the guest house to shower, sleep and change. But how hard did he really try? I convinced myself that my points were genuine and felt better for the decision. Delusion is not always a bad thing in life.

In the late afternoon I turned up at Jansher's house. His two policemen were there to greet me and they found it very amusing when I started to speak to them in Pushtu, the regional language. Atlas Khan and his sons had been teaching me a few words the day before, concentrating on parts of the body. I was happy to show off my new-found knowledge of Pushtu. In typically childish fashion, the strongest man in the world had taught me the Pushtu word for penis, which, when repeated to the policemen, was met with loud and raucous laughter. Jahangir's colleague – I never managed to grab his name – began to show off his limited knowledge of the English language. 'London,' he would say, followed by 'hello, goodbye, okay, thank you very much'.

Then he leant over, kissed my hand and said, in a rather disturbing way: 'I love you.' I gave him the benefit of the doubt and presumed he was getting his words a bit muddled, but, as I edged away to another chair, it hardly improved a day that had already seen me thrashed by his boss on the squash court.

Jansher appeared in his regulation *kameez* and *shalwar* and announced that he wanted to show me around his house. Walking across the garden he told me how he owned 50 properties, a shoe factory and clothes shops. Inside the house I met his wife, Naseem, again, whom I had not seen since arriving at Peshawar Airport. There then followed an extraordinary process in which Jansher showed me every single room in his house, from the trophy-adorned main living-room to his bedroom, his bathroom and even his toilets. At one point he opened a door and Mohibullah, who was lying on his bed watching television, leapt up in surprise. 'That's Mohibullah's bedroom,' Jansher said. Later on he insisted on fetching some keys and opening a cupboard full of children's toys. 'That's a toy cupboard,' he informed me, just in case this had not registered.

At the end of my guided tour I felt like saying: 'Well, I have two more houses to go and see, but I'm definitely interested.' I did not, of course. Instead, I just told him how nice his property was.

That evening we were all to go to his uncle's house back in Nawakille. Jansher, Naseem, who covered her face with a veil to hide herself from the night air, Ayaz, Sidra, Sana, Rabia, who sat on her father's knee while he drove the mile-long journey, and I all piled into his jeep. 'You can't do this in England, no?' Jansher asked me, as I looked nervously at Rabia.

His uncle's house was as basic as any in Nawakille. Made of mud, it consisted of just two cluttered rooms. We all crowded in one, where a black-and-white television was broadcasting a programme in Urdu. Despite the conditions, it was a happy household. His uncle had just returned from making Hadj, a pilgrimage to Mecca, the birthplace of Muhammad, and he was in an understandably joyous mood. He insisted on taking my bag and sitting me down next to Jansher, who stretched his long, wiry frame across the floor.

Within moments a plastic sheet had been placed on the floor and a mountain of food was brought in. Once again, Melmastia was in force. They may be poor in Nawakille, and indeed in many parts of Peshawar, but there was always food, and good food, on the table or, in this case, on the floor. His uncle gestured to Jansher's family and to me. 'Eat,' he said. And so we did. As I helped myself to some chappali kebabs, curry, rice and vegetables, I looked around and surveyed the scene. We were all sitting cross-legged on the floor, eating food as good as any I had tasted, using pieces of nan bread instead of cutlery. I had eaten a few curries in my time, I reckoned, but never in such natural and ethnic conditions.

While Jansher conferred with his uncle and cousins, I talked with Naseem. She was born in west London and had lived there for the first ten years of her life. She had met Jansher at a squash tournament. 'I was interested to see him play. Then, after I saw him, I was interested just in the man. But I don't think he was keen on me.'

Well, he must have been, I suggested. He married you and now you have four children. 'That's true,' she giggled, rather coyly. 'And now he wants more. Maybe two more children. But I've told him he will just have to wait until I am ready.'

Later that night, my last in Peshawar, the whole street had a power cut. People poured out on to the dirt track, conversed in a neighbourly manner and watched as two hapless engineers went to work up a nearby pylon. I felt like any other neighbour, with my new-found knowledge of Pushtu and my local fame, earned by playing squash against the master.

In the morning Jansher was leaving for Lahore and I planned to visit the Khyber Pass, in the name of further research. We sipped a last tea together in his garden and Jansher talked of how he hoped his son, Ayaz, would follow his lead and become a squash champion. If not, he reasoned, then surely one of Mohibullah's, Atlas's or Mehboob's sons would keep the Khan flag flying. Or maybe one of the two further children he wanted, I suggested.

'How do you know that?' he asked, a little sharply.

'Because Naseem told me last night,' I answered.

A broad, possibly even self-conscious smile appeared all over his face. 'Ah, you and Naseem talked,' he said. 'It's true. I love children. I hope, Inshallah, I have more.'

With that he left for the airport. He had shaken my hand all week on greeting me, but this time, on departing, he hugged me. He added that he would provide me with Jahangir, the policeman, for my trip to the Khyber Pass. 'You might need him,' he said, as he waved and drove away.

I was already feeling uneasy about my proposed Khyber Pass trip. It was something I had to do, especially as it was less than an hour's drive away, but tales of how the tribes up in the mountains, who enjoyed autonomy from the government, tended to kidnap tourists and hold them for ransom were far from comforting.

Rahimullah Yusefzai hardly helped matters. 'You would be a prized catch,' he told me the day before. 'You don't get too many Westerners with your colourings in the pass, and if they knew you worked for the BBC, that would make them very interested.'

Terrific! Rahimullah, I think, meant it as a compliment. I did not quite translate it that way. Still, it had to be done, so we obtained a special permit from the town's political agent – who needed records of foreigners visiting the pass, just in case they failed to return later in the day – and we headed off into the wilderness. *En route* we picked up a special guard, provided by the political agent. He came armed with an AK47 Kalashnikov and was required because of the dangers and sensitivity over drugs and guns in the region.

As Jahangir drove, Rahimullah continued to talk about the dangers. 'Now we have entered the tribal areas,' he explained. 'From now on, we could be kidnapped at any time.'

'What, here?' I asked, as I looked around from the back of the car.

'Oh yes,' said Rahimullah. 'Here, or anywhere else. It doesn't happen too often. But it does happen.'

'But we have an armed guard, Rahimullah,' I reasoned.

'Oh, there's no way he will shoot that rifle,' he answered. 'If he did that, he would be killed. No, if they want to kidnap us, then they can. There is nothing we can do about it.'

He did not seem in the slightest bit bothered. Neither did Jahangir, who, driving the car, looked at my uncomfortable expression in the wing mirror and laughed. 'Ian is a little worried,' he announced in Pushtu. Rahimullah translated this to me.

'No, no, I'm fine,' I insisted, but my face told a different story.

After a series of checkpoints, camel trains and small frontier villages, we entered the heart of the pass, which was littered by old British forts and pickets. Sides of the mountains had steel plaques revealing the names of a series of British army regiments. Afghan boys rode by on bicycles, towing two more. They were making the 60-mile journey from Kabul to Peshawar in order to sell the bikes and thought nothing of the feat. It made me wonder, if you placed these lads on a racing bike, presented them with the relevant attire and entered them in a professional cycling race, how they would fare.

The bikes were, technically, contraband, but the border guards turned a blind eye. Compared to the large opium fields nearby, the bikes were harmless. As we reached the last point of our journey, we all left the car and walked up the side of a hill to gaze at the scenery.

There, before us, stood the Afghan/Pakistan border. In the distance the 'White Mountains' of Afghanistan could be seen quite clearly, in all their snow-capped splendour. Behind us, much of the Khyber Pass remained as it has done over the centuries, the gateway between Northern Asia and the Indian subcontinent, and a crucial strategical point.

It may seem odd to link all this to the squash-playing Khans of Peshawar and Nawakille, but in order to place the last piece of the jigsaw, I needed to see the Khyber Pass. The great armies of the world have tried to quell these people. Alexander the Great and Genghis Khan were no match for the Pathans. Nor were the Huns, the Turks, the Aryans or the British army. The Pathans remain the one undefeated tribe in the history of war.

The Khans will tell you that many have now replaced the rifle with another potent weapon, the squash racquet. Where they once fought like demons in the hills, they now do the same on the squash court. A rare defeat must be avenged. An opponent, even an opponent like me the day before, is the enemy and must be beaten. More often than not, they are.

To see the Khyber Pass is some experience. To return to Peshawar, and away from kidnappers' country, provides a moment of great relief, which, in the company of Rahimullah, Jahangir and our AK47-carrying guard, I failed to disguise. They found the whole episode highly amusing. I was just glad to share a last tea with Atlas Khan before heading off for Peshawar Airport.

That night and, indeed, the following morning, the standing of Jansher Khan in Pakistan proved, once more, to be effective. The Midway House Hotel in Karachi was full. The hotel manager apologised for the inconvenience, but added that there was nothing he could do.

As a desperate last throw of the dice, I informed him that I had been a guest of Jansher Khan, I had played a game of squash against him in Peshawar and I had used the Midway the week before with the Khan family.

'One moment, sir,' the manager said and scuttled off. He returned a minute later. 'Follow me.' We went up to the first floor, where the manager led me into a large double room.

After a good night's sleep I arrived at the PIA check-in desk at Karachi Airport to be informed that, contrary to my belief, my seat had not been confirmed, I was on the waiting list and the flight back to London was completely full.

I used the Jansher Khan line again. 'Are you a squash player too?' the check-in clerk asked.

I thought about this for a split second and answered: 'Yes.' It was not exactly a lie. I am a squash player, albeit a very average one. And I did play the great man in Peshawar. The check-in clerk fell into a deep discussion with a nearby senior figure. They talked in a close huddle and every so often would both turn round and look at me. Eventually the check-in clerk sat down again on his chair.

'What would you prefer, sir, a window or an aisle seat?'

This, as they say, is not something you should try at home. In Pakistan it is different. Jansher Khan and his family are revered. He and his predecessors have created a force, from the social and economic ruins of Nawakille, like no other the world of sport has ever seen. I thought I knew this story before I came to Pakistan. I did not.

And as I was transported back across Asia and Europe to my own country, my own people and my home, I realised how fortunate I had just been to experience this for myself. Those four points against Jansher Khan in Peshawar, in full view of the most incredible sporting family on the planet, will remain forever etched in my memory.

KENYA

Train Hard, Win Easy

I had little time to relate my adventures to my wife and children, carefully playing down the Khyber Pass dangers and playing up my efforts on the squash court in Peshawar. Within days I would be off and away again, this time into deepest Africa performing a sport which required a totally different form of fitness and technique and which, quite frankly, had been one I had spent much of my life performing with little love.

I used to hate running, even though I found myself doing it rather a lot. Most sports contain the vital ingredient of moving your legs forward at a quicker-than-walking pace. I've never minded doing this with a bat in my hand, or a ball in my arms or at my feet, but with nothing else to occupy your mind, running itself was, well, boring, hard work and no fun.

Maybe I am scarred by the horrors of my annual school cross-country run, staged each February around the grounds of Burghley Park in Lincolnshire, where the famous three-day equestrian event is held, when the ground is at its muddiest, dirtiest and unwelcoming worst. I can't recall many of my friends looking forward to this dreadful afternoon either. If we could find a way to cut a few corners out of the five-mile course, we would. One year a few of us attempted to record the slowest time ever, in the hope that the teachers, who patrolled the grounds like prison guards, would give up and go home. Then we, too, would return to a warm house somewhere, regardless of how many miles we had covered in the race. But no, the teachers stayed until the bitter end, when the late winter's day had turned into a gloomy twilight and the rain had turned to sleet.

I can still feel those hot baths after the race had finished. My legs were so red and raw, so cold and so plastered in mud and rain, that they positively fizzled as they were submerged in the water, tingling like an electric shock to the extent that it often took three attempts before I could fully settle back into the bath and close my eyes.

In my last year at school a strange thing happened. Perhaps struck by a belated attack of pride – after all, I did well in all my other school sports – I actually tried. I adopted a tactic that, to my great surprise, worked out rather well, a strategy that I would continue to use in later life. At the start I sprinted, just so that I could say I led the race. At any moment I expected a horde of eager runners to swoop past me, but as the feet turned into yards, and the yards turned into a mile, I found myself still out in front. My 'devastating' turn of speed at the start seemed to have blown most of the others away, and although seven caught me in the last couple of miles, and I vomited within moments of crossing the finish line, I recorded an eighth place in my final school cross-country race. 'Nice to see you can run when you want to,' observed one knowing teacher.

When I was 20 and playing three games of squash a week at my university halls of residence in London, a friend entered me into the Lambeth Half Marathon, a 13-and-a-bit-mile race that meandered through the streets and parks of south London. Young and foolish, I agreed to do it, but when I received the entry form it asked me to write down my fastest time for the distance. As I had never staggered further than five miles in my life, I took what I thought was an educated guess.

On arriving at the race start, I discovered that the time I had stated on the entry form was good enough to place me in the top ten. I found myself in the company of serious runners, who belonged to clubs with such athletic names as the Herne Hill Harriers and who looked the part, with their headbands and weedy bodies, puffed-out cheeks and on-the-spot jogs. Bizarrely, a London radio station interviewed me about my chances, and the other 'top' athletes shook my hand and wished me luck.

I decided to adopt the same tactic I had used with some success at school. As the start gun exploded, I sprinted at full pelt, and even though it was somewhat unnerving to discover my fellow 'élite' athletes jogging beside me, I nevertheless led 3,000 runners for half a mile. As is often the case with any marathon or half marathon, those runners at the back would spend the first three or four minutes of the race walking, until the numbers had thinned out sufficiently to provide enough space to run. By then the rest of us were long gone.

Of course it would not last. Fitter men than me began to teem past, prompting a total change in strategy. As anything beyond five miles was alien territory, and as I could not imagine me actually completing the course, I slowed right down to a slow jogging pace to preserve some energy. A friend of mine jogged by, chanting in mock fashion the words of the Queen song 'Another One Bites the Dust', but as the miles stuttered past and the crowds in the street gave encouraging cheers, I discovered that I was not only still going strong, I was also beginning to enjoy myself. At the 11-mile stage I began to pick up speed again, passing my Freddie Mercury-quoting friend, who by then was wobbling in an exhausted, inebriated manner, before sprinting across the finish line in around 300th place.

Six months later a university colleague of mine showed me a small paperback book with a photo of the Lambeth Half Marathon on the front cover. The book was entitled *Fitness: Training Tips for Distance Runners*, and there, in one of the most blatant cases of fraud I can think of, was me, pumping my arms, with my head back, ahead of the field.

I have been running ever since, at least in spurts, and I still do not particularly enjoy it. Occasionally I am able to forget about the physical exertions of running and sort out a problem or two in my head whilst pounding the pavements, but normally I spend my time passing self-appointed landmarks and milestones and working out how much further I need to go. I do it because running is not only free of charge but also the simplest form of exercise, where no facilities are required and where you start and finish the chore the moment you reach your front door.

Watching athletics, however, is a far more enjoyable pastime, and you will not find a more avid viewer than me when it comes to an event such as the Olympics. I have been fortunate enough to have been present at a number of Olympic Games and to have seen some of the great, or misguided, athletes at work. I was there to see the unnatural Ben Johnson break the records and the rules in Seoul. I was there to see Linford Christie defy the odds and Father Time in Barcelona. And I was there to see Michael Johnson burn up the track in Atlanta.

Throughout these Olympics – indeed, since the late 1960s – a small, poor but immensely proud country has dominated middle- and long-distance events, throwing up new and unheard-of names seemingly at will to take on and beat the best the rest of the world can muster. That country is Kenya, and from the moment Kip Keino appeared at altitude in Mexico City to see off the American favourite, Jim Ryan, in the Olympic 1500 metres final with his smooth, languid stride and his engaging smile, the Kenyans have created a production line of world-beaters.

Just how have they managed to do this? And just how could I possibly hope to save face by running with these boys? I always felt I stood a chance of redeeming myself playing football in Brazil and squash in Pakistan. Those are sports I can play. But running? Long-distance? In Kenya? Then I remembered the Lambeth Half Marathon. It was hard work, but the finish line provided an incredibly sweet moment. Maybe Kenya could do the same for me? Maybe not. Either way, I would not know unless I tried.

I contacted Kim McDonald at his Teddington office in south-west London. McDonald is an athletics agent who specialises in middle- and long-distance running. This invariably means his client list is predominantly Kenyan, boasting the likes of Moses Kiptanui, three-times World 3,000 metres steeplechase champion, and Daniel Komen, a five-times world record holder. He listened attentively to my proposal, paused long enough for me to try and figure out whether he thought I was some sort of sado-masochist, and then announced that he could arrange for me to join his group's training camp at Nyahururu, a three-hour drive north-west from Nairobi.

He needed to know, however, if I intended to actually feature in a race. If so, what, and where? The what part was not too difficult to decide. The Kenyans have been winning Olympic, World and Commonwealth gold medals from the 800 metres up to the 10,000 metres, as well as the world's premier marathons, road races and cross-country races, but there is one event in which Kenya have proved so strong that it is a wonder nobody has reported them to the Monopolies Commission.

When it comes to the 3,000 metres steeplechase, no other country gets a look-in. Not content with winning all six Olympic titles they have competed in since 1968 (Kenya boycotted the 1976 and 1980 Olympics), Kenyans have also taken every world title and every Commonwealth gold medal since 1974. As a rule, compatriots usually fill the second and third placings as well, resulting in clean sweeps for the Kenyans. In 1996, nine out of the first ten steeplechasers in the world rankings came from Kenya. Technically, there are better hurdlers. Kip Keino once described his hurdling style as that of an old horse, but it did not prevent him from winning the 1972 Olympic gold medal in Munich in only his fourth-ever attempt at the discipline. What the Kenyans may lack in textbook hurdling style, though, they more than make up for in the strength and stamina required for the distance, the speed and the added task of hurdling.

Despite never having attempted the 3,000 metres steeplechase, I told McDonald this would be my race. 'Well, if that's what you want to do,' he replied, nearly disguising his doubts. He gave me the telephone number of David Okeyo, the Kenyan Amateur Athletic Association's Secretary, and suggested I try to persuade him to enter me into a Kenyan athletics meeting.

Okeyo listened to my impassioned pleas, asked me to repeat the other sports I had either completed or planned to participate in, and then, without a further moment's consideration, told me it sounded like a wonderful idea. Sending me a long fax listing all the domestic events in Kenya, he suggested I plump for the Kenyan AAA's weekend meeting at Kapsabet. I asked him why. 'Because you will be running in the heart of Kenya's athletics country,' Okeyo replied. 'Every famous Kenyan runner has featured there, from Kip Keino to Daniel Komen, and all of them live nearby. If you really want to get a feel for our country and our sport, then you must run at Kapsabet.'

My next call was to Ibrahim Hussein, the Kapsabet meeting promoter and organiser. Ibrahim happens to be the first African to have won both the New York and the Boston Marathon. In fact, he won both the Boston and the Honolulu Marathon three times each, as well as a host of road races, and therefore dollars, on the American circuit. Now he was emerging as an influential local and national sports politician, both in his role as chairman of the local Nandi District Amateur Athletic Association and as assistant secretary in Kenya's national federation.

Like David Okeyo, Ibrahim was very supportive. 'Thank you for choosing to run with us,' he said. 'You can enter the 3,000 metres steeplechase, no problem. In fact, I will give you a bye straight into the final. I will tell the Kenyan media about you and this will help me promote the meeting.' It was the first hint of things to come. I stressed to Ibrahim that there was more chance of Elvis Presley winning such a race than me, but there was to remain a certain belief in western Kenya that a top British athlete was coming to town.

'It will be good for the other athletes, and for the crowd, to see a British runner,' Ibrahim added before hanging up.

'Yes,' I thought. 'If they fancy a laugh.'

I left for Kenya just five days after returning from playing squash with Jansher Khan in Peshawar. This, in itself, posed a problem or two. Although you need great stamina for both disciplines, the fitness requirements for squash and long-distance running are very different. To play squash, you need to be able to accelerate, like a car, from 0 to 60 in a few seconds. You must have the ability to turn at acute angles at speed and you must be able to stretch and bend. To run any distance, and particularly with Kenyans at altitude, you need to possess great strength in your legs, your lungs and your head. The mental side of running is a crucial element. What you do not need is ligament trouble in your left foot. Running, because of the monotonous pounding of the foot, is the hardest sport of all for such an injury to withstand.

I did my best in the little time I had between the two sports, running round my local park in my woolly hat and tracksuit, being chased by dogs, normally the little, fluffy, yappy varieties, who seemed to take it more personally than the superior Alsatians and Rottweilers whenever I stepped on a patch of grass normally reserved for their bathroom habits. It was not enough preparation, but it would have to do. As I set foot on the tarmac of Nairobi Airport, I felt a greater sense of trepidation over the ensuing sporting challenge than before. Who knows what was going to happen next?

What immediately happened was that a driver named George collected me and then drove to the offices of a travel and touring company run by William Tanui, the 1992 Olympic 800 metres champion. George would then be taking me on to Nyahururu, but a curious Tanui wanted to meet me first.

'Can you run?' he asked, as his eyes surveyed my body. I told him about my other adventures, about my runs in the park, my previous efforts in the streets of London and my determination to do my best. 'Yes, but . . .' Tanui never finished the sentence. Instead he offered some advice.

'Eat lots of *ugali*,' he said. 'That's our staple diet. And green vegetables. We call them *sukuma wiki*. And just try and finish the race, hey?' As I left, I heard the sound of laughter behind me in the office. Tanui promised he would be looking out for news about me during the week.

The drive from Nairobi to Nyahururu took us up from 5,000 feet to 9,000 feet above sea level, past fields of grazing zebra and a sign denoting the equator, and beside the magnificent Rift Valley, this huge, 30-mile-wide dent in the earth's surface that runs from Somalia in the north down to Mozambique in the south of Africa. Ramshackle villages and villagers passed by, schoolchildren in their uniforms, save for their bare feet, and women bearing huge weights of clothing and wares on their heads. Most stopped to stare at the van as it negotiated the various potholes in what were supposed to be main roads, with this strange Englishman lurching around inside.

Eventually we came to the Kawa Falls Hotel on the edge of

Nyahururu, where McDonald's group of élite and wannabe élite athletes spent their days relaxing in between gruelling training sessions. There, in the dining-room, in his camouflage army jacket, sat Jimmy Beauttah, a man who would play a valuable part in my life over the next three days.

He ordered tea for us both – Kenyan chai, which, as in Pakistan, is brewed in a mixture of hot milk and water before being poured – and listened passively to my plans. Occasionally he threw in a question. 'How heavy are you?' he asked, looking at my waist. 'How many times have you run the steeplechase before?' came next, his face full of enquiry. 'When are you going to run?' As each answer was digested, so the smile on his face broadened, until he felt compelled to slap me on the back.

'Well, you had better go easy for the rest of the day,' he advised. 'You can't just arrive at 9,000 feet, after a long flight and a long journey in a van, and expect to be able to run. You will do yourself harm, and you don't have enough time to do that. Remember, my friend, up here in Nyahururu, altitude must be respected. But you know what's more important? Attitude.'

He repeated this last point like a mantra. 'It's attitude and altitude, attitude and altitude.' His eyes suggested I should copy him, so I repeated his own phrase back to him. 'Attitude and altitude, Jimmy, that's what it's all about.'

Jimmy was in his mid-forties, a self-styled jack of all trades who used to box and play handball before turning to coaching both these sports and then, latterly, athletics. He was also a useful physiotherapist and masseur, certainly good enough for the world's top middle- and long-distance runners to entrust with their care.

As he talked to me, I noticed his large, bony hands and his incredible fingers, fingers that looked as strong and as wide as African baobab trees. I mentioned my ligament troubles and the fact that my right calf muscle still felt a little tense after my exertions in Pakistan. Jimmy's eyes lit up. 'Come and see me later in the physio room,' he said. 'I'll put you right.'

That evening I mingled with a group of athletes at the hotel, most of whom turned out to be high achievers. All seemed interested in my plans. 'So you are training with us tomorrow, then?' asked Paul Ruto, the 1993 World 800 metres champion. 'We'll look after you,' added Laban Rotich, three-times former Kenyan 1500 metres record holder. 'Did you say the steeplechase?' enquired Joseph Keter, the 1996 Olympic 3,000 metres steeplechase gold medallist.

This last question had a tone of 'Do you know what you are doing?'

about it. Keter, the man who surprised Kiptanui in the final few metres in Atlanta to become Olympic champion, sat me down and decided to talk the idea through.

'You know, if you are not used to the altitude, and even after a few days here, it won't be enough before you run in Kapsabet; running 3,000 metres to a good standard is not easy. ['Who said anything about a good standard?' I thought.] But then you have the barriers to clear as well, you know.'

'Yes, but they are not that high, are they?' I replied, with false bravado. Keter smiled, in a disturbingly caring fashion. 'Maybe not at the beginning, no. But by the fifth, sixth and seventh laps, when your legs are tired and you are running out of breath, they grow to this height.' He stood up and raised his hand to his head in an exaggerated manner. I took his point and wondered what I had let myself in for.

Dinner consisted of *ugali* and *sukuma wiki*, just as William Tanui had advised. Maize is the main crop of the Kenyan farmer and, once harvested, is removed from the cob and ground into maize meal flour. This is then cooked into large orbs of *ugali*, eaten by the Kenyans in the same way that Europeans eat potatoes, or Asians eat rice. I would like to say that *ugali* is delicious, I really would. After all, it would be the one meal I would definitely be eating every day whilst in training. The truth is that it tastes like papier mâché and is only acceptable when mixed with other food. The other athletes swore by it, insisting that the nutritional value of *ugali* helped to make them strong, rather like the magic potion dished out by Getafix to Asterix and his chums in deepest Gaul. Maybe, but it still looks more like the kind of substance you buy in a tube and use to fill cracks in the walls.

It was always an early bedtime for the 40 or so athletes based at the Kawa Falls. They would be rising at 5.45 the following morning in order to start their training, with a mere 90-minute, 20-kilometre road run dead on six o'clock. I felt tired after my travelling, but before retiring I visited Jimmy Beauttah for his promised physiotherapy session.

'Welcome,' he said, in dramatic fashion, 'to the House of Pain.' It was hardly the most comforting introduction to Room 28 of the Kawa Falls Hotel, but never has a truer word been spoken. Within moments the man had me writhing around in agony as he dug his hands into my feet, ankles and calves. Through my muffled cries of pain I heard a knock on the door and an athlete entered.

'Hi,' said Moses Kiptanui, arguably the most famous Kenyan athlete currently on the circuit. He extended his hand and added: 'Welcome to Nyahururu.' I tried to talk back but at that precise moment, almost as if Jimmy did not want me fraternising with his athletes, another surge of pain hit my calf muscle. Moses looked at me sympathetically and, as he left Jimmy to get on with the physical abuse, muttered: 'We've all been there before.'

Next came the ice. Jimmy packed so much on to my calves, rubbing a bag of crushed cubes vigorously up and down, that I felt as if my frozen legs would snap cleanly into two pieces. Then he positioned my body into various contortions and told me to breathe in and then out, at which point he pulled me in opposite directions. There then followed an observation as I tried to regain my composure. 'Man, you are tight.'

Eventually, as I rose groggily to my feet, towelled myself down and put my trousers back on, Jimmy delivered his verdict. 'Well, you're never going to be a four-wheel drive, but I can make you into a saloon.' And with that he went off into the night, with his torch shining ahead of him, across the road and back to his nearby home.

On Jimmy's advice I missed the early-morning run. My foot was not up to too much wear and tear on the roads, especially if I hoped to race four days later, and I was still tired. 'Your body normally knows best,' many of the athletes would echo during the week. But I made it to the second training stint of the day at the Nyahururu track, a five-minute walk through the town from the hotel, with my stomach still full of the previous night's *ugali*.

Nyahururu is a small but thriving highland centre, full of noisy buses sounding their hooters and gushing out thick volumes of dirty smoke, makeshift churches and chapels blaring out gospel music, chattering market-stall holders, and children, seemingly hundreds of children, who had grown used to the sight of 40 top athletes trudging their way to the track, but not this white newcomer. On the way I chatted to Luca Morogo, an 800 and 1500 metres specialist. 'Let me see, now,' Luca said, as he looked skyward and did a few sums in his head. 'There are seven and three-quarter laps in the 3,000 metres steeplechase, right? [This measurement makes an allowance for the corner of the track you cut in having to clear the water jump.] I think you will be lapped ten times.'

The Kenyans, as I discovered throughout the week, had a habit of delivering such soul-destroying verdicts.

The grandly named Nyahururu 'stadium' had seen better days. It was run-down, with a small, hole-ridden stand for spectators, a dirt track with smudged white lines painted on the surface to denote the individual lanes, and cows grazing nonchalantly in the long grass alongside, and it seemed incredible that the world's finest athletes should have to put up with such facilities. Moses Kiptanui guessed my thoughts.

'We need altitude, diet, the right nutrition, but most of all we need the attitude,' he told me. 'Hard work. That's what we're all about. You'll see for yourself when you spend time with us. We don't need a modern track. This will do for us. It's in here that counts,' he added, pointing to his head and his heart. As he and his fellow champions went to work, it was obvious that such conditions had hardly dented Kenya's performances over the years.

Joining the group for 12 laps of grassy field surrounding the track, I found their easy pace to my liking. Despite the thinness of the air, something I began to notice after a couple of circuits, I moved up to head the field with Kiptanui. This was more like it. Here I was, in Kenya, leading perhaps the finest group of middle- and long-distance runners in the world. Kiptanui was ahead, but I was right on his shoulder, ready to pounce in the home straight. Okay, so it may have been all fantasy, but it still felt incredibly good.

I soon slowed down, allowing others to run past, until I was joined by the stragglers. I was beginning to tire, and by the time Kiptanui, the self-imposed leader of the training group, stopped after 12 circuits, I was exhausted.

'Is there much more training?' I asked everyone, in total innocence, as I lay on the grass sweating profusely. A number of the runners laughed. 'That was warm-up, my friend,' Moses replied. 'Just warm-up.'

There then followed a series of 1,600-metre work-outs, with the last lap sprinted, interlaced by just three-minute intervals, in which the group regained their breath as they walked round the track to the start of another race. I joined in with the stretching, jumping and general aerobic exercises that followed, before the warm-down process, another jog around the field, ended the proceedings.

Dieter Baumann turned up just after the start of the warm-up. The 1992 Olympic 5,000 metres champion from Germany, one of the few athletes, and certainly a rare white man, to have defeated the Kenyans, had decided that the only way to beat his main rivals again was to join in their training methods. This way, he hoped, he would become one of only a few athletes to compete in four separate Olympic Games by featuring in Sydney in 2000.

I did not get off to the best of starts with him. Approaching a man named Pascal from the sportswear company Puma, who had just turned up to film the Kenyans they sponsor at work, I said: 'You must be Dieter.' Pascal looked somewhat surprised and pointed to a man standing next to him. 'No, that's Dieter.' I compounded the situation further by muttering something about how similar they looked. As Pascal had a full head of blond hair, whilst Baumann sported a crew cut to help disguise his receding hairline, a pair of round glasses and a thin, wiry body, this was hardly the case. Still, Baumann ignored the *faux pas* and happily chatted away.

'For me, training hard is the secret of beating the Kenyans,' he told me. 'They make running look so easy. Kenyans are the best distance runners in the world today, of that there is no doubt. I found today's training tough, very, very tough. They are talented, but they work for their victories too. The world of sport needs them.'

The Americans, so it transpired on returning to the hotel, would not necessarily agree with this last sentiment. There was quite a commotion outside where some of the athletes had obtained copies of the two national newspapers, *The Nation* and *The East African Standard*, and were reading reports stating that the American athletics authorities were so fed up with Kenyans winning their races on the US road-running circuit that they would be reducing the numbers of foreign athletes allowed to enter, a general policy clearly aimed at the Kenyans, and increasing the prize money for Americans, even if they were to finish outside the major placings.

'We don't want American sprinters banned from competing in Europe just because they are the best,' seemed to be the general view at the Kawa Falls. 'Kenyans won't refuse to run against Michael Johnson just because he's going to win.'

Kiptanui then spoke. 'The whole point about sport is being missed here,' he offered. 'What do you do if you are faced with a better opponent than yourself? You work harder to find a way to beat him. The Americans should stop complaining about us and instead try and beat us. It's as simple as that.' The others nodded their heads in agreement.

In an attempt to lighten the mood, I told everyone of Luca Morogo's comment about the number of times I would be lapped at the Kapsabet meeting. 'That's a good joke,' said Godfrey Kiprotich, one of the top road-racing and marathon-running Kenyans who enjoyed rich pickings in the United States. 'Maybe the Americans will let you race in their country,' he added, with a wry smile.

Spirits were further raised by news of Kenyan success in, ironically, America. Moses Tanui had just won the Boston Marathon for a second time, making it eight successive Boston triumphs for Kenya. Meanwhile, Tegla Lorupe had just set a women's marathon world record in winning in Rotterdam.

I lunched with Moses Kiptanui – or rather I slumped, full up and exhausted from my morning exertions, as my guest devoured chapattis and meat. Since first winning the world title in 1991, this 30-year-old man, lean, proud and bearing wide, alert eyes filled with conviction, had become one of the biggest draws in athletics and certainly one of the most famous figures in Kenya. Richer than he had ever imagined he could be when, as a young man, he began teaching as a profession, he had been introduced to his undoubted natural talent for running during a stint with the army, and for most of the 1990s he has graced the European athletics circuit with a series of world-class performances, mainly over the barriers at 3,000 metres.

As he hungrily attacked his food, I asked him why he did not seem to mind having a man like Dieter Baumann, an arch-rival to the Kenyans, amongst his training group. 'Why should I mind?' he replied, with genuine surprise. 'It's no problem for us. You see, we have no secrets. We have nothing to hide. It's just hard work. Anyone who wants to match us in athletics has to work as hard as we do.' He paused, to gain maximum effect. 'Few do, or want to.'

He was at pains to stress the point about the work put in. 'You know, we have a saying here in Kenya,' he continued. 'Train hard, win easy. That's our philosophy. People from elsewhere believe that if you are born a Kenyan, then you are a natural runner. That's not true. Yes, it helps that we are used to altitude, that we have a natural, nutritious diet and that, without even being aware of it, we have been training since early childhood when we used to run to school each day. But we would achieve nothing in sport without the work we put into training. That's why the racing is often the easy part.'

At the age of seven, Kiptanui used to run 12 kilometres a day, just to attend school and to eat. 'It was three kilometres from my house to school,' he recalled. 'I ran there in the morning, back home for lunch, back again for afternoon school and finally returned home after school. I wore no shoes until I was 12 years old. After school I used to play football with my friends. We used a ball we made out of string.'

I asked him if, in a perverse way, these deprived conditions helped. 'Yes, I think they do,' he answered, quite passionately. 'In England the children are not hungry enough. Their lives are too easy. That's why you failed to find true successors to Sebastian Coe, Steve Ovett and Steve Cram. In Kenya the kids want to follow me, just as I wanted to follow people like Kip Keino, Ben Jipcho and Henry Rono. They know that running is the only way they can make lots of money. You're not going to get too many international businessmen from most of the farming villages in my country.'

I thought of the Pakistani village of Nawakille. A different village – indeed, a different world – but a similar sporting environment. Both sets of people had discovered a sport in which they could escape from the poverty of their upbringing and which they could maintain as almost their exclusive right. The motivation was the same, as, indeed, were the results.

Kiptanui changed the subject as he poured out the first of numerous cups of chai. 'Did you try some *ugali*?' he asked. I told him it had filled me up for the whole night and morning. 'It stays in your stomach for a long time,' he replied. 'It digests slowly, and that's one of the reasons why it is so good for us.'

I asked him about the Olympics. Despite all his World Championship success, the Olympic gold medal had somehow eluded him. In 1992 Kiptanui finished fourth in the national trials after suffering from illness. Only three were to qualify, but the Kenyans still offered him a place at the expense of one of the initial qualifiers. Kiptanui refused, and the three Kenyans went on to record a clean sweep of the medals in the 3,000 metres steeplechase.

'I couldn't go because I would be taking the place of a friend and colleague,' Kiptanui explained. 'We try and give everyone a chance to compete in our country. We are all good enough to win. It does not matter if I do or not, as long as a Kenyan does.'

So he didn't mind finishing second to Joseph Keter in the 1996 final either? 'I was disappointed, but not too bothered,' he said. 'God makes the decisions. I am a human being, but I don't know why I am here. All I know is that if you knock hard enough on the door, God will open it.'

Kiptanui went back to his room to sleep. I had already learned two important facts about the Kenyan training regimes. They worked hard, very hard, but they also knew how to rest. This is as important an aspect to training as any physical exertion. Besides, Kiptanui would be going on one final run later in the afternoon, making it three separate sessions in total for the day.

As he went he promised he would inspect my hurdling technique before I left for Kapsabet. 'Maybe I can finish the race in ten minutes,' I suggested. Kiptanui smiled politely. 'I think more than ten minutes,' he replied.

Whilst Kiptanui slept, some of the others seemed content to bask in the afternoon sunshine, sitting in the modest dining-room sipping tea and talking, or merely standing around outside watching the world go by. This may not sound too exciting, but the Kenyan athletes saw it as valuable relaxation time and had got it down to a tee.

One of them turned out to be Martin Keino, the 25-year-old 1500-metre runner whose father only happened to be the greatest athlete in Kenyan history. 'What's it like being Kip's son, then?' I asked him, immediately regretting introducing a subject which, I figured, was hardly original. Martin smiled.

'Everywhere I go, all over the world, people say to me: "I know that surname. I don't suppose your father is Kip Keino, is he?" It amazes me how well known my dad is. On the whole it's good being the son of Kip. It has a lot of positive connotations, but, on the other hand, people expect a great deal from me.'

I suggested that perhaps he wanted to be seen as Martin Keino in his own right. 'Yeah, you're right there,' he replied with enthusiasm. 'I run for my own purposes, not because my father used to. And I've surpassed a lot of his times. I feel that I'm close now to achieving things in my own right.'

Others later agreed with this assessment. Martin Keino's only problem, apart from his surname, is that he is Kenyan, which means that to compete for his country he has to come through the toughest of apprenticeships. Never mind the Olympics or the World Championships. When it comes to middle- and long-distance running, the hardest race in the world to win is undoubtedly the Kenyan trials. Still, young Keino was beginning to look good, and he hoped that the days of merely pace-making for the likes of Daniel Komen would soon be over.

'Don't get me wrong,' he insisted. 'I don't mind pace-making. I like helping Daniel break world records and it pays well, but I want to be the man breaking the records. Sometimes I get the urge to continue in the race, even though I'm supposed to step off the track once my job is done. I think my days of pace-making are nearly over now. Somebody will have to do it for me.'

That night Moses Kiptanui and Godfrey Kiprotich took me into the town for dinner. Kiptanui had squeezed in some work with his sponsors as well that afternoon and was looking rather dapper in his checked sports jacket and shiny shoes. Kiprotich, in contrast, was in regulation baseball cap and tracksuit. As we ate our meal using our fingers and large clumps of *ugali*, the conversation turned quite serious.

Kiptanui had sent a fax to Lamine Diach, an influential African member of the International Olympic Committee and International Athletics Association, complaining about the Americans' stance over Kenyan athletes. 'I don't care if it leads to Kenyans boycotting athletics events,' he said. 'We can't allow this to happen.' Kiprotich leant over and added: 'Moses is a powerful man, you know.'

But didn't it hurt the Kenyans when they boycotted the 1976 and 1980 Olympics? Think of all the lost chances for the best athletes in the world. 'Doesn't matter,' Kiptanui retorted. 'We must make sacrifices. Our country is more important than the wishes of an individual. We will always produce more athletes to replace us and win medals.'

Kiprotich was concerned about a passage in an American newspaper report in which he is quoted talking about the American decision to reward Americans who may well finish below him. 'What does disillusioned mean?' he asked. 'That's how they described me. Are they criticising me?'

I explained that they were not. Disillusioned was the right word to describe Godfrey's mood when he realised he would be earning less than an American finishing three places behind him. 'Oh, that's all right then,' Kiprotich replied, cheered by this news.

The conversation then focused on how Kenyan athletes lack sufficient education when it comes down to finances. 'It worries me,' Kiptanui admitted. 'We have too many cases here of Kenyans making a great deal of money and losing it all. They don't know how to invest it properly and they don't seem to realise that your first cheque could be your last.'

He, naturally, had no such problems. Kiptanui had invested much of his earnings into land, recognised in Kenya as a more valuable commodity than cash. On this land, near the large town of Eldoret, he had built homes for his wife and three young children and for his father. The discipline of running, however, meant that he had to be away in Nyahururu, a three-hour drive away, at the London base of Kim McDonald or on the athletics circuit for much of his time. 'It's a sacrifice I have to make,' he explained. 'I don't like it, but I have to do it, and I've been rewarded for doing so. My family understand this, but I still like to telephone them as often as possible, even my nine-month-old baby son, though he can't talk back to me. I miss them, but it helps to make me hungrier for success.'

As we made our way back to the hotel I suddenly remembered I was supposed to be visiting the House of Pain that night. As I knocked on Jimmy's door, he was about to leave. 'Where were you?' he asked. I apologised and told him that Kiptanui had taken me out to dinner. I hoped I managed to hide my delight at missing an agony session.

'You'd better come first thing in the morning, then, before training,' Jimmy said, with a knowing glint in his eye. 'That's if you are serious about running in Kapsabet.' As he switched on his torch he turned round and added: 'Oh, and you'd better have another session after training as well. I've got a lot of work to do on your calf muscles.'

'Muscles?' I shouted, as he disappeared into the gloom of the night. 'I've only got a problem with my right one!' But he was gone, leaving me to think about his baobab hands for breakfast.

The debate over the Americans' stance raged on the following morning. Ibrahim Hussein had stepped into the fray, suggesting in the national press that what they were doing was tantamount to surrender to the Kenyans. 'They're giving up,' he announced. 'What kind of a response is that?'

Jimmy Beauttah went to work on my saloon-car body, this time in the presence of David Kibet, a former Oslo 'Dream Mile' winner who was attempting a comeback in international athletics. A huge figure of a man who resembled a young George Foreman, Kibet was interested in physiotherapy and liked to practise his own questionable methods whenever given the chance.

A happy-go-lucky personality, he liked to joke with anyone in his company. 'Does it hurt?' he asked me, as my face went purple and I gripped the edge of the bed with my clenched hands. 'How come we don't shout when Jimmy's working on us, then?'

It reminded me of a story I had once read about the high pain threshold of a Kenyan, which was later confirmed by the athletes in Nyahururu. Many, if not most of the top Kenyan runners are from the Kalenjin tribe, who circumcise by traditional methods. The teenage boy sits in silence, without anaesthetic, as the elders perform the ceremony. The moment, and the pain, is never forgotten by these athletes. So, whenever they are hurting in training, or, for that matter, on Jimmy Beauttah's physio table, they remember the day they were circumcised. After that, they reckon, they can face any pain barrier.

It is a story to make your eyes water, but not an example I was prepared to follow. I may have been living and training at altitude with the Kenyans, but there were limits, believe me, to how far I was prepared to go. Method journalism in Kenya could be a dangerous game to play.

Back at the track, Kiptanui led another of his 'easy' warm-up sessions. I surged ahead once again, fully intent on enjoying running shoulder to shoulder with Kiptanui and Komen. After five minutes or so, Pascal from Puma asked me if I would mind running at the back of the group. 'We only want to film the good athletes,' he explained, in an unintentional put-down. I went and joined the 'not-so-good' ones at the back.

I tried to disguise my tiredness at the end of the warm-up as we all trotted to the middle of the field surrounded by the Nyahururu stadium's dirt track for a series of stretching exercises. The athletes took turns to step out in front and bellow out instructions to the rest of us, like an aerobics teacher at a health club. We then lined up and jumped over a series of wooden planks, before finding a partner and wrapping a large rubber band around us and running hard in opposite directions. This produced a few giggles, especially when my partner began to drag me all over the grass.

The temperature had reached 30 degrees, but one of the athletes completed training still in his full tracksuit and baseball cap. I, in contrast, was down to a T-shirt and shorts, which revealed the full extent of my perspiration. 'How can you train in all those clothes?' I asked him.

'It keeps me warm,' he replied, looking at me as if I had just asked a stupid question.

At the end of training we all sat on the grass whilst Kiptanui made a few team announcements. At one stage he called out the names of those athletes from Nyahururu who would be making a trip to Qatar to race in a meeting. As he finished the list I asked him why my name had not been mentioned. Kiptanui smiled and replied: 'If you win in Kapsabet, you can come to Qatar.' It was a promise that caused great amusement within the ranks.

Daniel Komen had arrived that morning, sporting a flashy pair of alternate-coloured training shoes. He, at least at the time of writing, was the top athlete in the world. Just 21 years old, he was already the 1997 World 5,000 metres champion and world-record holder, as well as the holder of a further four outdoor and indoor world records.

'I still have so much time to do so much more,' he told me over lunch, his shy look and quiet voice disguising the confident man on the track. 'But already people expect me to win in every race. I'm not like a car. I can't just fill myself up with petrol, you know, and then run.'

It sounded as if too much had happened too soon. 'It can be difficult for me,' Komen acknowledged. 'I'm still trying to get used to the fame. I never thought it would happen so quickly. I used to play football, and then I nearly became a soldier. But I looked up to John Ngugi [a former world cross-country champion and Olympic 5,000 metres gold medallist] and I realised that if I became a runner I could look after my family.'

He can certainly do that now. In the previous 12 months Komen had earned $500,000, a vast fortune to a Kenyan, and this kind of money enabled him to lead the life he had dreamt of since childhood days. 'My aim now is to win the Olympic and Commonwealth gold medals to add to my World title,' he confirmed, still in his softly spoken voice.

I told him of my plans at Kapsabet. He smiled 'Do you think you can do it?' he asked. I told him I was not sure. 'If you really want to, you can,' he replied. 'That's what running is all about.'

Before dinner I visited the House of Pain again. Despite the horrors of Jimmy's hands, my foot and calf muscles always felt better after these sessions. My main problem was just getting through them, especially once Jimmy had declared himself a devout Christian. Aware that the odd f-word, shouted out in pain, might not be too well received, I had to make up my own, similar-sounding words instead. So, as Jimmy's fingers bored into my bone, I would yell 'fick', 'sheet' or anything else that came to mind.

Joseph Cheshire came to town that evening. Cheshire was the chief coach of the Nyahururu training camp, having been a top, if rather unlucky, 1500-metre runner for many years. A five-times national champion – which in Kenyan terms took some doing – he was placed fourth in three global championships. The only medal he had to show for all his exertions was a bronze at the World Indoor Games in 1985. He remained, however, a highly respected figure in Kenyan athletics.

'It just wasn't to be,' he said over dinner. 'I remember the 1992 final at the Barcelona Olympics. I was in the best shape of my life, but the race was just too slow for me. When Fermin Cacho [from Spain] kicked for home at the end, I knew I would not have the speed to catch him.' Cheshire finished fourth.

He, like everyone before him, listened to my plans with amusement, before revealing the daunting news that the other Nyahururu athletes would be concentrating on an athletics meeting in Nairobi in a fortnight's time. 'So you will be our representative in Kapsabet,' he said. 'Make sure you do well.'

Mwalimu Kimeli, a 1500-metre runner who took great pleasure in watching me trying to keep up with my new-found colleagues in training, sat down next to me. 'I tell you what,' he said. 'I will give you $50,000 if you win in Kapsabet.'

I mentioned this to some of the other athletes later. Kiptanui rushed off, saying he was going to make Kimeli sign a contract. Godfrey Kiprotich and Sammy Nyangichi, a fellow marathon runner, devised a cunning plan.

'Why don't you pay the other runners in the final 5,000 Kenyan shillings to let you win the race?' they suggested. 'Then you will take the $50,000 from Kimeli and make a huge profit. But we want 10 per cent.'

Much of the ensuing talk that evening centred on my race. 'Why don't you run under the barriers?' someone suggested. 'Don't forget your swimming trunks,' said another. 'You'll be needing them for the water jump.' It provided a good laugh for all of us, but also underlined the growing realisation that my day of reckoning was almost upon me.

By the time I had made some late-night phone calls, the other athletes had long retired to their beds. The busy road outside was quiet and only the sound of the crickets and the flies buzzing around the lights broke the silence of the clear African night. There, sitting by himself, was Joseph Cheshire. I asked him what he was doing.

'I can't sleep,' he explained. 'I only have four hours a night.'

I asked him if this was enough for him.

'Oh yes, I am not tired. Four hours seem to do.'

I told him he was a lucky man.

'Lucky?' he replied. 'I think I am sick. Why am I lucky?'

I explained my theory that too much of our lives is spent in bed. Cheshire's lack of sleep meant he was living a longer life than the rest of us and could achieve more with his extra time. 'Maybe,' he said. 'But I still think I'm sick.'

As I went to my bed, leaving Cheshire to his insomnia, I wondered if finishing fourth on so many occasions had something to do with it.

By the time I emerged in the morning, changed and ready for my last training session before leaving Nyahururu for Eldoret, most of the other athletes had seen *The East African Standard*. Godfrey Kiprotich was the first to break the news to me.

'So, now you are famous,' he said, with a broad smile plastered all over his face. 'You are a top runner and the paper talks about you.'

'Oh yeah, sure,' I replied, enjoying his joke.

'No, no, I mean it,' Kiprotich replied, his eyes growing larger by the second. 'Come, look.'

He grabbed a copy of the newspaper and thrust it into my hands. There, in the centre of the sports page, ran a headline: 'Top runners for Eldoret.' Underneath, a piece informed us that Daniel Komen was expected to highlight at the big meeting that weekend at the Kip Keino stadium. The concluding paragraph added: 'Ian Stanford from Britain will feature in the 3,000 metres steeplechase.'

I looked at this last line again, just to make sure I was reading it correctly. There was no mention about this British guy being a writer and not a professional athlete, just that he would be featuring in the

3,000 metres steeplechase. As far as the newspaper's readership was concerned, the British had sent me over to take on Kenya's best. Then the name registered. 'Ian Stanford.' They had spelled my surname wrong.

During training I tried on my new pair of spikes for the first time. Whilst the others performed a series of gruelling 600-metre and 400-metre sprints, I ran as fast as I could up and down the 100-metre straight. My strange shoes felt uncomfortable and my right calf muscle pulled each time my foot left the track's cinder surface. Urged on by the others, I joined in for the final 400 metres race and trailed in a distant last, beaten by everyone else in the race including a 14-year-old boy called Julius. He seemed particularly pleased with himself. He had just beaten the *mzungu*.

'Mzungu' was a word I had just learnt that morning. It is the Swahili term for 'white man', and it was something I had heard repeatedly during the week. Some of the athletes who were unaware of my name referred to me as 'mzungu'. This was not a racist term and I did not take it as such. It merely stated what I am, a white man, which in western Kenya, despite many years of British colonisation, is something of a rare sight these days.

At the end of training Moses Kiptanui showed me his hurdling technique and then stood back to watch me. I had not got round to telling him this, but I had never actually jumped over a 3,000 metres steeplechase barrier before. Still, with a final in a major athletics meeting to compete in in two days' time, I figured it was better late than never.

I expected Kiptanui to say something along the lines of 'Not bad, but you have to lift your left leg more', or perhaps 'Try and run a little faster as you approach the barrier'. His response, as I cleared the barrier, was a little more direct.

'No way!' he shouted, causing a couple of athletes to look over in our direction. 'No way.'

'I'm sorry?' I said.

'You can't appear in the steeplechase final,' he replied. 'You're going to damage yourself. You only just cleared the barrier. I'm telling you, if you race on Saturday you will definitely hit one of the barriers, and when you do you may injure yourself. It's not worth it, especially as you have all those other sports to do for your book.'

This was not what I wanted to hear. 'I thought I cleared the barrier okay, Moses,' I reasoned.

The three-times World steeplechase champion shook his head. 'No, you didn't. And another thing. That barrier is for the women's race.

The men's ones are higher than that. No, you must do something else. What about the 5K?'

The 5,000 metres. I gave it some thought. It would mean running for a further 2,000 metres, another five laps, at altitude. But at least I would not kill myself falling from the barriers. It would have to be the 5K.

I told Jimmy Beauttah of my decision during my final visit to the House of Pain. I had noticed how Jimmy would often use his hands to end a sentence instead of actually uttering any words. So, instead of saying 'Today we will run up a hill', he would merely state 'Today', and follow this with a series of upward hand movements whilst making a 'swishing' noise with his lips.

This morning, he was at his manual best. Denoting the absence of barriers in the 5K but more laps, his hands went up and down in short bursts before following a smooth line across his body, all accompanied by small noises. Occasionally he would throw in a word, but not when a hand movement would suffice. This 'conversation' went on for minutes. He then shook my hand, wished me luck and returned to his home.

Godfrey Kiprotich would be driving me to the town of Nakuru, a third of the way to Eldoret, before I was to catch a Matatu, a seven-seater taxi, to take me the rest of the journey. Before I left, I went in search of Kiptanui. I found him in his room, preparing for an afternoon's snooze.

He told me he would only be running for a further two years. 'There's only so much the body can take,' he reasoned. 'There's no point in me earning all this money if I am going to drop dead and never have the opportunity to enjoy it with my family.'

Why two years though? 'Because the Sydney Olympics are in 2000,' he said. Of course. There was still that elusive Olympic gold medal to win. 'It keeps getting away from me,' he added. 'I'd like one more chance.'

As he bade farewell, Kiptanui shook my hand and pointed his finger at me: 'Remember, do the 5K.'

I promised him I would.

Kiprotich took me to a central market square in Nakuru, where we spent the next hour haggling with taxi drivers. I was all for jumping into the first car, but Kiprotich was thankfully there to stop me. 'You can't do that,' he said. 'You don't know who these people are. Some might drive you into the bush, take your bags and leave you there. They might even do something worse! No, we must find a friend.' I didn't bother to ask him what he meant by 'worse'.

Eventually a friend turned up and Kiprotich went home to his family. It was to take a further three hours to reach Eldoret, a journey punctuated by pot-holes and a violent thunderstorm just as we drove through a large forest. 'It's dangerous here,' my driver informed me. 'This is where many robbers hide out. Sometimes they come on to the road and if you drive on they shoot.' It felt like the Khyber Pass all over again. For the second time in less than a fortnight, I was in a dangerous part of the world and feeling rather vulnerable. The night sky was lit by dramatic forks of lightning, and as we drove through the wilds of Kenya, Tammy Wynette blasted out of the radio. It was just another day in this bizarre series of adventures I had chosen to experience.

I arrived at the Kip Keino stadium in Kapsabet just before lunch-time. I use the word 'stadium' advisedly. Most of the crowd stood around the grassy verges, or sat on top of buses parked at the back, to gain a better view. It was a basic facility but, after five days in Kenya, just as I had imagined it to be. What it lacked in standard, it more than made up for in atmosphere and in a deep appreciation of athletics.

Wading through the crowd, I tried to find Ibrahim Hussein, going on a photograph of him in a book in which he sported a moustache. It was Hussein who found me. This smiling man, without any hair on his upper lip and a great deal bulkier since his days of winning international marathons, led me to the VIP stand, slightly less rickety than the other stand on the opposite side of the track, and sat me down. I shook hands with a number of local and national athletics dignitaries, treasurers and assistant secretaries, vice-chairmen and *ex officio* members, and started to read the official programme.

'All are invited to come and witness records being broken. Internationalists to feature,' it stated on the programme cover. Inside a further message read: 'The organising committee wish to thank all the volunteers for assisting in this great event and, on behalf of the meet, would like to assure you that pretty soon an event of this magnitude will be held in your village before you know it. Thank you, and God bless.'

As I read all this I heard the stadium announcer begin a long speech. 'Ladies and gentlemen,' he said. 'I am pleased to announce that one of the world's greatest sportsmen is here today in Kapsabet.'

I carried on reading.

'He's played football with Brazil, he's played against the world squash champion, Jansher Khan, in Pakistan, he is in the South African international rugby team . . .'

At this point the penny dropped. He was actually referring to me. One of the world's greatest sportsmen! Ibrahim Hussein's wife sat down next to me and laughed.

'Yes, I'd like you all to show your appreciation for IAAANN STANNNNFORD.'

A ripple of applause sounded from around the stands for Ian Stanford and my embarrassment battled in a war of emotions with my irritation at the sound of my name being mispronounced. I sank further into my seat, but the announcer suddenly looked across and added: 'Ian Stanford, please stand up so that we can all see you.'

Reluctantly, I rose to my feet and delivered a rather limp and self-conscious wave around the stadium, prompting a second burst of applause. 'It's actually Ian Stafford,' I muttered to an official on the other side of me. 'Oh, sorry,' he said. A few minutes later he introduced me to another dignitary. 'This is Ian Stanford,' he said. 'He's running in the steeplechase final tomorrow.'

This reminded me of Moses Kiptanui's advice. I mentioned it to Ibrahim Hussein, who shrugged his shoulders and said it was not a problem. I could run in the 5,000 metres final instead. I then pleaded with Hussein to ensure that, by the time of the race, the announcer had made it clear to the watching public that I was not an athlete but a writer, and that I would undoubtedly finish last. He shrugged his shoulders again. 'Don't worry,' he said. 'It's not a problem.'

I went for a walk around the stadium in search of Brother Colm O'Connell, who, after me, was just about the unlikeliest person to be there at the Kapsabet stadium, and the only other *mzungu*. With his pot belly, baseball cap, permanent red face and twinkly Irish eyes, he is the last person you would expect to be a successful athletics coach, especially when you consider the fact that he first came to Kenya in 1976 to teach at St Patrick's High School knowing absolutely nothing about the sport.

At the age of 17 in Tullow, County Carlow, he had joined the Patrician Brothers, an order whose mission is to work with young people. Much of their work is done in the Third World, where the long white robe and emerald sash worn back home in Ireland is abandoned in favour of ordinary clothes. Ten years later he left for Kenya. Following a couple of years of careful observation, Brother Colm took over in charge of training at St Patrick's. Ibrahim Hussein is one of his former pupils. So is Wilson Kipketer, the Kenyan-born Dane, who broke the 800 metres world record. He coached Peter Rono and Matthew Birir, both Olympic gold medallists, and a host of other Kenyan champions too. His latest talent, Japhet Kimutai, is already the world 800 metres junior champion and, according to Colm, 'definitely one to watch'.

Which is more than he could say for me. I told him of my race plan the following day. I intended to sprint at the start, just as I had done during the Lambeth Half Marathon, so that I could at least say that I had led a top race in Kenya. Then I would slow down to my own pace. Colm felt this was too dangerous. 'If you start like that, you'll never finish,' he advised. 'Don't forget, the other athletes will also start quickly, because they'll all be wanting to get to the front. Just go at a pace you are comfortable with. Otherwise, the altitude will get to you.'

It was sound advice. I joked that I had to go and collect my $40,000 appearance money. Colm replied: 'Is that to get on or get off the track?'

I watched the 5,000 metres heats on top of Colm's bus. You made the precarious climb up the side of the bus using a ladder. Most of the St Patrick's pupils skipped up the ladder like a cat climbing a tree, but I clung on to the side as if I was challenged by the north face of the Eiger. I did not feel any more comfortable having reached the summit. The bus seemed to lean at the side, and every time another body climbed up I felt the vehicle lurch forward.

The track officials used tactics that begged for no debate. As soon as a struggling athlete was lapped in one of the heats, they would be removed swiftly from the race, rather like the 'hook' used in stand-up comedy clubs for those failing to gain sufficient laughs. There must have been close to 300 athletes in the 5K heats. In one race, I counted 55 participants, many of whom ran in bare feet. It was just as well I, as one of the world's greatest living sportsmen, had been granted an automatic place in the final. There was absolutely no way I could have qualified otherwise.

Later, back in the VIP stand, I talked with a middle-aged man for ten minutes or so. He asked me where I lived and I told him quite near to the Crystal Palace stadium, for some time England's premier athletics track. 'Oh yes, I've raced there many a time,' he replied. 'Oh, are you an athlete?' I asked, in all innocence.

'Yes,' he said. 'My name's Ben Jipcho.'

Ben Jipcho just happens to be one of the most famous runners in Kenyan athletics. Largely credited for helping Kip Keino around to a steeplechase gold medal at the 1972 Olympics, Jipcho had helped himself to an Olympic silver, as well as two Commonwealth gold medals, a silver and a bronze. His word of advice for the big race the next day was simple: 'Make sure you finish.'

At this point the biggest name in Kenyan sporting history arrived and was immediately surrounded by well-wishers and hand-shakers.

A smiling Kip Keino, now 58 years old but still looking lean and fit, finally made his way over to the VIP stand. We were introduced. 'This is Ian Stanford,' said one of the officials. I was beginning to get used to my new name by now.

'Good luck for tomorrow,' he said, which immediately worried me. Even Kip Keino had heard that this great British runner would be competing in Kapsabet. I explained who and what I was, and he laughed. 'This I must see,' he said, before echoing Jipcho's words. 'The most important thing is to finish. Nothing else matters. It does not matter how you do it, but just finish.'

Those words reverberated around my mind as I spent a predictably sleepless night back in Eldoret. 'Just remember,' I kept telling myself, 'this time tomorrow, it will all be over.'

The Saturday morning went very slowly. I saw no point in arriving early at the meeting, so I paced up and down my hotel room, ordering endless cups of chai from room service. Despite having bought a brand new pair of spikes for the big race, the resulting tenseness in my calf muscles told me it would be unwise to wear them on the Kapsabet track. I packed my reliable trainers instead and called for a taxi.

On my arrival at the stadium, I sensed that the crowd had increased from the day before. Ibrahim Hussein told me later that it was close to 15,000 people. This made sense. After all, this was finals day, and only the top athletes like me would be featuring. A race was taking place. As I made my way over to the VIP stand in order to find Ibrahim Hussein, I asked a passing athlete what event was on show.

'5,000 metres,' he replied, and walked on.

5,000 metres? I looked frantically at my programme. Yes, I thought so. The 5,000 metres was not supposed to start until 2.05 p.m. I checked my watch. It was midday. But the race looked like the 5,000 metres. The athletes looked like 5,000-metre runners.

Ibrahim Hussein ran up to me. 'Sorry, sorry,' he said. 'They brought the race forward. I tried to stop the referee, because I knew you weren't here, but he refused.'

'But it's over two hours early,' I reasoned.

Hussein gave yet another shrug of his shoulders and replied: 'This is Kenya.'

There was only one other final I could appear in, the very race Moses Kiptanui had advised me to avoid. 'I'd better go for the 3,000 metres steeplechase, then,' I said to Hussein.

'I'll tell you what,' the chairman of the Kapsabet meeting said, his face suddenly brightening. 'We will allow you to run in the steeplechase final, but you don't have to jump over the barriers. Just treat it like an ordinary 3K.'

'Will anyone mind?' I asked. 'I mean, you will make sure the crowd are fully aware, won't you?'

Hussein smiled. 'No problem.'

The steeplechase was, according to the programme, set for 1.05 p.m. At 12.30 a man with a loudspeaker started calling for the steeplechase finalists. I was still in my tracksuit and had barely had time to change in the middle of the grassy pitch when my fellow finalists lined up. A young lady called Selina, from the St Patrick's bus, threw me a baseball cap to protect my red scalp from the heat of the midday sun, and I tagged on to the back of the group as we jogged over to the VIP stand.

We were then ordered to stand in a wide line whilst our names were introduced to the crowd. Finally, they came to me. 'And now, from London, England, please welcome Ian Stanford.'

I raised my hand and waved, feeling a little like Forrest Gump. A few weeks before this same figure had been seen kicking a football with Romario. A few days before he had been witnessed on a squash court with the greatest player in the sport's history. Now he was lining up with some of the best Kenyan athletes. People observing photographs might have come to the conclusion that my head had been superimposed on to someone else's body. But no, it was me, on every occasion. Besides, nobody else had a body like mine.

We lined up in an arched row at the start of the race. I managed to secure lane two and began to jog up and down on the spot, puffing my cheeks out and wringing my hands out and down by my side, as if they were wet. This, so I had often observed, is what athletes do moments before they run. The starter raised his gun and we all crouched low, with our arms raised upwards as if they created a tactical advantage.

BANG. I started quicker than I intended, carried along by the rush of Kenyan feet around me. For 100 metres I stayed with the pack, but I knew I would have to slow down if I stood any chance of completing the race.

We ran around a complete circuit before the first barrier came upon us. By now I had already dropped back to a more comfortable pace and I found myself lagging some 20 metres behind. If the crowd were expecting something special from this top European athlete, they soon realised this would not be the day.

Their next surprise of the day occurred seconds later. I ran towards the first barrier with intent, before producing a rugby-style side-step which sent me around and past the barrier. A large gasp was audible, followed by laughter.

I reproduced this action at the second barrier. This time another section of the crowd had a closer view of this strange *mzungu's* tactics. They had never seen a 3,000 metres steeplechase final before where one of the athletes was deliberately omitting to jump the barriers.

The water jump was always going to provide the major point of interest. The crowd was particularly deep at this barrier, in the hope that a few splash landings would be on show. I had inspected the water jump with great suspicion before the race. The dirty brown water looked deep and uninviting, and I was sure there were creatures living in it beneath the surface.

To clear the water jump, you need to take a slight diversion off a corner of the track and across a small muddy stretch. I ran right up to the jump before producing another side-step, shaking my head as I passed by. This caused some consternation, both with the water-jump officials and with the nearby spectators. This *mzungu* was clearly not going to win the race, but he was providing some entertainment.

I don't know what the other finalists thought of all this. I had a chance to ask them, as they lapped me for the first time after three laps, but they were past me in a flash, a wave of Kenyan legs eating up the track, leaving a plodding Englishman to his own devices.

Midway through the fourth lap, I began to develop stomach cramps. This was a potential disaster. I knew I was at altitude, but I expected to be able to run eight laps of the track. I changed my breathing pattern, inhaling and exhaling heavily after each stride. For a while it was pretty painful and my screwed-up face revealed my discomfort.

'Come on, you can do it!' someone shouted from the crowd. 'Go, English, go!' said someone else. 'Don't die on us!' another wag yelled, to surrounding merriment. 'Come on, Ian!' cried out the Puma team's cameraman.

The other finalists surged past me again during the sixth lap. This time I noticed they took longer. Some were struggling behind – but they did not really know the meaning of struggling. I was way ahead in that department. As I ran past the VIP stand I heard further shouts of encouragement. This spurred me on. Looking around the track, with two laps to go, I realised I was now out on my own. Everyone else had finished the race.

At this point the crowd seemed to unite in support. The pains in my stomach disappeared and as I began to pick up a little speed, so I started to enjoy myself. It became a wonderful, beautiful three minutes. The people of Kapsabet could see I was no athlete, at least no serious athlete, but they also recognised that I was trying my best. That was good enough for them. Their pure love of athletics meant, as I was told later, that they respected anyone who gave it a go, even me.

As the bell sounded to denote my last lap, I decided to hurdle the barriers. Aware of Kiptanui's words, I vaulted each barrier, placing my left hand on top and lifting both legs over at the same time. It was ungainly, and slow, but the method worked.

As I rounded the final bend I came face to face with the water jump. My lungs felt ready to burst and I was hot, dreadfully hot, but I just knew I had to tackle the water, if only in gratitude to that section of the crowd who had helped me round the track. Hoisting both legs over the barrier, I plummeted straight down into the murky water until it swilled around my waist, and I let out a loud gasp as the cool water contrasted against my hot, sweaty skin.

A burst of laughter erupted from the stands as I staggered out of the pit and water poured from my trunks, followed by more applause. In the final straight I felt my feet squelching, but I still mustered up a sprint finish in front of the VIP stand. I could hear, above the noise, the tannoy announcer commentating on 'Ian Stanford's sprint to the tape', before I employed an extravagant dip on the finish line.

I collapsed on to the grass beside the track. I did not feel too bad and merely wanted a few seconds to regain my breath, but four track officials ran up and lifted me back on to my feet in a rather ostentatious manner. 'You must stand,' they said, treating me like a serious hospital case.

After a few shaky steps, I staggered over to the VIP stand, where a grinning Kip Keino leant over and shook my hand. 'Well done,' he said. 'Well done. I want you to come to my house in the morning.'

I nodded my head as the commentator waved for me to come and join him. He then conducted an interview, the only interview of the day with a finalist who finished last. 'Ian Stanford,' he began. I saw no point in correcting him at this point. 'How did you find the race?'

'Easy,' I replied, in between gasps. 'I was coming on strong in the end. A few more laps and I would have caught the others.' Those who appreciated the humour laughed. Others just looked at me in bemusement.

'Was it tough?' the interviewer asked. I talked about the thin air and then looked across at an attentive Keino. 'Kip Keino told me I had to make sure I finished the race,' I said. 'Well, Kip, I finished.' He laughed and started to clap, prompting the others in the VIP stand to follow suit.

For the record, I completed the race in a forgettable time of 14 minutes, 22 seconds. Richard Limo and William Koech took the first two places, some five and a half minutes ahead of me. These are names you may well not have heard of. But you probably will. They, and many more, are waiting in the wings to follow the likes of Moses Kiptanui and Daniel Komen to global sporting success. They train very hard, you see, but they win easy.

Later, Brother Colm made the point that, regardless of being lapped twice, I was still the best white athlete in the whole athletics meeting. Okay, so I was also the only white athlete in the whole athletics meeting, but it still sounded good. Some of the junior winners were then presented, in a rather awkward ceremony, with cows and goats in front of the VIP stand. The cows refused to stand still on top of the winners' podium and one of the goats relieved himself on an official's shoe.

'Where's my animal, then?' I asked Ibrahim Hussein.

'We're going to give you a fish,' he answered.

'Why's that?' I said.

'Because you spent so much time in the water jump.'

I was to leave for London that Sunday morning, but before beginning the long journey back to Nairobi Airport I took up Kip Keino's offer and drove round to his farm, eight kilometres outside Eldoret.

As I waited in his living-room for Kip to return from walking his cows, I gazed at all the trophies and trinkets, photographs and plaques, all marking one of the finest careers in the history of sport. This, without any doubt, was the man who opened the door for Kenyan athletics.

Now, 25 years on, he has established an orphanage in the grounds of his own farm, where 70 grateful children are fed and accommodated. 'It gives me as much pleasure to see these children grow up to become doctors or lawyers as winning a gold medal,' he explained on his arrival. And you could see, without any doubt, that he meant it.

The smart suit of the VIP stand had been replaced by a casual shirt and slacks, and he had been transformed from the greatest living Kenyan sportsman to a modest farmer. 'I still like to run,' he told me, with a proud expression on his face. 'I like to stay fit.'

If he were running today as an international athlete, he would be a millionaire. 'Maybe,' he said. 'But money does not buy you happiness. It is what I have achieved in sport, and in life, my memories and my family.' He nodded his head and smiled, a man at peace with himself. 'I am content.'

Kip took me into his fields, showed me around his land and then picked some self-produced passion fruit for my journey home. Never has a passion fruit tasted sweeter. He seemed pleased by my reaction as we returned to the house.

'You did well yesterday,' he said once we were inside another room. 'You are a tough guy.' And with that he handed over a beautifully made milk gourd, with multi-coloured beads around the lid and a leather strap. 'This is your prize for finishing the race,' he said, and shook my hand.

It was, to my surprise, a rather emotional moment. This was not just a simple milk gourd. This was a present from someone I would class as a truly great sportsman and a truly great man. You cannot place a price on such a personal possession, however simple it may seem. It is something I will cherish for the rest of my life.

In this age of winning at all costs, Kip Keino reminded me of what sport used to be like, before the money men and the corporate sharks gatecrashed the fun with their hospitality suites and their cheque-books. Running around the Kapsabet track had produced a similar feeling. The crowd clearly felt they were not watching an imposter, some English media figure who had no right to be there. Far from it. The people of western Kenya, even if they never grasped my true name, were supporting someone whom they accepted as a kindred spirit.

For that afternoon, at least, I had become an athlete in a part of the world where it matters the most.

SOUTH AFRICA

The Springbok Boys Are Happy . . .

Running in Kenya was always going to be physically demanding, and I returned drained and a great deal leaner from my athletic exertions. My ligament-damaged foot was causing some serious pain now and as I flew back home to London I fantasised about the mountains of food I would soon be demolishing. *Ugali* would definitely not be on the menu.

After requiring a slimline body for the long-distance running, something which I went only some way to achieving, I now needed to beef myself up quickly to stand any chance at all of surviving my next sporting fantasy. Past experience, together with the lessons I had already learned from my recent travels, had taught me that I needed to be correctly prepared if I was serious about playing rugby union at the highest level.

I used to be a half-decent rugby player, but when I played for my school first team the game always seemed to be more fun when we were winning. The tackles did not hurt so much and you weren't beaten up so badly either. But when we were losing, rugby suddenly turned incredibly arduous. You felt the cold, the wind and the rain more, and for some reason you always ended up collecting some kind of injury.

Today's coaches would have been unimpressed with my 'fancy dan' style of play. I was a flanker, or wing forward, and I did not see much point in hurling myself into a scrum or loose ruck only to end up at the bottom of a huge pile of heavy forwards. No, it was much better to loiter around the fringes of the pack, where no personal harm could be done, and wait for the ball to pop up. Then I would be away with a sudden burst of speed, gaining ground for my team, with half an eye on the crowd to make sure they were being attentive.

I only tackled when I really had to and when there was nobody else around to do the dirty work. I remember once finding myself totally out of position on the pitch but being the last player between a rampaging, long-legged winger and the try line. A quick glance around confirmed what I already feared. I was required to stop this oversized teenager. People later told me it was a memorable tackle. All I can recall is throwing myself at him, his knee smashing against my thigh, and the worst dead leg of my life. It prevented a certain try, but as I was stretchered off the pitch I felt, all in all, that a missed tackle might have been a better option.

Once, just once, I captained the school team. This was only because four other contenders were all injured. It took me approximately four seconds of my captaincy debut to join the injury list. The opposing team kicked off, I jumped up in the air to catch the ball, landed awkwardly and hobbled off the pitch with a sprained ankle. That was it. On my return to the side, I was reduced to the infantry again.

After a couple of months of living it up at university, a sudden twinge of guilt persuaded me to offer my services to the rugby team. I took the commuter train down to the King's College playing fields in Motspur Park, a typically leafy suburb of south-west London, to discover that I would be playing against a rival London University college that same afternoon. I was introduced to the college captain, told I would be open-side flanker and promised a lengthy spell in the team if I produced the goods.

I had a nightmare. Five minutes before we were due to run out on to the pitch, the captain called the whole team into a small circle in the dressing-room. He asked us all to jog up and down on the spot in our boots, pumping our knees upwards and shouting 'Kings' every second. This, he believed, would spur us on before we entered the fray. Unfortunately, my knee inadvertently smashed into the captain's knee. The point of impact must have favoured me, because whilst I experienced only slight discomfort, he collapsed to the floor holding his knee and shouting expletives whilst in obvious agony. Non-playing colleagues rushed him to the local casualty department, where a large plaster cast was fixed on to the injured area. I made my debut for my college in the knowledge that I had just severely injured my own team captain before the match had even started. It proved to be my first and last game for King's College.

My only other appearance on a rugby pitch occurred many years later when I took part in a television film in which I was asked to spend a couple of days training with the Sheffield Eagles rugby league team. The film's director demanded a certain sequence where I was to run straight at the Eagles' forwards. I was to try and burst through their tackles whilst they – and I still remember the glint in their eyes when this was explained to them – had to stop me, using any method they saw fit. The first effort felt as if I had just played British Bulldog with a brick wall. The second effort resulted in a severe pain in my chest. In order to avoid a further mauling, I decided to adopt a cleverer approach. As I ran towards the Sheffield pack, I chipped the ball over them with the intention of running past, collecting the ball on a lucky bounce and scoring. The first part of the plan went well. I produced the perfect lofted kick which sailed over the opposition into unguarded territory. Unhappily, the opposition decided to take me out in any case, whether I had the ball in my hand or not. The tackle on me was worse because I was looking up in the air at the ball at the time and was not prepared to be hit. When I eventually rose from the mud, my chest felt ten times worse. The director insisted on another four takes, an X-ray later that day confirmed two cracked ribs and I decided that if I was ever going to play the game again I would have to be physically up to the task.

Time, as always, eases the pain, and when I decided to approach the best rugby team in the world I had conveniently forgotten the negative memories and the fact that rugby players had somehow all grown considerably in size since my day. It was always going to be a straight choice between the New Zealand All Blacks and the South African Springboks. No other international team at the time, save Australia, were even close to the skills and power of these two, and no other country treated rugby as a religion.

South Africa, the defending world champions, just got the nod. I had been impressed by the quiet but ruthlessly efficient manner in which they had destroyed British and French resistance in the winter of 1997, their much-improved off-pitch image and the new coaching set-up headed by Nick Mallett, an Oxford-educated, English-speaking former Springbok, who I felt might well appreciate what I was attempting to do.

There was one final reason. The remarkable sight of President Nelson Mandela wearing François Pienaar's number six Springbok jersey on the day South Africa won the 1995 World Cup final in Johannesburg was still fresh in my mind.

I spoke to John Dobson in Cape Town. Dobson was the editor of *South Africa Rugby* magazine, one of the various international publications I occasionally make contributions to. Always helpful, he said he would have a word with Mallett, a personal friend, on my behalf. I followed this up with a fax to the national coach.

Mallett, so it transpired, went straight to the Springboks captain,

Gary Teichmann, to seek his approval. 'If the players did not want it to happen, then it would not have done,' he was to tell me later. Teichmann had successfully followed the hard act of Pienaar as South Africa's captain. Although quieter in nature than his predecessor, and as a result less comfortable in the media spotlight, he was nevertheless as astute a captain and as inspirational a player, and he commanded the total respect of all his team. What Teichmann says normally goes.

To my amazement, Teichmann agreed. Alex Broun, the South African Rugby Football Union's Media Liaison Officer, made contact shortly afterwards and a date was set in our diaries. I would be flying down to Johannesburg immediately after South Africa's first Test match against Ireland in June to spend the week training with the 'Boks, culminating with the second Test against the Irish in Pretoria. No promises could be made about how much I would be permitted to do. We would just have to see how the week panned out and how the players responded to my intrusion. Broun had made a good point there. After all, I was English and I was a journalist, two rather unavoidable ingredients which would hardly endear me initially to a close-knit group of South African rugby players. I would face not only a tough physical challenge, but a mental one as well. I would need to tread very carefully indeed.

Within a few weeks the whole trip looked likely to be cancelled. SARFU's then President, Dr Louis Luyt, was accused of racism and mismanagement by South Africa's National Sports Council, who called for a boycott of South African rugby unless Luyt quit. For a while it seemed as if the summer tours of South Africa by Ireland, Wales and England would not go ahead and rugby would be plunged back into crisis. Luyt, an intransigent figure whom I had crossed a rocky path with before when I last visited the country in 1994, finally resigned, saving himself the humiliation of being forced out of his own executive, who were all set to oust him. The rugby world breathed a collective sigh of relief and my tour of South Africa, together with those of the home unions, of course, was back on.

In the remaining three weeks before departure I became obsessed about the training required to handle a week with the Springboks. It got to the stage where I was spending one hour a day on my exercise bike (normally in front of the television in the living-room, which caused great irritation to the rest of my family), 45 minutes a day on my ergometer in the garage, half an hour more pumping my biceps with a pair of dumb-bells and, on alternate days to rest my injured foot, a further 45 minutes running around my local park. I visited Sarah, my physio, in the week I was due to leave for South Africa. She told me I was overdoing it and there was no point arriving in South Africa tired out by my exertions. I would need to be fit and fresh to last a week's training.

By now we had discovered another problem with my foot. My condition had been diagnosed as an osteo-condrial defect with lateral ligament instability. In short, this meant that I needed surgery. The whole process, from the day of the operation back to full fitness, could take as long as four months, four months I did not have if I wanted to complete my sporting fantasy. We decided I could get by for a few months but my ligament needed to be reconstructed sooner rather than later. If not, then arthritis could begin to set in.

If this concerned me, so, too, did the thought of losing my teeth. A dentist friend of mine therefore sculpted a mouthguard for me in green and yellow, the colours of the South African rugby strip. I thought the gesture might go down well in Johannesburg. I bought a new pair of rugby boots and shorts, and tried them out the day before I left for the southern hemisphere, running up and down the length of my garden with my guard in my mouth, pretending to pass an imaginary ball to my colleagues. If the neighbours saw me, they might well have wondered if I had been hitting the alcohol again.

It was my son's fifth birthday party on departure day, and he had decided he wanted to have a pirate party. This meant that I had dressed up in my stripy Breton jersey and spent a couple of hours prancing around pretending to be Captain Hook. Within half an hour of the party finishing, however, I was sitting in a taxi *en route* to Heathrow Airport. As we drew near and I watched 747 after 747 climbing laboriously into the clouds, I wondered what fate befell me. After experiencing three sports in three totally contrasting regions of the world, I knew there was no point even trying to guess.

Moments before boarding I caught a glimpse of a television set in the departure lounge. The half-time score of the South Africa versus Ireland first Test match flashed up. South Africa were leading by just 13–10 in a match they were expected to win at an easy canter. Oh dear! If the score stayed as close as this then my questionable participation during the following week would probably be the last thing the Springboks needed.

Twelve hours later I found myself confronted by a passport-control officer at Jan Smuts Airport, Johannesburg. 'What was the score?' I asked him. I knew that any further details, such as using the words 'rugby', 'South Africa' or 'Ireland', were unnecessary in a country where the people breathe the sport. '37–13,' he replied. Much better than at half-time, then, but still not quite what was assumed of a rugby-playing nation almost burdened by such a high level of expectation. 'You're English,' the officer said, breaking my thoughts. 'Not staying for the England game, then?' I shook my head. 'Probably for the best,' he replied. 'It might be too painful for you, eh?' And with that he laughed and waved me through. This, as I was later to find out, was indicative of the general attitude of many in South Africa. The team, certainly against the less-powerful nations, were almost in a no-win situation. A hefty victory merely meant that the opposition were too weak. A narrow win resulted in criticism. Either way, Nick Mallett and his men found it difficult to satisfy the public and the media.

After a short sleep in my hotel room in Sandton, a smart suburb of Johannesburg yet still close to the slowly improving Alexandra township, I ventured downstairs just in time to meet Nick, who, together with the Springboks, had just arrived from Bloemfontein. Inviting me to join him and his management team for lunch, he introduced me first to his assistant coach, Alan Solomons, otherwise known as 'Solly', and then to Jake White, the team's technical adviser.

As he picked at his salad, Nick, a big brute of a man who has also lived and coached rugby in France, said how flattered he was to have been chosen ahead of the All Blacks. Not half as flattered, I thought, as I was when he and Gary Teichmann had agreed to the week ahead. He then explained how under the old Afrikaner Springbok management regime I would have stood no chance at all of training with the team. 'You would have heard two words only,' he said. 'And the second word would have been "off".' Then his tone changed as he laid down a few of the ground rules.

'You must go very easy with the team at first,' he explained. 'You must remember what an honour it is in this country to be a Springbok and to wear the Springbok jersey.' I asked if they had any Springbok kit I could borrow for the week.

'You're going to have to earn it first,' came the reply. 'If I'm honest, I have to admit I'm nervous about your participation. I don't know how you are going to behave and I don't know how the team will react. But I do know that if you become a distraction to the team, you will be out and on your way home by Wednesday.'

I got the message. In fact, I had already worked most of this out for myself. I had already intended to lie low for a day or two and try and impress on the training field. I knew I would be expected to fail and was determined to surprise a few people, gaining their respect and trust in the process.

Nick then invited me to the management-team meeting that

evening before introducing me to Kevin Stephenson, the fitness trainer, and Wayne Diesel, the physio. 'I've got a feeling you'll be getting to know Wayne quite well this week,' he added, with an ominous smile on his face.

Some of the players had joined us for lunch. I introduced myself to Gary 'Teich' Teichmann and in the course of the conversation happened to mention that I had a green and yellow mouthguard. Mark Andrews, the big lock forward, looked up from his plate. 'Gold,' he said. 'It's green and gold. That's what we play in.' It wasn't said in an unfriendly way. Yet it served as an instant reminder of what the Springbok colours meant to these boys.

That evening I attended my first ever Springbok management meeting in Nick Mallett's room. We were joined by Jake, Solly, Kevin, Wayne and the remarkably efficient Alex Broun. Wayne had produced fitness and injury reports on various players following the previous day's Test match against Ireland. The list was so long and detailed it resembled a casualty list following a small battle. Incredibly, despite the severity of some of the injuries, nearly all the players named were considered definite starters for the following Saturday's match.

As I suspected, the management team were far from happy with their side's performance against Ireland. 37–13 seemed, to me, to be a pretty conclusive victory, but it wasn't in Nick Mallett's book, nor in any other of the management team's. 'We're going to have to make them work hard tomorrow at training,' promised Solly. They decided to add a specialist prop coach to the team for a day or two to sort out the evident problems the front row had experienced against the useful Irish props, and then went through the week's itinerary. As we all stood up to leave, Nick looked across at me and added: 'Maybe we'll put Ian in an Irish jersey tomorrow. That should pump the boys up.'

At dinner I introduced myself to some of the Free State players who had arrived late after staying over in their home town of Bloemfontein after the Test match. André Venter, Johannes 'Rassie' Erasmus, Werner 'Smiley' Swanepoel and Naka Drotské all listened attentively to my explanation and wished me good luck. On first impressions they all seemed very pleasant, but I was left wondering what they meant by 'good luck'. I would find out in the morning.

I joined Jake White and the big Natal prop Ollie le Roux in the team room. The Springboks always have such a communal room wherever they stay. In this a pool table and a table-tennis table is provided, together with a refrigerator full of energy drinks, a video screen, massage tables and rows and rows of seats. Jake was reviewing the Ireland match on video, editing out all the passages of time where the ball was dead. A concerned le Roux was trying to ascertain what had gone wrong against the Irish front row.

'I won my first cap in 1994 and was then dropped,' he explained. 'Yesterday was only my second cap. I've waited that long for a recall. I hope it's not going to happen to me again.' He seemed genuinely worried and sought reassurance from Jake. Despite his huge, rounded body, Ollie had been a former schools squash champion. When he heard I had played Jansher Khan in Pakistan, he peppered me with questions. 'How much did he beat you by?' he asked, making the natural assumption that Jansher had, indeed, won the big match. 'Do you think he's the best ever? What's he like, then?' It later transpired that he, together with Mark Andrews, had also been a national water-polo player.

Jake challenged me to a game of table tennis. In my youth I had collected a few cups playing in the little-known Stamford and Rutland table-tennis league, but I had rarely picked up a bat since. Consequently Jake beat me, but I told him that I would shake off my rustiness and that he would not take another set off me all week. We went for a beer and talked about Nick Mallett. 'He's the first coach ever to apply for the job, rather than just be elected,' Jake explained. 'Nick chose his own management team, which is why I am here now.

'In the past, under the Afrikaner rule, the players were made to feel as if they were in the army. Nick's big on psychology and man-management, though. That's why most of the players have gone to the cinema tonight. They are trusted and encouraged to participate as much as possible. There's a lot of interaction in the squad now between the players and the management. We're a happy team.' He explained how he and Nick had since their appointment trekked around the country looking for new talent in areas previously left alone by selectors, especially in the black and Coloured communities. 'We've been trying to secure college places for people who otherwise would just return to their townships,' he said. 'It's wonderfully exciting. Just think what this country can do in rugby terms now that we truly have the whole population to choose from.'

I mentioned that I had seen highlights that afternoon from the Emerging Springboks' victory over Wales, a performance dominated by black and Coloured talent. 'That's right,' Jake enthused. 'And the guy who scored a hat-trick is joining us for the week in what we call our "Rising Star" project. He'll be doing some of the training alongside you.' He downed his drink and stood up. 'Come on. You'd better get some sleep. You've got a hard day ahead of you tomorrow.'

Jake, as I was to discover during the week, was an affable man.

Often the good-natured butt of Nick's jokes, the former teacher was nevertheless seen as an integral part of the management team and represented all that is good about the new Springbok set-up. Yet his serious manner at the very end of our conversation suggested he meant every single word he had just said.

I left early in the morning with Jake, Solly and David Dobela, an Under-21 Development Officer from Border who had come to learn some of the Springboks' coaching methods. We drove ahead of the rest of the squad in a combi to the St John's College playing fields, a public school in the Houghton district of Johannesburg, in order to prepare for training. 'It's crucial that no time is lost once the boys arrive,' Solly explained as he ran about the field placing cones and markers down on the grass. Jake followed suit, whilst I limbered up. Despite the fact that Johannesburg is situated some 5,000 feet above sea level, I felt comfortable. After running at 9,000 feet in Nyahururu and Kapsabet, Johannesburg was easy in comparison.

The rest of the squad arrived shortly after ten o'clock in the team bus. One or two, just as the Flamengo players had previously done in Rio, commented on my new boots. They looked at my shiny, long studs and then at the hard South African ground. Despite the fact that June is supposed to represent winter down in Johannesburg, the temperature was a pleasant 20 degrees. 'You're going to get major stud bruising,' they predicted.

Training got under way. We began with ball skills. Facing each other in two lines, we had to pass a series of balls to each other in quick succession until the last one had gone cleanly through our hands. Then we had to run back to the front of the line and go through the whole process again and again. So far, so good. My handling skills have always been reasonable in all sports, and I managed to complete the exercise without dropping a ball. Mark Andrews told me later that he had been waiting for me to make a mistake so that he could give me 'a verbal kicking'. He was surprised to see me come through.

After further exercises, in which we had to enact diagonal runs across each other's paths whilst passing the ball to each other, we came to the tackle bags. Here we had to run, with the ball, through two players holding padded tackle bags. Once I had managed this, it was my turn to hold the tackle bags, together with McNeil 'Mackie' Hendricks, a popular black winger from the Boland district. We stood together and waited for the lock forward, Krynauw Otto.

On first impressions, Krynauw Otto is one of the scariest sights in international rugby. He stands, with his crew-cut hairstyle, a mere six foot seven tall and weighs approximately 260lbs. Incredibly, despite his huge bulk, he records just 11 per cent body fat. The rest of this mountain of a man is muscle.

Krynauw started to run towards us. I stood there holding the tackle bag, braced myself and tried not to think about what was to happen. At the last second Krynauw dipped his shoulder, missed Mackie and ploughed straight into me. There was an audible gasp as I felt my breath leave my body, my feet depart from the ground and my body fly – and I use the verb in a literal sense – backwards before crashing to the ground a couple of metres behind. Krynauw, despite his physical appearance, turned out to be a quiet, well-mannered gentleman who, off the field, seemed to possess a permanent and friendly smile. Stooping down to ground level, he hauled me back up to my feet, apologised profusely for having helped me break the world backwards-long-jump record and explained how he had tried to barge into Mackie in order not to hurt me. Meanwhile, in the turf, an Ian Stafford-sized divot remained.

'That's okay, Krynauw,' I told him, aware that a few of the 'Boks were watching with interest. 'Who's next?' I do not know if this false show of bravado worked or not, but it provoked a couple of chuckles from my new-found colleagues.

The squad was split up into five groups and I found myself with Teich. The object of the next exercise was to run up and down the field passing to each other diagonally, and when our group won the competition, the captain enacted high fives with everyone in his group. Slowly I began to feel part of the squad.

Nearby was standing Joost van der Westhuizen, who, together with Mark Andrews, was one of just two survivors from the 1995 World Cup-winning team. He revealed later on in the week how he still liked to watch a video of that unforgettable match. 'My wife shuts the door and leaves me to it,' he said. 'She knows it's my special time again.' Arguably the best scrum-half in the world, he was also one of the better-known Springboks, although he was later to play this down. 'The good thing about this team is that there are no superstars or egos. We play for each other and we are all equals.' He promised me that during the course of the week I would become fit.

A smiling James Dalton approached with his hand extended towards me to shake. Dalton is the fiery Springbok hooker. After Andrews and van der Westhuizen, he is the most capped player in the squad, a big name and a colourful character in South African sport. A short man, with a shaven head and a bad-boy image made worse after his sending off against Canada during the World Cup which cost him his place in the final, I was interested to discover what he was really like. It emerged that Dalton was full of positive surprises. 'Hi, I'm James,' he said, by way of introduction. 'I've heard what you are doing and I think it's awesome. You must tell me all about the other sports you've done or you're going to do some time this week.'

To say I was taken aback would be an understatement. Here was one of the biggest names in South Africa bending over backwards to be accommodating to me. James then insisted that I joined him and Ollie le Roux in the next exercise that required groups of three. Ollie was in a good mood by now, having learned that morning that Nick had stuck with exactly the same side to face the Irish that coming Saturday.

James placed a large rubber belt around his body and, rather like the exercises in Kenya at Nyahururu, proceeded to drag me along for 22 metres, before turning round and running back to the try line. Then it was my turn to pull Ollie. As I did this, some of the team began to shout out words of encouragement. They realised that dragging Ollie le Roux was like trying to shift a house.

Having taken my turn punching a tackle bag using boxing gloves, I was then asked to jump ten times on to a bench, side-step a few cones and then hurl myself at another tackle bag as if I were tackling an opponent. We were all required to do this for a good five minutes or so. After one such tackle Nick Mallett shouted out: 'Tackle it, man, don't mount the bloody thing!' This produced a few sniggers. I shouted back: 'Don't forget, I've been away from home now for a couple of days,' which produced more laughter.

After two and a half hours of heavy training, we all clambered back on to the team bus and motored back to the hotel. I had mixed emotions. I was delighted that I had survived a full training session and had been treated so well by the team, but I was also concerned. My troublesome right calf muscle had tightened up again, just as it had done prior to playing Jansher Khan in Pakistan. As we drove back through Johannesburg, I wondered if I would be able to last the rest of the week.

Over lunch Nick and Solly were complimentary. 'You did very well,' they said. Nick added: 'I was impressed by your attitude and the players' attitude towards you. It's a compliment to all of you.' Then he looked me up and down and smiled. 'You'll be feeling it in the morning, though.'

Never mind the morning, I thought, as I made my way straight up to Wayne Diesel's room. I'm feeling it now. Wayne seemed to be expecting me. A former South African Olympic squad physiotherapist, he had only joined the Springboks the previous week for the first Irish game but, with his easy nature and quiet but reassuring manner, had immediately blended into the set-up. Wayne identified a muscle tear in my calf and confirmed that my left foot needed surgery. After treating the damaged area with interferential therapy, he gave me some anti-inflammatory tablets and promised me that, providing I made sure to stretch properly before training, I would not be troubled by my muscle tear again. I found this statement difficult to believe, judging by the pain I had felt during the morning's session, but Wayne proved to be right. I was never bothered by it again throughout a hard week's training.

After an optional weights session in a Sandton health club that afternoon, for which half of the team turned up to expand their already huge muscles, I managed to beat my first Springbok at the table-tennis table, Ollie le Roux. Teich and the big former Zimbabwean prop forward Adrian 'Garvs' Garvey were playing pool. I noticed how the Natal Sharks team-mates were prodding each other with their cues each time either produced a bad shot, resulting in a small blue chalk dot on their clothes or, sometimes, on their faces.

That night Nick held a video-nasty team meeting. The whole squad sat in the team room as the first Test against Ireland was reviewed on the big screen. It proved to be a fascinating insight into the pursuit of excellence. At the very height of his power, Jansher Khan would, on winning 15–2, wonder why he had lost two points. The Brazilians, no doubt, would be asking why they had not won 3–0 instead of by just two goals. Pete Sampras in the early 1990s would have been upset if he had lost one set at the Wimbledon tennis championships. Here, in a room in Sandton, the Springboks were undergoing a similar post-mortem.

Nick Mallett produced a staggering performance. This had been his first Test match on home soil and he was far from satisfied. Pacing up and down in front of the screen and continually asking Jake to stop the film to allow him to make his point, the man hardly stopped talking for nearly two hours. His long narrative was full of rants, criticisms and cutting observations about both his team and the Irish, who had produced a robust, if not violent, style of play to thwart the Springboks. 'It's giving me ulcers,' he would shout. 'Look at you three,' he would say, pointing at the front row. 'You look like the three stooges.' Later he added: 'This is like something out of *The Goon Show*.' Many sentences also included the word 'kak', the Afrikaans word for 'shit'.

Yet this display of perfection-seeking was not all about a verbal bashing. Mallett was astute enough to intersperse his criticisms with compliments, both individually and collectively. He also found time to highlight moments of humour. Once, he freeze-framed Ollie le Roux as the big prop jumped upwards to try and block an Irish kick up field. Allowing the film to be played in slow motion, he pointed out how the ball had landed 50 metres further on before Ollie's feet had touched the ground again. 'Look,' Nick said, with a wide grin on his face. 'Ollie should be landing any moment now.' It reduced the room to giggles, and even Ollie himself, wearing his rather studious-looking rounded glasses, broke out into laughter.

There was just enough time for a few more games of table tennis. Having seen off the big, friendly centre Pieter Muller and the self-assured utility back Franco Smith, I then faced the confident challenge of the coach himself. I had been warned about Nick Mallett. Jake, among others, had told me that Nick did not like to lose in anything to anyone. It was questionable if it would be in my best interests to beat the man. Possessing a similar competitive nature myself, however, and thinking that I might be able to make up for some of my training-ground deficiencies on the table-tennis table, I went on to record a comprehensive win. I was about to thank him when Nick walked to the other side of the table and said: 'Come on, next game.' This time he changed his game plan, turning from attack to defence. These tactics resulted in a much closer set, but still another win to me. 'It may be 2–0,' Nick said as we shook hands, 'but there's a long way to go yet.'

I expected to be stiff and sore in the morning but, apart from my aching shoulders, felt remarkably fresh. Downstairs in the lobby I bumped into Stefan Terblanche, the speedy winger who had marked his debut that weekend with a four-try blitz against the Irish. This, for a Springbok debutant, was a record. The rest of the squad were eating breakfast in T-shirts and shorts, but the Boland winger was dressed up in what was termed his 'Number Ones', the full Springbok green blazer, black trousers, shirt and tie. On top of his head sat his first cap which, with his teeth brace, made him look like an overgrown schoolboy. I half expected a chocolate bar to be sticking out of one of his blazer pockets, with perhaps a catapult in the other.

On guessing my thoughts, Stefan explained how it was a tradition for a first-time international to wear his 'Number Ones' and cap until the end of the Wednesday night. Did he mind having to get dressed up all the time? 'No way,' he replied, bristling with pride. 'It's an honour. When I was a kid I used to pretend to be a Springbok with my friends. We'd all pick a player, and I'd be Naas Botha. It was pretty emotional when I heard I'd made the squad and then the team. My dad died when I was eight, but my sisters and mother have followed me everywhere and given me as much support as anyone could have. It meant as much to them as it did to me.'

I went early to training again with Jake and Solly. They spent half the journey talking about playing me at hooker for some of the forthcoming session. 'It will be okay,' Solly said, putting on a consoling expression. 'We know a good neurologist in Cape Town.' He and Jake burst out into great guffaws of laughter. I shared the joke, wondering just what fate might befall me later in the morning.

After the usual ball skills and stretching exercises, the backs sprinted off to a corner of the field, leaving the forwards to their own devices. Nick invited me to join the pack for the rest of the session. At first we practised loose forward play and rucks. The 'Castle' move was when one player would roll three times on the ground in possession of the ball before making it available to his supporting players. Teich lobbed the ball over to me and called for a Castle. I set off, threw myself to the ground and proceeded to roll three times. Unfortunately, instead of rolling in a straight line I rolled in a curve, forcing the whole Springbok pack to run after me in a wild, lateral chase across the width of the pitch. Teich would keep mentioning the Castle to me for the rest of the week in a series of friendly digs.

For the remaining 40 minutes I played in the number eight position, which suited me fine. As a former flanker, I understood the rudiments of back-row play and happily slotted in to the back of the pack as we pushed against scrum machines and worked with the ball. It was hard work, of course, but at least I knew what I was doing.

Two problems, however, arose. First, I had to squeeze my head between the large, tree-trunk legs of André Venter, the big Free State flanker who was trying his hand at being a lock forward, and those of a newcomer to the squad, Selborne Boome. After great effort I usually managed to do this, but occasionally my head became lodged, as if in a vice, and my ears rubbed furiously against two rock-solid thighs. On resurfacing I felt my red, raw and throbbing ears. For the rest of the week my ears would be flaky and peeling, as if, like a snake, I was shedding my skin. It was easy to see how rugby forwards soon develop cauliflower ears. Mine, in the space of one morning, had already become florets.

The second problem was a little more embarrassing. As number eight I had to grab the shorts of Venter and Boome in a tight grip whilst pushing my head through the minuscule gap between their thighs. After one forward thrust, the whole pack collapsed to the floor. Losing my balance, my right hand inadvertently pulled down Venter's shorts and my head all but disappeared up his now bare backside. It might have taken the rest of the morning to have extricated my head from André's buttocks. Thankfully, it was a near miss and André hoisted his shorts back up with one hefty tug as if it was nothing more than an occupational hazard.

As training drew to a close, a delicious smile suddenly appeared on Nick Mallett's face. Wagging his finger towards me, he shouted out: 'Ian, now it's your turn to see what it's like to face the Springbok pack.' In front of me stood the front row of Adrian Garvey, James Dalton and Ollie le Roux. I shook their hands in a mock farewell, took up my position as opposition hooker, hoisted my arms around Naka Drotské and prop Robbie Kempson, and scrummed down. The initial impact was bearable, but as soon as the first-team pack began to push I felt Adrian's head furrowing into my chest. The pain was instant and I was made fully aware of the awesome power of a pack of eight players weighing some 870 kilos. At any moment, I feared, the boys could snap my body in half with just one concerted shove. When we all resurfaced I felt as if Adrian Garvey had left an imprint of his face on the left-hand side of my chest, like the Turin Shroud.

Some of the team spent the afternoon playing golf. I was teamed up with two of the younger reserves, Robbie Kempson and flanker Bobby Skinstad. Both had highly promising futures and were expected to become permanent fixtures in the Springbok side before long. Their golf, incidentally, was a far sight better than mine on the day. Despite having had a practice round with a friend the week before in England in the knowledge that there was every chance of playing golf with the 'Boks, I ended up looking as if I was trying to putt every shot, including my drives off the tee.

On the 30-minute bus journey home I talked to Teich. At the age of 31, he had been handed the unenviable task of not just taking over the captaincy from François Pienaar but also leading a disjointed side fraught with internal and off-field problems. Defeats on home soil to both New Zealand in the Tri-Nations series and the British Lions might well have spelled the end of his leadership, but he had battled on and now, with a succession of impressive victories under his belt in France and Britain, Gary Teichmann enjoyed the full support of both his confident team and his management.

'It was very tough after the Lions, though,' he admitted, as he sipped a drink on the bus. 'As you can imagine, the defeat didn't go down too well in South Africa. I was lucky to survive. What made it so frustrating for us all was that we knew we shouldn't have lost that series. The Lions were a good side and they developed over the weeks into a strong, well-bonded team, but we were our own worst enemy.'

Since then, however, under Nick Mallett's guidance, the Springboks had returned to winning ways. 'It's a different style of management and it works very well,' Teich said. 'We're all playing for each other again, and there are no distractions or problems deflecting our purpose.'

Was it easy being the leader of a group of men the whole country aspires to be? 'I don't mind it on the field, but it can be difficult sometimes off it. It can affect your privacy, of course, and it means I have a great deal more to do than most of the other players. But it's also a great honour and something that came about quite unexpectedly. I never dreamed of being the Springbok captain. In fact, I never dreamed of being a Springbok. I was born in Zimbabwe and only really got into rugby when I came over to South Africa as an 11-year-old. My first cap took a long time coming, so I've never taken anything for granted.'

The bus pulled into the Holiday Inn Crowne Plaza Hotel. 'We'd better hurry,' Teich added as we stepped off the vehicle. 'It's the "Kontiki" in 15 minutes, and I've got a feeling you're going to play a part in this.'

'Kontiki' is the Afrikaans word for 'court', a tradition in rugby teams that still, despite the advent of professionalism, goes on, albeit in a diluted version. Not that long ago players deemed to have done something silly were 'punished' by a kangaroo court of team-mates. Various stories have emerged over the years, such as the two England lock forwards forced to hold hands with each other for a whole day and another England player tied naked to a lamppost outside a top restaurant. The consumption of large quantities of beer has always played an important role in all these shenanigans.

The Springboks have their own version of this. Part of the Kontiki was designed to honour new caps. This used to take the form of a beating. The whole squad would line up and hit the new cap's backside with a wooden stick until it became quite painful. Nick Mallett, although enthusiastic about the team-bonding element of this process, had frowned about the brutal aspects of the Kontiki. As a result, the beatings and the drinking had been toned down. After all, they all had another Test match in four days' time.

Werner Swanepoel stood attending the door. The rest of the squad sat in a circle in the team room, but new caps Stefan Terblanche and fly-half Gaffie du Toit, uncapped Robbie Kempson and Selborne Boome, and myself and David Dobela from Border were asked to stand outside. Gaffie had already endured a bad day. After making a reasonable start to his international career, he had been forced to withdraw from the second Test with an injury. Franco Smith would be replacing him and Gaffie was flying home in the morning for a ten-day recuperative period.

As if this was not bad enough, he and Stefan, resplendent in their tassled caps and Number Ones, trekked nervously up and down the hall outside the door. They kept asking us what we thought might happen to them. As none of us had ever been in a Springbok Kontiki before, we could only guess. Robbie Kempson told Stefan that he was bound to be in big trouble for scoring four tries on his debut. 'The judge will accuse you of showing off,' he said, which brought a smirk to our faces but a worried frown to Stefan's as Smiley opened the door and asked him to join the rest of the team.

This left Gaffie to his own thoughts. He started to let out huge sighs, stood jangling some money in his pockets, stared down at his shiny shoes and finally began to go on walkabout again. The sound of a sharp crack broke the silence. 'What was that?' Gaffie asked. 'Sounds like a beating to me,' Robbie replied, looking relaxed. He knew that he and Selborne, as uncapped players, would escape any such punishment. I assumed I would be spared too.

Gaffie then made an announcement. 'When I'm called in, I'm not going to look at anyone,' he said. 'I'm just going to stare dead ahead.' At this point, the door opened again, Smiley looked gravely at Gaffie and the Griquas stand-off set off at a measured pace as if walking to the gallows. The sound of further cracks could be heard, followed by chanting and applause.

Now it was our turn. Robbie, Selborne, David and I were asked to walk through the circle of seated players and stand in a row, as if we were facing a firing squad. Robbie and Selborne were asked to sit down. 'Your time will come,' said Joost van der Westhuizen, the leading judge of the panel of three. Alongside him at a table sat Mark Andrews and James Dalton, the three most-capped Springboks in the side. I was about to take a seat too. 'Ian, you stay there,' Joost shouted out. 'We haven't even started with you.' It was at this point that the palms of my hands began to sweat.

Joost asked me to say who I was and what I was doing. I had just begun my answer when Mark Andrews pointed accusingly at me. 'He's crossed his hands over,' he shouted, with evident glee. At this point I was handed a tall glass of beer and told to drink it all in one go without taking a break. As I slowly downed the alcohol, the Springboks started to chant:

'Cheers to Ian,
He's so blue,
He's a drunken through and through,
He's a bastard, so they say,
Tried to go to heaven,
But went the other way.'

Then, as I took measured gulps of my beer, they began to count.

'One, two, three, four, five . . .'

As soon as I finished the drink, various players started to point their fingers at me again. My crime this time had been to hold the glass with my right hand. They had conveniently forgotten to tell me I had to carry out my punishment holding the glass in my left hand. This constituted a further penalty. I took the second glass of beer in my left hand and began the whole process again.

'Cheers to Ian,
He's so blue . . .'

Joost demanded an answer to his initial question. I explained that I was writing a book about my experiences playing sport with the world's greatest sportsmen. Nick Mallett interrupted me. 'Is it a crime to have three of his jacket buttons fastened?' he asked.

A collective 'yes' signalled yet another beer. This time they started their chant even before the glass had been handed to me. By the time I had finished, the 'Boks had counted up to ten and had moved on to the months of the year.

'. . . eight, nine, ten, January, February, March . . .'

Joost asked me how I had found the experience so far. I told him and his fellow kangaroo jurors that I had enjoyed training with the boys immensely. James Dalton had been unusually quiet up to now. One of his various nicknames was 'Cyrus', after the evil John Malkovitch character 'Cyrus the Virus' in the film *Con Air*. I'm not sure whether James looked like this baddie, acted like him, or both. On hearing my reply, however, he swivelled his head round, looked at me with a particularly evil expression straight out of the Malkovitch repertoire and said: 'You're telling us you find training easy, are you?' By now I had realised that I could never provide an acceptable answer in a

Kontiki session. Another glass of beer was handed over to me and, for the fourth time, I was required to down the drink in one go.

The jury asked if anyone on the floor had anything to add. Teich stood up. 'Does the jury know that in the course of a conversation I had earlier today the accused kept asking me questions about the Lions defeat?'

This time Joost, Mark and James all looked at me. I knew what was coming. Beer number five was handed over to me and I poured the glass down my throat, again giving a gleeful Teichmann a look in the process. The squad had reached 'May' by the time I had finished.

Still the fun was not finished. Joost asked me to step forward, remove my jacket and bend over. This was definitely not in the script I had read, and as I obeyed his orders I was unsure if he really meant to carry out his threat. Joost picked up the beating stick, moved towards me and then smiled. 'It's okay, Ian, you can put your jacket on again now. We all welcome you to the Springbok squad and hope you continue to have a memorable week with us.'

I tried to act cool, but my heart had been pounding inside. The judges leapt down to the floor and asked the whole Springbok squad to form a circle in the room, link arms and sing the team song. Stefan had taught me the basics during his nervous wait outside, so I managed to keep up with the rest of the boys as we sang the following:

The Springbok boys are happy,
The Springbok boys are we,
We never never quarrel,
We never disagree,
For the motto of the Springboks,
Is come and drink with me,
The motto of the Springboks,
Is come and drink with me.

Forwards form the scrum,
Half-back puts it in,
Half-back to the centre,
Centre to the wing,
Wing scores a try,
The Irish begin to cry,
Hurrah, Hurrah,
For we can sing and play,
Hurrah, Hurrah,
For we can sing and play.

And then we returned to the first verse again. By the end of all this everyone was laughing, slapping backs and enjoying a beer, whilst Stefan and Gaffie, looking immensely relieved, smiled and rubbed their backsides. It was, to say the least, an unusual evening, but one that revealed a little more about the seemingly unbreakable team spirit of this new Springbok squad. And for me, as I stumbled off to bed, it was a sign that I had been fully accepted by the boys. For the first time that week, I felt a warm glow inside me. Of course, the beer might have had something to do with this.

Henry Honiball had joined up with the squad by Wednesday morning. Known as 'Lem' (the Afrikaans word for 'blade') because he could cut through opposition defences at will, he had been out with a neck injury, and although it was felt he was still not 100 per cent fit, Nick wanted him to sit on the bench for the Ireland match as cover for Franco at stand-off and any of the other backs. An experienced and quietly assured farmer from Natal, he seemed to command the respect of the whole squad. He was also a useful table tennis player, and later we fought an epic set which I eventually took 29–27 after both Lem and I had played as if our lives depended upon winning.

Training consisted of more ball skills and heavy tackling before the squad concentrated on specifics. Line-outs proved to be one area. Under the new rules, the jumpers in the line-outs are now allowed to be assisted by two colleagues. The ever-enthusiastic and friendly Bobby Skinstad volunteered to lift me up from behind for me to catch the ball. Unfortunately for him, each time we enacted this move my right foot would inadvertently jerk up behind me and land full on his private parts. A red-faced Bobby would then run around clutching his shorts. After four successive collisions he suggested I did the lifting.

As if the day before had not been enough, I was then invited back into the scrum. This time André Venter was in the opposition and as we packed down he playfully but repeatedly punched me on the forehead. As my hands were round the back of my two props, I was completely powerless to react. Emerging from the scrum, I told a smirking André that next time I would cite him and get him banned from international rugby.

Nick Mallett wanted to see a little more action. He asked Mark Andrews if he would tackle me. Andrews, on 43 caps, was close to breaking the Springbok record for number of appearances. A huge man, probably the second largest in the team behind Krynauw Otto, his balding pate and large gap between his front teeth provoked endless material for his teasing colleagues, but he remained one of the most popular and passionate members of the team. It also transpired that he had a great love of art and, in particular, furniture. I had told him how I had recently spent a weekend in an area of Suffolk where in each village rows and rows of antique warehouses could be found. 'Oh, I'd be in my absolute element,' he replied.

Now, however, he stood on the try line, slightly crouched, and waited for my attacking foray. He did not, it has to be said, look particularly concerned. Bobby Skinstad suggested that as Mark tackled me I flick the ball across to him to score a try. I was supposed to run straight at Mark, but my natural instinct to live forced me to side-step at the last minute, causing my knee to crash into his cheek. Bobby collected my pass and ran on to score.

'No, no, do that again,' barked out Nick. 'And run straight at him this time, Ian.' Mark's expression, as he rubbed his cheek, had grown unnervingly serious. As I approached him he was more than ready. What happened next remains a blur. One moment I was running with the ball in my hand, the next I was lying in a crumpled heap on the ground. It felt as if I had just been attacked and devoured by some large wild beast. The beast in question was standing in front of me, looking rather pleased with his kill. Nick Mallett was laughing. 'Now that's what I call a tackle,' he said, having clearly enjoyed the cameo performance we had just played out.

By now I really needed to see Wayne the physio again. *En route* to his room I stopped off on the first floor of the team hotel to pay Mark Andrews a visit, just to make sure there were no hard feelings. He shared a room with Adrian Garvey, and neither will mind too much if I state that someone had clearly let a large bomb explode inside. Finding a small piece of carpet not covered by bags, kit, newspapers, strapping and orange peel, I observed the scene of destruction. Adrian lay on his bed watching CNN on television. 'Garvs likes to catch up with what's going on in the world,' Mark explained. 'And I like to read a lot.'

He showed me what looked like a personal file. 'This is a passage I read before every game I play,' he explained, handing over the book. It read:

> To believe you can win is like any other kind of faith. You can think about it, talk about it, write about it, dedicate your life to it. But it doesn't matter. Belief is a simple thing. The Springboks believe they will win as simply as the sun shines, and even if you match their training, to beat them you will have to match their faith. In my mind, I am a winner.

It must mean a great deal to be a Springbok, then, I suggested to this player who was a hard man on the field but a thoughtful, intelligent soul off it. 'It means everything,' he replied. 'Nothing else in my life matters. It's all-consuming. I remember when I won my first cap. People's perception of me changed overnight. My friends, even members of my own family, no longer saw me just as Mark. They saw me as a Springbok. To me, my debut meant more than winning the World Cup. If I can make it to 50 caps, it would be the most wonderful thing I can ever imagine.'

I had to keep to an appointment with Wayne. Franco Smith was also in the physio's room and he immediately commented on the size of my chest. It had, indeed, become swollen. Wayne carried out a few exercises and diagnosed a sprained left pectoral muscle. 'I'm afraid all you can do is rest it,' he said. 'But as you're training with us, it's going to be painful.' I left with yet more anti-inflammatory tablets.

That night the whole squad played a full role in the annual SARFU banquet at the Sandton Sun hotel. After being individually introduced on stage, accompanied by their favourite songs, the players then all hosted tables crammed with corporate rugby fans. These fans were later to pay vast amounts of money for signed Springbok jerseys and balls. Some of the team also had to play a couple of games up on stage. In one, entitled 'Check Your Mate', room-mates had to answer questions about each other. Mark Andrews, for instance, was asked what was Adrian Garvey's most annoying habit. He replied: 'Garvs likes to strut around the room naked.' A film recording of an earlier interview with Adrian was then shown on a large screen on the stage. The same question was put to Garvey about himself. 'I know Mark gets annoyed when I walk around with no clothes on,' he said. This was accompanied by a huge cheer from the audience.

On the way home that night, Nick Mallett congratulated the squad on a good public-relations performance. 'You all did very well,' he concluded. Public relations, so the coach recognised, was a new and extremely important aspect to the Springboks. 'I know very well how boorish and arrogant South African rugby had seemed to the rest of the world when we were first readmitted into international sport,' he told me later. 'That's why there's much work to be done to reveal the true picture. I hope the process has started.'

One of the 'Boks had stayed back at the Holiday Inn. James Dalton had woken that morning with a sore throat. His condition had grown worse during the day, and there were now major concerns that flu-like symptoms would rule him out of the Irish Test on the Saturday. It had seemed a quieter day without his bubbly personality.

I was to spend much of Thursday with the coach. As we cycled on exercise bikes in the morning during the optional gym session, he talked of his family. 'I'm married, with two children,' he said, with a satisfied look on his face. 'My daughter's eleven and my son is nine, and they are the most important things in the world to me. I went to boarding-school as a child and sometimes my wife accuses me of being unsympathetic towards them as a result. I hope I'm not. What I do know is that I never let rugby overrule my family.'

We then talked about his current position. During the first Test in Bloemfontein he had been heckled by some of the Afrikaner members of the crowd. There were even a few of the old national flags from the days of apartheid on show. 'I was very frustrated afterwards,' he admitted. 'I'd say 85 per cent of this was down to the fact that we didn't play well against Ireland. But the crowd didn't help. It was pretty depressing.'

What sort of things were they saying to him? 'Oh, really stupid things like "Can you speak Afrikaans, Mallett?" or "You're a shit team". Do you know, I receive abusive phone calls and faxes at home and in the office from a few of the Afrikaners. It's water off a duck's back, really.

'People elsewhere mistakenly believed that when we won the World Cup in 1995 it was the birth of the new Rainbow Nation. But to some it simply confirmed what they had always believed. We were the best, and other world cups did not count because we had not competed in them. It was a lost opportunity, but you can't change some people overnight. Only now can I see changes taking place.'

I asked him why it had taken him some time to become the national coach. 'Because I was too much of a hot potato before,' he replied, without batting an eyelid. 'It had been hard enough making the Springbok team as a player. Two caps for an English-speaking player back in the mid-1980s was a feat in itself. That's why, when I took up this job, I insisted on doing things my way. I have a contract until after the World Cup, regardless of results, I had the right to appoint my own management team and I have sole responsibility when it comes to selection.

'Other coaches, you see, just have to coach and select a team. I have to please a whole country riddled with division. I have to pick on merit, and that means I'm going to upset someone all the time. I also have to ensure that real development is taking place in this country. I know how disbelieving the rest of the world has been in the past. Well, now it's happening, and South African rugby will soon be bearing the fruits of the sport, and top coaching, being made available to everyone.'

Jake White turned up, prompting Nick and Solly to tease him about his phantom drinking problem. I reminded Jake that I owed him one on the table-tennis table. 'You won't get me back on the table,' he said. 'You're really cooking now.'

Nick overheard this. 'That's the only reason why I'm scared of Jake ever beating me on the golf course,' he said. 'If he does, I know he'll never play me again.' We returned to the hotel table-tennis table, where Nick finally took a set off me. 'That's 2–1, and I'm coming back strong,' he chanted, clearly pleased with his efforts. I suggested we played the best out of five over the remaining couple of days. 'We'll keep on playing until I'm ahead,' Nick replied.

That afternoon the squad travelled to the Loftus Versfeld stadium in Pretoria, where the second Test against Ireland would take place. It was a tradition for Teich to take charge of what was termed 'The Captain's Practice'. This meant that the test team would carry out various drills on the field and get more acclimatised to the pitch and stadium. The reserves, and I was deemed to be one of them, would have their own training session on the pitch, overlooked by Kevin Stephenson, the fitness trainer.

After various ball-skill exercises, sprints and boxing spells on the tackle bags, we had to line up with a small parachute tied to our backs. The idea was to sprint the width of the pitch, take a 20-second breather, and return. The faster you ran, the more the parachute opened up, supposedly making it harder for the player to sprint. Having now collected two battered and bruised knees to go with my sprained pec, I ran in such a laborious fashion that my chute barely opened at all. Teich broke off training up field to watch my efforts. Turning to Jake, he said: 'You watch over there. In a minute that parachute's going to overtake Ian.' He wasn't far wrong, either.

The physio's room was crammed full of players that evening. Mark Andrews was having his back seen to, Nick Mallett and Teich both required a hard massage, the full-back, Percy Montgomery, wanted his ankle looking at and Ollie le Roux was in need of some ankle work. The US Open golf was on television, and Ollie, the all-round sportsman of the squad, spoke of his plans after rugby. 'I want to join a senior professional tour,' he said. 'I'm an eight handicapper, and I can soon knock that down. I also want to play some American football. I've got contacts at the San Francisco 49-ers and the Dallas Cowboys. I'm really serious about it.'

I suggested he should try the decathlon. That would test his all-round sporting skills. I meant it as a joke, but as I left Wayne to his work, Ollie looked in deep thought.

Friday, the day before the big game, was a rest day. The players were advised to stay off their feet as much as possible. A smiling James Dalton had emerged feeling a great deal better. 'It's amazing what the thought of missing out on another cap can do to a cold,' he said, letting out a hearty cackle. That morning the players would be given their team shirts. This would be an unusual occasion, mainly because the Springboks would be playing in predominantly white jerseys in order not to clash with the green of the Irish.

Ampie le Roux, the team's kit man, saw me wandering around the hotel lobby and beckoned me over. 'Come,' he said. 'I want to show you something special.' He led me to a room, unlocked the door and gestured me forward. 'You'll enjoy this,' he said in a hushed tone, opening the door as if we were about to enter a church. There, in front of us, lay the 15 jerseys of the Springbok team to face Ireland the next day. To Ampie, and no doubt to a great many of the South African population, this had become a sacred room. 'This is my place,' he said, with pride written all over his face. 'And there, before you, are the Springbok jerseys.'

Shortly afterwards Nick Mallett fronted a small ceremony in the team room. The coach handed a jersey to each of his Test team, shaking their hand and congratulating them in the process. 'Never forget what it means to wear this,' he said to all and sundry. We all posed for team photographs. I was allowed to lie down in front of the team in a Springbok tracksuit. When the photographer asked the team to look relaxed, they promptly started to pull each other's ears. The end result was a hilarious débâcle.

Most of the squad relaxed that afternoon, but I drove back to Loftus Versfeld in the combi with 'Monty' (Percy Montgomery), Franco and Lem for kicking practice. All of them could be required for place kicking against Ireland in 24 hours' time, and all therefore wanted some last-minute practice. As we strode on to the pitch, preparations were being made for the big game. Groundsmen were marking out lines and sponsors' logos on the pitch with paint, and the stadium tannoy system was continually being tested.

We began by punting the ball to each other up and down the field, before I took my position behind the posts and waited for the conversions to start flying over. Over the course of the next hour or so I caught ball after ball as Monty, Franco and Lem kicked from all angles and from all lengths. The hard ball crashing down on my fingers soon took its toll, and a trip that evening back to Wayne's room confirmed ligament damage in my left ring finger, just to add to my long list of other Springbok-related injuries. At least the kickers were grateful for the service I provided, but as I left Wayne's room he confirmed what I had suspected. No one had been treated more for injuries that week than me, and I wasn't even a proper Springbok. Still, I looked at it as confirmation of my efforts during the week. But, as the old Red Indian saying goes, 'It's not the man with the scars you should fear, but the man who gave them.'

The team had their own words to memorise that night. All had been handed a reminder of the Springbok Code of Honour. The players scuttled off to read what amounted to yet more evidence of the true meaning of being a Springbok in South Africa. I was given a copy too. Its remarkable passage reads as follows:

I, —, hereby undertake and pledge my word of honour in support thereof, to honour and abide by the following code:

That I shall at all times and in all places wear the Springbok colours with pride and dignity.

That I shall at all times, and at every occasion, conduct myself in a dignified manner and with pride, so as to ensure that all my actions are worthy of the proud traditions of Springbok rugby.

That whilst wearing this jersey, I shall at all times be gracious in victory and honourable in defeat, yet never shall I surrender whilst enjoying the privilege of wearing the green and gold.

That the Springbok team and its interests shall always be placed above my own ambitions, and my contribution will serve only to enhance the proud history of Springbok rugby.

We are clearly talking about much more than just a rugby team here. In Brazil they may have their footballers, but in South Africa few believe anyone can achieve more in life than becoming a Springbok.

Saturday, the day of the match itself, began bright and early for me. I went to the gym with Kevin Stephenson and Selborne Boome for a work-out and some plyometrics. For the next hour or so we jumped up and down on benches before moving on to weights. On my return I saw a fully recovered James Dalton, who invited me to join him for a late breakfast. He was evidently excited about events to come that afternoon in Pretoria.

'It still means just as much to me now to be a Springbok as it did when I started back in 1994,' he admitted, in between spoonfuls of yoghurt and muesli. 'I can't tell you how concerned I've been this week over this cold. It's bad enough missing an international with a proper injury, but with a blocked-up nose . . .!' He shook his head and smiled.

I told him he was different from the public perception of him. 'You're right, I am,' he replied. 'I head one of the leading chemical firms in the whole country, so I can't be that stupid, can I? I've done a few bad things on and off the pitch in my time, but I generally know where to draw the line.'

His problem was that the red card he received during the 1995 World Cup in South Africa was in full view of a global audience. 'Yeah, I know,' he said. 'It takes no time to get an image, and an eternity to lose it. Do you know, it insults me when people come up to me and say: "Now, you are going to behave yourself, aren't you James?" I mean, I'm a professional sportsman!'

James retired to his room for some last-minute relaxation. For an hour or two, the players were nowhere to be seen. When they emerged for lunch, consisting of the usual players' diet of pasta, rice, chicken and fish, their demeanour had changed. The conversation was quieter, the expressions on their faces far more serious. Their thoughts had begun to turn elsewhere.

Nick and Teich delivered short speeches in the team room afterwards, reminding the players of what they are, who they represent and how well they can play. Then we all piled on to the team bus. I had been given a full Springbok tracksuit and was going to sit on the reserves' bench for the actual match. I was excited about the prospect, but quickly realised that this was not the time to share my jovial mood.

The contrast between this journey and any other taken during the week was extraordinary. Normally the team bus was full of shouting, laughter and jokes. Music would often be played, the odd banana skin would be lobbed across the aisle and people would be swapping seats as if they were playing musical chairs. This time, the silence became almost excruciating. In the 45-minute journey from Sandton to Pretoria, I barely heard two words spoken. I would occasionally look around at the players. All stared either ahead at nothing in particular or out of the window. Some took swigs from a water bottle, others tried to close their eyes. Even the management team behaved in exactly the same manner. Nick and Solly, who sat in front of me, normally never stopped jabbering on about rugby. This time, both remained mute.

Followers of sport would be forgiven for believing that sportsmen such as the Springboks may find it difficult to pump themselves up for matches that are considered to be foregone conclusions. Certainly no one gave the Irish any chance of winning this game. The evidence of the bus journey, however, painted a totally different picture. The Springboks knew they would be in for a tough, physical encounter. Bad blood remained from the previous week's tussle and national expectation weighed heavily on everyone's shoulders. Whether it was their second cap or their forty-third cap, the players acted the same: tense, serious and motivated up to their eyeballs.

Once the bus had finally cut its way through cheering punters waving their flags and banners on the streets close to the stadium, the team walked purposefully straight to their dressing-room. The reserves, including me, enjoyed a quick run-out on to the pitch, where we practised a few passes. On a given signal from the tannoy system we were all required to punt a rugby ball into the crowd. Once again, just as in Rio, Peshawar and Kapsabet, a great many people must have wondered just who the hell I was. A television crew proceeded to interview me on the touchline, creating more confusion within elements of the crowd close by.

Back in the dressing-room, Wayne, Kevin and François, the other team doctor who had joined the group later in the week, went to work. Mark Andrews had his shoulders and back strapped up, André Venter rubbed 'Deep Heat' cream all over his tree-trunk thighs, and backs André Snyman and Pieter Rossouw wrapped bandaging around their gnarled fingers. Krynauw Otto had his feet and ankles taped up, Teich enjoyed a massage and Lem started to throw the ball around. James Dalton just sat on a bench, his Springbok baseball cap lodged on his shaven head, staring down at the floor.

Motivational messages were displayed all over the dressing-room walls. One read: 'Success comes to those who become success-conscious.' Another stated: 'For glory gives herself only to those who have always dreamed of her.' I tried to keep myself to myself at this point. Nick and Solly were pacing up and down the dressing-room in opposite directions, and this was clearly not the time for any small talk.

Jake shouted out: 'Three minutes to go, boys!' This prompted Nick into a last-minute pep talk. 'It's your team,' he said. 'Controlled aggression. Play for each other.' Teich looked up and asked for the time. 'Two minutes, Teich,' said Jake, in a comforting manner.

At this point I was witness to an extraordinary, moving and almost frightening scene. The Springboks team, led by Joost van der

Westhuizen, huddled together and prayed. Fifteen men stood silent, with their heads bowed, moments before entering the lion's den. They then shook hands and delivered warm, almost passionate, hugs as they wished each other luck. It made me shiver with a mixture of awe and anticipation. The narrow glaze in their eyes as they ran out on to the pitch will never leave me. I wanted to be part of it. Instead, I looked across at the Irish team and pitied them.

I took my place on the reserves' bench next to Lem, who appeared to be the coolest customer on the park that afternoon. Beside us sat Robbie Kempson, Bobby Skinstad, Werner Swanepoel and Naka Drotské. All but Bobby and Lem would get some play that afternoon.

At half-time the 'Boks led by 19–0. The game had been brutal, the aggression often boiling over into mini-battles on the pitch between opposing players. The Irish had clearly set their stall out. The object of their game was to limit the damage. Their defensive, physical approach was not pretty, but it had kept the home side's score down. I particularly remember one moment when Eric Elwood, the mercurial Irish stand-off, began a darting run. Then he met Pieter Muller. Elwood was carried off after a perfectly legitimate but massive hit delivered by the Springbok centre. In the dressing-room during the interval, Elwood's blood was still all over Muller's shirt.

'That's much better, lads,' Nick said to the team, slapping every player's back as they trudged back into the dressing-room. 'The first ten minutes of the second half will decide whether we win 37–15 or 50–0,' he added. Joost and James added their rand's worth before Teich chipped in with a final word of advice. 'Don't even look at the scoreboard,' he said. 'From now on it's a new game again.' And with that the Springboks ran back out into the full glare of the Loftus Versfeld floodlights.

The second half followed a similar pattern to the first. The Irish never went close to scoring themselves, but their tactics prevented the floodgates from truly opening. South Africa ran out winners by 33–0 in a match marred by violence from both sides. Robbie Kempson and Mackie Hendricks both won their first caps that afternoon, whilst Stefan Terblanche hobbled off injured a couple of minutes after half-time. The man who had scored four tries on his own debut the week before was reminded of how the sporting fates can change so quickly. Rassie, James, Joost, Teich and Pieter Rossouw all managed to cross the Irish try line to rubber-stamp a comprehensive victory.

The general feeling in the dressing-room afterwards was one of satisfaction with a job carried out in a thorough fashion. Once all the players had been assembled, a further prayer took place. Then the mood lightened. Joost called for a rendition of the Springboks' song and the home dressing-room soon became filled with the noise of 'The Springbok boys are happy, the Springbok boys are we.' Some of the Irish appeared at the door wanting to swap jerseys. One of the reserves came up to me. I started to explain my story and then gave up. It was too long and confusing right then, so I just said I did not have one to give away.

After a cocktail function full of official speeches that neither team seemed happy to attend, we were off and away again in the team bus back to Johannesburg. As a new cap, Mackie Hendricks was asked to provide a song. Clasping a microphone at the front of the bus, he delivered a touching, if slightly painful, rendition of 'I Believe I Can Fly'. The rest of us tried to accompany him as we drank from cans of beer.

Back in the hotel team room, we all assembled for a final time. The players would be leaving for their respective homes early in the morning. Nick was allowing two days off before they all had to return to Sandton to prepare for yet another Test match the following Saturday, this time against a weakened Wales. 'It's like being on tour in your own country,' Nick explained. He, in particular, was desperate to see his family. The next day was Father's Day, and he was booked on a 7 a.m. flight out of Jan Smuts Airport back to Cape Town. Teich, too, was keen to get home. He was wondering what present his little girl had bought him.

A small Kontiki session took place. The two rising stars, who had trained for much of the week, were ordered to knock down a couple of drinks. Joost then congratulated everyone on the afternoon's work before asking us, once again, to perform the Springboks' song. For the third time that week, we all linked arms and swayed together as we sang boisterously.

I knew that this would be the last time I would ever be in the company of one of the greatest sports teams in the world. I wanted to thank the Springboks for my week and Nick gave me the chance. 'Boys, before you all go, Ian would like to just say a few words.'

I stood up and was immediately handed a glass of beer by a beaming Mark Andrews. 'Oh no, here we go again,' I thought, as they all started to chant again: 'Cheers to Ian, he's so blue, he's a drunken through and through.'

'What have I done now?' I asked.

'You're giving a speech,' Mark replied, handing Smiley another glass. 'And your hands were crossed.'

Smiley Swanepoel tried very hard to give me the beer in my right hand, but if there was one lesson I had learned above anything else that week it was that it was correct to drink with your left hand during a Kontiki session. I downed the beer in one and then asked if it was now okay to say something.

The Springboks sat down and waited. I thanked them for the week and then expressed my disappointment at failing to get a game against the Irish. I made it clear that I was sure the fact that I had beaten the coach 2–1 in table tennis had not come into his selection policy. The players laughed, prompting Nick Mallett to stand up and shout: 'It's not over yet. This is just one leg. When we come over to England in November, we'll carry on the series.'

I then went through my injuries obtained during the week and thanked those responsible. Adrian Garvey and Mark Andrews seemed particularly pleased to have their names read out. I finished by revealing my new-found knowledge of the Afrikaans language, including a swearword taught to me by James Dalton that I could not possibly repeat now, and finally wished them good luck.

With that the boys were gone. Some went out for a quick drink with their families, others retired in readiness for a very early start in the morning. Nick and Solly sat through a video of the whole Irish match again, still not satisfied with the eventual outcome, before also taking the hotel elevator to their rooms.

As we bade a final farewell, Nick patted me on the shoulder. 'You did well, you know,' he said. 'And now I think you understand a little more about the Springboks.'

Indeed I did. And as I, too, went to bed, a certain sadness overcame me. It was the end of something I suspected I had always wanted to do. A week was not enough. Not even training and sitting on a bench would do. I wanted to be a Springbok, or an English international player, or, at the very least, some kind of top sportsman. For the past week I had almost been a Springbok. I realised it would be the closest I would ever come to such an honour.

In the morning the whole squad had gone. The team room was bare and silent, and it seemed as though I had the whole hotel to myself. I gave the boys a silent toast as I sat at the bar and waited for my taxi to take me to the airport. It was only when I had finished my beer that I noticed something very odd. I had been holding the glass in my left hand.

STEVE REDGRAVE AND THE
GREAT BRITAIN COXLESS FOURS

The Thames Dipstick

When I first hit upon this rather deranged idea of mine, I had it all neatly worked out. I would perform a different sport each month with the best in the world, allowing plenty of time for recovery and practice before attempting the next challenge.

In principle this would have been just fine. In reality, however, I was dependent on other people's schedules. This explains why, on returning from playing squash with Jansher Khan, I was allocated four days back home in London before leaving for Kenya and the high altitude of the Nyahururu training camp. Yet this was easy in comparison to my next two sports. Initially I was down to play rugby in South Africa a week earlier, in June. The Springboks, clearly nervous about some unknown Englishman joining their ranks, decided to delay my visit by seven days, allowing Nick Mallett and his merry men to notch up their first win on home soil under the new management regime against Ireland in the first Test match.

On completing my spell with the Springboks I was to have enjoyed a fortnight at home before joining Steve Redgrave and his coxless fours partners in Henley for what I imagined was going to be a demanding week. It was a far from perfect arrangement, but at least most of my rugby-related cuts and bruises would have healed and I could have spent some time rehearsing on the water.

This failed to materialise. In the end, my week's rowing with Redgrave and co. began the day after I returned home from Johannesburg. I knew it would be a tall order, but I had little choice in the matter. If I really wanted to mix it with the world's greatest sportsmen, I knew I had to put up with all the obstacles placed in my way. It would prove to be a real test of my resolve.

I suppose I really ought to have known better. I knew rowing was a tough sport. People have told me so. But it's easy to say that rowing is tough. I didn't really know this for certain. I mean, I had no first-hand experience. I had never rowed for a school or a college, in a University Boat Race or any kind of official head-to-head. I had never collapsed, exhausted, in my boat at the end of a two-mile sprint, with sweat cascading down my face and my lungs struggling to find oxygen. I had only ever seen this from the comfort of a towpath, with a notebook in my hand, or from my own armchair watching television. This looks tough, I would think, and then immediately forget about it.

In short, I'd never actually rowed to any reasonable degree in my life. At least in football, rugby and squash, I had performed at a decent level when I was younger. Like most people, my experience of rowing had been gained merely on various lakes in parks, water-filled gravel pits and on the sea. Now I was expecting to slot casually into the working pattern of the best coxless fours team in the world for a whole week. If I had given this some serious thought, I might have reached the conclusion that, this time, I was pushing my luck too far. But I swept such considerations under the proverbial carpet. Besides, I had the rugby to concern myself with first.

I have known Steven Redgrave for over ten years now. He, in my humble opinion, is the greatest current British sportsman. He is not, perhaps, the best known and he is definitely not the wealthiest. Yet who else can lay claim to winning four gold medals at four successive Olympic Games? Who else has remained at the top of his sporting tree for over 15 years? And who else, over such a long period of time, has had to endure such physical and mental hardship as he continues to push himself to the limit in order to remain the best?

Over the years I have come to Henley on many occasions to see Steve. I have stood by the Thames at seven o'clock on a December morning, when frost has plastered car windscreens and ice has frozen parts of the river, and witnessed a weary-looking sportsman clamber out of his boat whilst steam rises from his hot and sweaty body. I have been in the weights room after a heavy circuits session to watch Steve lie prostrate on the floor, clutching his whole body in agony. And I have sat in the warmth of the Leander Club in Henley, waiting for the man to finish yet another two hours on the river, wondering why, and how, he can work himself so hard when the Olympic Games is still three years away. 'Doesn't seem that long to me,' he would always reply.

Some people have found him difficult to talk to, or even relate to, in the past. Even some of his former rowing colleagues considered him to be hard work, especially if they actually partnered him in a boat. His constant striving for perfection and his assumption that others who worked with him shared his hunger for success sometimes made life intolerable for those attempting to keep up with his own standards. Unbelievable success, age and fatherhood has undoubtedly mellowed the man and in the past five years or so he has grown used to, and even become comfortable with, the public spotlight. But one ingredient remains unblemished. Steve Redgrave, CBE, seventeen times winner at the Henley Regatta, six times world champion, three times Commonwealth gold medallist and, of course, four times Olympic champion, is still not satisfied with his lot.

Never mind the fact that by winning the Olympic coxless pairs title in Atlanta with his partner, Matthew Pinsent, he became the first rower in history to win four Olympic gold medals. Never mind the fact that it also made him the first sportsman in Olympic history to win four golds in four consecutive Games. Never mind the fact that his Atlanta gold meant that he became the top British medal-winner of all time. And never mind the fact that, seconds after winning the coxless pairs final in Atlanta, he slumped his head down to his knees in total exhaustion and gave his express permission that if anyone saw him near a boat again they could shoot him.

That was then and now long forgotten in Redgrave's book. The dawning of the new millennium may be a major historical moment to most people, but it means just one thing to this particular rower. The year 2000 spells the Sydney Olympic Games and Steve Redgrave, at the age of 38, will be attempting, this time with Pinsent, Tim Foster and James Cracknell in a coxless fours crew, to win his fifth gold medal.

It was with all this in mind that I travelled to Henley with some trepidation in late 1997 to discuss my idea with Steve. I say some trepidation because, although we knew each other well and, I think, trusted each other, we had only ever really enjoyed a journalist/subject matter relationship. In other words, I knew he was the best in a boat and he understood that I could turn my hand to journalism. Now I was proposing to cross the great divide, to be his partner, to train with him and the guys, and to race with him against top opposition. I knew how seriously he took his training, his sport and his winning. Would he really countenance such a daft proposal?

My timing could have been better. News had just leaked out that he had been diagnosed a diabetic and various scare stories were doing the rounds that his condition would render a fifth Olympic challenge nigh on impossible. Typically, Steve dismissed the notion. 'It's not an issue,' he said, munching through a small mountain of toast after a morning's training. 'I don't know why everybody's making such a fuss. If I had twisted my ankle, would people be making such a big deal of it? That's how I see my diabetes. As far as I'm concerned, it's business as usual.'

He took a large gulp from a mug of tea and stared at me. For a short while I stared back. Steve has a track record of not allowing medical adversity to stand in the way of his relentless pursuit of Olympic titles. A terrible bout of colitis hampered him for four months just before the 1992 Barcelona Olympics, leaving him so critically ill that at one point Matthew Pinsent even feared for his life. It still failed to prevent him and Pinsent taking gold. One formed the opinion that the guy could be run over by a steam-roller and still stand up to say defiantly: 'Didn't hurt.'

I told Steve what I had in mind. I promised that I would not in any way be a hindrance and that I would try my hardest to keep up with him and the boys in everything they did. I wanted to know what it was really like to be a top rower and I would be prepared to suffer for my art. Then came the *pièce de résistance*. I proposed partnering him in any race he suggested.

I tried to study his eyes as I delivered my speech, but they gave nothing away. When I had finished and sat back waiting for the verdict, Steve plonked his tea mug down on to the table. A rather wicked smile slowly developed and the previous weariness resulting from his training seemed to desert him. 'All right, you're on,' he said. 'But don't think it's going to be easy for you. If you're going to do this, then you're going to do it properly. I can tell you now, Ian, we'll make it hell for you.'

Thanking him for his kind and encouraging words, I asked how we could arrange a race. 'We'll go for the Henley qualifiers,' Steve replied, referring to the most famous regatta in the world and one of the highlights of the English summer social scene. 'Let's see if we can qualify for Henley.'

His sudden enthusiasm became disconcerting. Mindful of his love of winning and his loathing of failure, I felt it necessary to make an obvious but crucial point. 'Look, Steve,' I ventured. 'You do know, don't you, that I've never really rowed before? I will take some lessons before we get down to the serious business, but we're clearly not going to win, are we?'

Steve Redgrave stood up, ready to begin the next stage of a typically punishing day's training. Fixing me with a determined glare, he uttered five words that sent a chill down my spine. 'I don't see why not,' he said, before striding purposefully back to his boat.

I drove back to London in a state of mixed emotions. I was delighted that Steve had agreed to my plan, but also apprehensive about the proposed week: just what had I let myself in for?

The next day I telephoned Peter Haining, the three-times former lightweight single sculls champion. I had met him a couple of months earlier and had been instantly impressed with his attitude and his successes achieved, like Redgrave's, in the face of adversity. This is the man who, as a small boy, fell into Loch Lomond during winter training and survived in the harshest inland conditions for five minutes. 'They reckoned I should have been gone after two minutes,' he admitted. This is the man who needed to win 42 consecutive races, which is still a record, to convince the southern-based rowing authorities to select a Scot. And this is the man who, during the 1993 lightweight single sculls world championships final, smashed his boat against a buoy and still recovered to win. Oh, and there's one more thing. Haining happens to be a chronic asthmatic. Amazing people, these rowers.

I had realised that Redgrave and I would be required to scull, in which we would each be using two oars. If we had attempted to row with one oar each, which is more in Redgrave's department, the results would have been farcical. His greater strength over mine would have sent the boat turning round and round in circles. Haining volunteered to be my sculling coach closer to my week's rowing with Redgrave. I had other sports to contend with first, but I hired a van and drove over to Haining's stretch of the Thames, at Putney in south-west London, to collect an old ergometer. This rowing machine would be housed in my garage for the next few months and I would use it three or four times a week to practise my basic rowing movements, as well as for general fitness purposes.

In March, Steve telephoned to advise me of a change in plan. His coach, Jürgen Grobler, was not happy about the Henley qualifiers. The German, recognised as one of the top rowing coaches in the world, felt it would hamper the British coxless fours' own attempt to win the Stewards Cup at the regatta. Redgrave had an alternative suggestion. 'If we had entered the qualifiers, we would have been racing against the clock,' he argued. 'Why don't we have a proper race? We will challenge Matthew [Pinsent] and either Tim [Foster] or James [Cracknell] to a head-to-head at Henley.' It sounded good to me, if rather a tall order. Redgrave would be facing Pinsent, a double Olympic gold medallist, and either Foster, an Olympic bronze medallist and world champion, or Cracknell, a fellow world champion. His partner in this unlikely meeting of champions would be me.

I managed not to dwell on the frightening spectre of this race over the next few weeks. I had the likes of Romario, Jansher Khan and Moses Kiptanui to contend with first. Yet as soon as I returned from Kenya I planned for the rowing. I knew I had no time after my week in South Africa to learn the ropes, so I began before I left for Johannesburg in the belief that any training I managed to complete for rowing would only serve me well for the rugby too.

There are various rowing communities found along the River Thames, stretching from London to Marlow and Henley and beyond, to Reading and into Oxfordshire. Just about the first pocket of activity is situated to the west side of Putney Bridge, where the University Boat Race between Oxford and Cambridge begins each year. Here, along the Thames towpath, can be found a long line of rowing establishments, including the Thames Rowing Club. In these villages small communities of water people lead their lives when others are either waking up or going home after a day's work. At ten o'clock in the morning, or at four o'clock in the afternoon, the shutters are up and there is not a soul to be seen. But in the summer evenings, or early in the morning, when the sun already glistens on the perfectly calm water and the only noise to be heard is the slap of an oar on the water as a sculler glides past, the Thames Rowing Club, and the others close by the Lower Richmond Road, suddenly become frenetic centres of activity.

Peter Haining was waiting for me at the Thames Rowing Club when, on the first day of June, I finally turned up to begin my crash course in sculling. 'I pride myself in never having put a newcomer through a first session without him throwing up at the end,' he had told me, using a phrase straight out of the Steve Redgrave 'Make Them Feel At Ease' manual. He and I were just about the oldest people there. The rest of the men all appeared to be big, muscular hunks and most of the young women were either larger than me as well or at least a great deal fitter.

After a 15-minute warm-up session in a weights room, Peter took me to a children's playground in a small park situated just behind the rowing clubs. A young mother was there with her two small sons and she was probably wondering why a grown-up was queuing patiently for one of her children to finish playing on the swings. Peter asked me to swing backwards and forwards without holding on to the chains, thus creating a balancing exercise. 'You will discover that sculling has a lot to do with movement and balance,' he explained, looking at my quizzical and, frankly, embarrassed expression. It took less than ten seconds for me to end up lying on my back on the carefully padded floor with my legs in the air and my head ducking frantically to avoid the swing on its downward return. The mother and her two sons started to laugh. 'I knew that would happen,' a satisfied-looking Haining concluded. 'Everybody falls off.' As we strolled back to the club I suggested that the little exercise had not exactly derived from the Amateur Rowing Association's coaching textbook. 'No, you're right there,' he agreed. 'Still, at least you passed the swing-missing-your-head test.'

Peter then took me inside to another large room housing two sets of oars straddling narrow strips of water. Guessing my impatience to get on the water, he said: 'It's technique, technique, that will make you a sculler, much more than strength.' For the next half an hour or so he had me sculling away in this contraption, moving nowhere inside a warehouse but getting to grips with the movement of my sliding seat, my bending knees and the oars. Whenever I lost rhythm and control he would shout out, 'Come on, Mr Redgrave wouldn't like that, would he?', thus helping to create an image in my mind of Steve Redgrave in the boat, looming menacingly over me and shouting out abuse at my inadequacies.

That was enough for day one. Haining, so he later told me, had only been winding me up about vomiting at the end. 'You didn't think about that, did you?' he asked me, a look of incredulity written all over his chiselled, rather weather-beaten face. 'No, no, of course not,' I replied. Only every day.

I got to sit in a boat on my second day of training, but still not in the water. Haining had positioned a single scull on top of two benches wedged in by matting inside the Thames Rowing Club's weights room, for all and sundry to see. It was here that I had to learn the rudiments of technique. Arms needed to remain straight for as long as possible, hands had to stay close together and my fingers and thumbs should always be found at the very end of each oar. My hands needed to stay still, with my wrists twisting up and down after each stroke to flatten out the oars. I had to lean back as far as I could during a stroke and then bend forward when preparing for the next stroke, so that my knees touched my chest. Then Peter and a TRC colleague would rock me from side to side as I sculled, my blades wafting through thin air, of course, just so that I could feel the effects of movement on the water. As the hunks gathered to watch, I felt faintly ridiculous. 'Now do it with your eyes closed,' my coach suggested. A few seconds later,

Peter, to his evident glee, tipped a bottle of cold water down my back, causing me to release the oars and swear. 'Now, now,' Peter rebuked. 'You can't act like that with Mr Redgrave during the race, can you? That's what it feels like when you're on the water. You'd better get used to it.'

One or two other coaches had heard the commotion and had joined the increasing crowd of voyeurs. When they were informed of what I proposed to do at Henley and my complete lack of previous sculling experience, they appeared to smile with sadistic anticipation. 'So let's get this straight,' said one. 'You've never sculled before, and you've got just over three weeks before you partner Steve Redgrave?'

'Two, actually,' I replied. 'I've got nine days to spend in South Africa during that time.'

He left the scene shaking his head and laughing, joining the growing list of people chipping away at my ego.

Haining gave me his tight-fitting, all-in-one rowing outfit. It had the red and blue markings of a Great Britain international rower all over it and, on the right breast, a Union Jack flag and the words 'Goodwill Games, St Petersburg, 1994'. At home that night I tried it on and was pleasantly surprised to see that it looked better on me than I had first feared. I went downstairs to reveal my new look to my wife. She was busy talking to a friend on the telephone and, on seeing me, burst out laughing. As I left the room I heard her explain to her friend: 'Well, he's no Linford Christie.' I'm not certain she was referring to my biceps, either.

I had to be in Putney for 6 a.m. for my next training session. It meant an appallingly early wake-up call, but a pleasant drive across an empty London which, at that time of the morning, seemed to belong all to me. 'I don't normally get up at this time just for novices,' Haining said by way of a first greeting. We carried a double sculls boat down to the river and, after I had negotiated climbing into the boat with some difficulty, stroked away from the water's edge. It had not occurred to me but Peter had positioned me at stroke, which meant I was in front and determining the nature of how we would scull. The boat felt alarmingly unsteady and I was surprised to find myself sitting so high above the water, as if I was on the boat and not in it.

Sculling for real is a different proposition to pretend sculling on dry land. It is hard enough trying to remember all the rudiments of the technique required to scull, without the added problem of choppy, wet water. I caught a number of crabs that morning. This does not mean I laid a number of lobster pots down in the river. 'Catching a crab' is a rowing term in which the oarsman makes a stroke where the oar either misses the water or digs too deeply, causing the rower to fall backwards. To make matters worse, dark clouds began to spill out rain, first in a steady drizzle and then in a downpour that left us both drenched to the skin. 'I've got to be mad doing this,' Haining muttered, just as I nearly lost an oar into the murky waters of the Thames.

Slowly I found some kind of a rhythm. We sculled up and down past Fulham Football Club's Craven Cottage ground, nestling in prime real estate on the banks of the river. As I began to feel more comfortable leaning backwards and forwards in my delicate boat, so I exacted more power from my arms and legs. A few people stood by the water's edge and watched the three-times former world champion and his partner, who tried to paint a picture of normality. 'Hey,' my demeanour was trying to exude. 'It's no big deal.' More often than not, such thoughts were swiftly followed by another error from the novice that brought the boat to a near halt.

Later, over a sausage sandwich in the nearby rowing community's local café, Haining revealed that he had never before asked a novice to stroke. 'I wanted to watch your every move,' he explained. 'It normally takes a couple of months for someone to reach your standard and, don't forget, it will be a lot easier with Steve Redgrave because he will be at stroke.'

For a split second I felt rather pleased with myself, that is until Haining destroyed my moment's pleasure. 'Don't forget, the difference between rowing and the other sports you try is that you can drown doing this.' I thought of my imbalance tipping the boat and, God forbid, Steve Redgrave over into the Thames. I imagined my feet strapped tightly to the shoes already provided and fixed inside the boat. I saw Redgrave's huge bulk forcing me under the water. And finally, I saw my body and the boat spiralling downwards to the bottom of the river. A little melodramatic, I grant you, but it represented the worst-case scenario.

I was to leave for South Africa on the Saturday evening. The morning before I drove to Henley to ensure that Redgrave and his crew had not come to their senses and changed their minds at the eleventh hour. 'Remember, Steve,' I said. 'No dispensations.'

Steve Redgrave shook his head and smiled. 'Oh no, don't worry about that. It's going to be the worst week of your life.'

I arrived back at Heathrow Airport from Johannesburg at 7 a.m. on a Monday morning sporting a sprained left pectoral muscle, numerous cuts and bruises and ligament damage in my feet and fingers. Peter

Haining was there to collect me and drive me to Putney. I was so concerned about my lack of sculling experience that I was happy to undergo one final lesson before my first day at Henley, even though I had just endured an overnight flight from South Africa. For the next hour the two of us would scull, rather unsteadily, from Putney Bridge to Hammersmith Bridge, backwards and forwards. It was not enough. I would have needed months to have even passed as a competent sculler, but it would have to do.

The next day would be my first with Redgrave, Pinsent, Foster and Cracknell. They were under some pressure. Foster, much to the annoyance of his team-mates, had somehow managed to put his right hand through a window at an Oxford University Boat Club party a few weeks before, damaging several tendons in the process. It meant his temporary withdrawal from the crew for the first round of the World Cup series of races in Munich. Leander's Luka Grubor replaced Foster, but the British coxless fours could only finish fourth. It was the first time that Redgrave and Pinsent had lost a championship race since 1990, and the first defeat for the four after a run of 11 wins which had begun a year before. Predictably, the British newspapers were asking if this was the end of an era. Foster made a miraculously quick recovery, no doubt spurred on by his colleagues' shock defeat and a certain degree of guilt. The crew had been back together for just a couple of weeks before I was due to join their ranks. The week afterwards they would be representing Leander in the Stewards Cup at the Henley Regatta. The series of races, hopefully culminating in a final, would confirm whether they had returned to the top or continued their slump in form.

I realised that I would be figuring in this scenario. Of all the weeks to have chosen, I had been told to join the Leander coxless fours at a moment of high drama. Now I was convinced Redgrave had meant every word he said. This truly could be the worst week of my life.

It did not begin well. Due to a pile-up on the M25 motorway, I arrived at the Leander Club 20 minutes late. Jürgen Grobler, the British national rowing coach since 1991, was just concluding his morning briefing. Steve saw me and then looked pointedly at his watch. 'I even got here early this morning because I knew you were coming,' he told me. I wasn't entirely sure whether he was joking or not.

As I stood next to the coxless fours crew, I felt dwarfed. All were considerably over six foot tall and three of the four weighed over 220lbs. Only Tim Foster carried a lighter weight, but at over 200lbs his large frame still contrasted heavily with mine. The muscles in my legs and biceps had grown markedly since I had begun this whole project, but they resembled molehills next to the mountainous arms of my new colleagues.

Matthew gave me a friendly nod. I had known him since just before he and Redgrave won their first gold medal as a partnership at the Barcelona Olympics. A jovial, friendly figure but with a raw, competitive edge, Pinsent had emerged from his partner's shadow since 1992 and now, at the age of 27, believed he stood on an equal footing. Nothing irritated him more than the suggestion that Redgrave would win a gold medal with any partner. Pinsent will be trying to secure a third Olympic gold medal in Sydney which, in normal circumstances, would be a staggering achievement. Yet he is the first to realise that the world's media spotlight will, once again, be on Redgrave.

Tim shook my hand and wished me luck, giving me a knowing look in the process. The last time I had spoken to him was in the immediate aftermath of the coxless pairs final at the Atlanta Olympics. He, together with Johnny and Greg Searle and Rupert Obholzer, had just won what was for them a disappointing bronze medal, having being edged out of first place in the final few metres. The whole crew had sat in a despondent state whilst, just a few metres away, camera crews and journalists fought each other to speak to Steve and Matthew. The contrast was striking. The following year Tim had lost in the University Boat Race when rowing for Oxford. Yet at least he had since enjoyed the status of becoming a world champion, courtesy of this coxless fours win. At 28 years of age, he was different from Steve and Matthew. With his long, rock-star blond hair, which he sometimes wore in a pony tail, and his interest in playing the guitar in a band, Tim Foster rather stood out.

The same could be said of the fourth member of the crew, James Cracknell. At 26 he was the youngest and he was extremely grateful to have been given the chance to row with the best. With his dyed peroxide-blond hair, earring and tattoos, James gave the impression of being the errant boy amongst the men. This, however, is an unfair description. James, as Steve readily admitted, more than deserved his place in the boat. People talked of James receiving instant payback when the crew took the world title in 1997. 'Yeah,' he said to me. 'It was a case of achieving overnight success after seven years of trying.' Now he had his chance and he had every intention of taking it.

He and the crew were about to go out on to the water for a row of a mere 16 kilometres. Steve told me I had to do the same distance on the ergometer. The distance, although seeming a long way, meant little to me. My neanderthal version at home did not possess anything as fancy as a distance gauge. But I knew that I had never rowed on an ergo for more than half an hour.

'It should take you the same time as us on the river,' Steve said, making his way down to the wooden jetty to join his crew members.

'How long's that, Steve?' I asked.

'About an hour and a quarter,' he shouted, as they pushed themselves away from the jetty and out towards the centre of the river.

I tried desperately hard not to reveal my true thoughts but palpably failed. Steve said later how concerned I looked. Faced with no other option, I sat down on the ergo's seat and began to pull. Ten minutes passed by and sweat started to glisten on my legs and arms. I reached five kilometres just as other Leander Club members joined me on nearby ergometers. They immediately began to produce stronger pulls than me at a slower, more measured speed. I followed suit, not wanting to appear too much of a weakling in such company. Once I saw the coxless fours sail past the jetty and up to Henley Town Bridge, where they turned round and headed back down the course again. I looked away, pretending to be concentrating on my work.

To my amazement, I reached the 16K mark in one hour, 14 minutes and 22 seconds. I felt tired and sweaty but triumphant. Moments later the coxless fours arrived back at the jetty. I was so pleased and relieved to have rowed the distance that I gave them a thumbs-up sign. 'Look,' Matthew shouted out. 'He's looking happy.'

I told them I had passed the first Herculean challenge. 'Only another 34 to go,' Steve chipped in. He asked me what my stroke rate per minute had been on the machine, and the average time it read for me to reach 500 metres. I told him 22, at two minutes, 15 seconds. 'That might just be good enough to make the women's lightweights team,' he added, as he and his colleagues headed off to the tea room.

After a quick breakfast of toast, jam and orange squash, we carried their fours boat to a trailer, piled into two cars and drove to Richmond, where the coxless fours were due to front a conference announcing that Lindemans Wines would be the official wine supplier to the Great Britain Olympic team for the Sydney 2000 Games. *En route* in Matthew's sponsored Range Rover, Steve examined the details of the agreement, knowing full well that he would be required to deliver some kind of speech. 'We could do without the break in training,' he said. 'But at least it's another sponsor for the Olympics. Until Lombard came in to sponsor us after Atlanta, my bank balance had been constantly in the red.'

The four duly conducted their row past the gathered throng of media folk before making themselves available for quick interviews. Four bottles of Lindemans were presented to each crew member, together with doggy bags full of the remaining vol-au-vents, chicken drumsticks and sausage rolls, and we were away again, back down the M4 to Henley. 'We've hardly started,' Redgrave said, rather ominously. 'There's a lot to do today. None of us woke up looking forward to this day.'

Half an hour later I began to understand what he meant. The crew, and their latest recruit, endured a circuit session in the weights room that lasted some 45 minutes. This was the programme:

Bench pulls: 55kg weights, 40 repetitions.
Knives: Throwing feet and arms upwards, 20 reps.
Sit up on incline: 10kg weight resting on chest, 20 reps.
Lifting weights on a box: 10kg each hand, 30 reps.
Dorsal rise: 15kg, 15 reps.
Leg curls: 30kg, 20 reps.
Angel (lie face down, lift arm and leg): 5kg, 20 reps.
Lateral pull: 50kg, 20 reps.

I could handle some of this almost as well as the guys. Other disciplines proved to be immensely difficult. The bench pulls, for example, tugged away at my sprained pec. In a surprise show of compassion, the four allowed me to lift a lighter weight. In the time it took them to complete five such circuits, I had struggled and strained my way through three. As we all slumped to the nearest seat we could find, our T-shirts were dark and our hair matted with sweat.

'We all hate this,' a panting Redgrave explained. 'But we know it's a necessity. This is where the work's done. If we want to remain the best, we've got to go through with it. You've got to be the fittest and the strongest in this game.' A few months ago, before I had begun to play my various sports, I would not have stood any chance at all of completing even one circuit. I sat in the Leander weights room exhausted, in the knowledge that there was still an afternoon's work ahead. Already I felt as if I had been there a week.

We made our way back into the Leander tea room, where more toast and jam was consumed. 'Why so much toast?' I asked the crew. 'Because it's free,' came back the reply in unison. Within a few minutes, other equally exhausted oarsmen joined us. The need for liquid replacement was so strong that these guys never bothered drinking out of a glass. They used a large jug instead. By the end of the week it had become second nature to me as well. I thought nothing of sitting upstairs in Leander, overlooking the Thames and Henley Town Bridge and knocking back a complete jug full of orange or lemon squash. I only hoped I would kick the habit before my next dinner party.

The fun – or rather the fun for my crew-mates – began after lunch. Steve explained that he and the boys would be rowing for another 16K on the river. He suggested I should hone my sculling skills. Hoisting a single sculling boat over his shoulder as if he had just picked up a small toy, he led me down to the water's edge, held the boat steady and told me to jump in. I, like a sheep led by a dog, obeyed. Only then did it occur to me to say something. 'Steve, there is one thing.'

'What's that?' he replied, as he pushed me out into the middle of the river.

'I've never been out in a single scull before.'

'WHAT?' The way he shouted was rather disconcerting. 'You told me you'd had some sculling lessons.'

'I have,' I reasoned. 'But always in a double sculls boat. That's what we'll be doing together, isn't it?'

Redgrave looked at me as I floated and wobbled out into the centre of the river. 'Oh well, it's too late now. You're out there on your own. You told me you're good at most sports, so you'd better just try and give it a go. We're going to do two laps of the course. See if you can scull one lap.'

Pinsent, Foster and Cracknell had emerged by now with their fours boat and seemed to be sharing a joke with Redgrave. 'There's no way you won't fall in,' Redgrave shouted, amid general laughter from the Leander jetty.

Moments later they rowed past me, still laughing as I pretended to appear not bothered by my predicament. 'Just about to start sculling, boys,' I shouted as they quickly disappeared upstream. Ahead of me lay two one-and-a-third-mile stretches of the Henley Regatta course.

The first time you attempt to scull is similar to your first ever ice-skating lesson. Ideally, you want to just get on with moving your oars, just like your feet with skates on, as quickly and as strongly as possible. This, when every sneeze sends your boat into a furious wobble, is difficult. Each time a motor launch chugged past, the resulting wash from the engines made me produce a drunken man's act in a boat. I looked at the uninviting and cold Thames water and decided I really did not want to be sucked under, with my feet still strapped to the shoes. I unfastened the strapping in the hope that if I were going to take that one crucial wobble too far I would be able to release myself quickly from the boat before I had drunk too many pints of the Thames.

It was in this manner that I edged my way down the river, past the Remenham Club to my right and various boathouses to my left. Just when I had built up enough confidence to attempt five or six steady strokes, I would catch one of my blades at a wrong angle in the water, sending both my boat and myself into a shaking, shimmering frenzy. My Great Britain international all-in-one compounded the situation. I became acutely aware of people staring at me from the towpath and from the water itself. Crews would sail past, gliding effortlessly across the surface. Most, if not all, would strain their heads and glance at Mr Wobbly. Why, they must have thought, was a British international sculler resembling a jelly in a boat?

To attempt a first ever outing in a single scull the week before the start of the Henley Regatta was akin to taking an inaugural flying lesson above Heathrow Airport's west runway. The Thames that afternoon was heaving with international crews rehearsing for the following week. Eights from American universities, such as Harvard and Yale, Princeton and Syracuse, would zoom past, their rowers grunting and their invariably female coxes bellowing orders. Coxless fours and pairs would overtake me in a flash, affording me a quick, and often derisory, expression as I tended to block their paths, not possessing the skill to remove myself in time. Coaches would cycle furiously up and down the towpath, past the white, swanky houses and the individual jetties, with their baseball caps and loudspeakers. Occasionally, a single sculler would sail by at a slower rate. I would give them a knowing nod, as if to say that we, as fellow water men, were kindred spirits.

Then it happened. I had been so concerned in maintaining my balance and sculling downstream that, with my back facing the direction I was sculling, I had not given too much attention to the white posts in the middle of the river denoting the race lanes. Suddenly I drew level with them. Although my single scull was a couple of metres to the left of them, my left oar did not have enough room to evade them. I desperately attempted to draw my oar nearer to me, but in doing so created an immediate and irretrievable imbalance. It was at that moment, for that split second, that I knew I would be taking a cold and wet ducking.

It was over in a second. My feet were out of the strapping in double-quick time and I found myself thrashing about in the water, shocked by the severity of the cold. It was supposed to be June, for goodness sake, but still the chill shot through my body. I began to swim to the river bank, pushing my capsized boat along in front of me like a beaver with a thatch of weeds. Just as I reached the water's edge, a coach cycled past on the towpath on the other side of the river.

'Sculler in the water,' he shouted out over his megaphone in a loud, plummy voice. 'Sculler in the water.' My demise was being broadcast all over Henley.

Oh God, that was all I needed. I looked around to see whether anyone else was watching. I wanted to tell him to shut up, but I was too far away, and still with just my head popping up above the surface. 'SCULLAH! SCULLAH! Are you okay?'

'Yes, yes, I'm fine. No problem,' I shouted back, trying very hard not to appear flustered – which, with my upturned boat and my cold body still in the River Thames, was unlikely. I looked back at the coach, who was still watching me. 'Just please go away,' I thought.

Placing my feet on some horrible, spongy moss, I turned the boat back to its proper state, leant against the river bank and sat back in. A middle-aged couple walking a small, yappy dog strolled past. 'You need any help there?' the man asked when he could see I had become stuck in the lilies and weeds. 'Is it that obvious?' I replied.

Grabbing my right oar, the man pushed me away from the river bank just as the Leander coxless fours crew rowed by. 'He's gone in!' they shouted with obvious joy as they fast faded into the distance on their return lap. I looked down at my shivering body. A large, brown weed had stuck itself to the shoulder of my British international all-in-one.

It's one thing failing to see some white posts. It is another to crash into an island. Further down the river I began to pick up some kind of rhythm. Intent on maintaining this sudden surge of technique, I ploughed my unsteady way through the increasingly choppy water until, suddenly, Temple Island appeared to my right. Just to my right. In fact, my course had taken me to a few feet of the island, once again allowing no room for my oar to manoeuvre. This time I knew what fate was about to befall me.

The Thames felt decidedly warmer the second time I went for a dip. That was the good news. The bad news was that this was a favourite turning point in the river for many of the crews. I found myself pushing my boat across the water just as half of Henley arrived on the scene. 'You okay in there, feller?' a member of the Princeton eights shouted out. 'Yep, I'm doing just fine,' I answered, still trying to appear unconcerned. I'm a sculler. These things happen.

I heard more shouts of glee from behind just as I tried to haul myself back into the boat. Yes, my friendly team-mates had returned on their final lap and had been lucky enough to witness my second ducking of the day. 'Now you know why we row, not scull,' Matthew said before stroking his crew back upstream. I lifted myself back into the boat, using the bank as ballast, and drifted gingerly back into the middle of the river.

Slowly the rhythm returned again and I eased my precarious existence up the river. Some time later I noticed Steve Redgrave, having clearly finished his row, striding back down the towpath. He was watching my efforts with keen interest. I pretended not to notice him, in the hope that he could see that I was succeeding effortlessly. This would work for 20 seconds or so, before a badly timed stroke would send me back into a jerking fit, as if someone had just plugged me into an electric socket.

Eventually I made my painful way back to the Leander jetty. Redgrave was waiting for me there and held the boat steady as I clambered out. It had taken me nearly two hours to scull my way from the Leander Club to Temple Island and back. He told me that the boys had just completed an extra 4K on the ergo, so that was now expected of me. I must have looked a rather pathetic, bedraggled figure as I sloped off to the ergo, sat down and began to heave.

When I finished, Pinsent and Foster had already showered, changed and left for home. James Cracknell was also *en route* to his car. 'Glad you got a ducking,' he said. 'Now you've been baptised.' Changing his tone a little, he added: 'You know, I fell in only last year when I went sculling. You can't avoid it, really.'

Steve knelt down beside my exhausted body and, for the first time that day, a look of sympathy developed on his face. 'Now, I think, you understand more about this sport,' he said, in a rather soothing voice. 'You can play football and rugby, but you can't just expect to pick up sculling, just like I can't expect to walk instantly into an ice-hockey team. You've got to be very strong, very fit, but you also need to possess the technique.'

He paused and surveyed the scene of wreckage in front of him, still panting from his final 4K. 'So that's your first day,' he added. 'You wanted to know what it's like, with no dispensations. Well, we haven't given you any. Now you know. It would have been difficult for anyone to have done what you did today. You did all right. Not bad at all.'

I think that was his way of admitting that I had passed the initial test. But we both knew I still had four days of this purgatory to come.

At this point a slightly built middle-aged man with a blue V-neck rowing club sweater approached me. 'Saw you in the water,' he said, in another rather upper-class voice. 'I think you win the Thames dipstick award, don't you?' He did not stay to hear my reply, but after he had disappeared through the Leander Club door, Steve leant over and whispered: 'Actually, I think he wins the Thames dipstick award.'

'How come?' I asked.

'Because it was his boat you were using and he doesn't know.'

It was the end of my worst day since I had started this whole caper. I had been relatively pleased with my efforts up to this point, on the beaches and playing fields of Rio, the squash courts of Peshawar, the running tracks of Nyahururu and Kapsabet, and the rugby pitches of Johannesburg and Pretoria. But this day had sent my spirits and my ego crashing back down to earth, or rather water. The physical demands challenged my determination to the full, whilst I found the whole single sculling experience to be humbling. I knew why Steve had put me through this and in a perverse kind of way I was grateful to him. Yet, as I rested my weary body into my bath that night and closed my eyes, I felt depressed. I could not even use my age as an excuse. I used to remind the Springboks and the Kenyans that I was the oldest man participating, just so that they could include this fact in their summarisation. Yet Steve Redgrave was nearly two years older than me. 'You're still a baby compared to me,' he would say. And that evening, as the bath water turned my skin into crinkles, I felt about as strong as a newborn child.

I'm not quite sure what happened during the night. Strange things must have gone to work in my subconscious state. When I awoke, I leapt out of bed ready for a new, bright day. I didn't ache as much and I didn't dread day two at the Leander Club. Far from it. It had become a challenge. For some stupid, male, competitive, face-saving reason, I decided I would take everything the coxless fours would throw at me and match them. I knew they could not see me lasting the week. I knew, one way or another, I would.

I arrived in Henley before Steve. This was a good start. We all went for a short 800-metre jog along the towpath. The boys grumbled at this, saying it was a pointless exercise. They did plenty of warming up in the boat, they argued, but Jürgen Grobler insisted on it. I took the lead and led the pack back to Leander. It was my way of showing that I was up for the day, however worthless a point it made.

Then we began a gruelling 10K session on the ergometers. It was not so much the distance that hurt, but the requirements of the exercise. The first 1,000 metres had to be achieved with a stroke rate of 18 a minute, the following 2,000 metres with a stroke rate of 22.

This pattern continued until 10K had been reached. I sat beside Tim, whilst the others rowed behind. In hindsight, I should have stuck to my own pace, which had improved to around two minutes and five seconds for 500 metres. Casting an eye over to Tim's gauge, however, I saw that he was pulling at a rate of one minute, 40 seconds. I tried to keep up with him and, for a couple of minutes, managed to do so. 'I was getting seriously worried,' Tim admitted later. 'I wasn't sure whether you had reached international standard overnight or I had turned into a crap rower.'

It couldn't and indeed didn't last. Exhausted by my early efforts, I slowed back down to 2.05, then 2.10 and finally 2.15. Steve, Matthew, Tim and James all seemed to finish at around the same time, their bodies now dripping with sweat. I had another 1,300 metres to complete and they, out of duty, sat around me and watched, adding the occasional word of encouragement. 'Nearly there,' said Steve as I passed the 9K mark. 'Keep it up,' added Matthew. As I drew near to the finish, my exertions caused me to let out loud grunts, rather like Monica Seles in mid-serve. Finishing with a grunting crescendo, I wiped the sweat from my furrowed brow and was rewarded with a 'Well done' from the boys.

Jürgen joined us for morning toast, squash and one of the most important points of the day. The coxless fours and their coach had been involved in a football World Cup sweepstake since day one of France 1998. Anyone who predicted the right score would immediately be paid 50p by the others. If everyone failed, then they would adopt a rollover system, rather like the National Lottery. The money may have been small, but the stakes appeared high. Matthew would produce a piece of paper with a carefully written-out table and all the matches and his crew's names. He would then ask for predictions for that day's matches, before announcing who had got it right from the day before. Fifty-pence coins would then cross over the table to the lucky recipient, who acted as if he had just won an Olympic medal.

The boys went back out on the river for a further 12K's rowing. I came to a bold and painful decision. I would complete the two outstanding circuits in the weights room from the day before, and then row another 11K on the ergo to make up for the distance I still owed the crew from completing just one lap of the Henley course the previous afternoon in my single scull. I had been invited back to Steve's house that afternoon but decided that afterwards I would return to Leander and row 12K on the ergo, to cover the distance the crew were about to row on the river that morning. It would mean a long and sado-masochistic day, but I wanted to go to bed that night in the knowledge that I had rowed, in some shape or fashion, exactly the same distance as the British coxless fours. Just as I had done with the Springboks, I was looking for recognition and realised that I would only really achieve it through blood and sweat.

The crew had finished and left for their homes by the time I climbed, sorely, off the ergo. Matthew and James lived in Henley, Tim a little further away in Oxford, and Steve, as he has always done, in nearby Marlow Bottom. I showered and drove the eight miles to Steve's new house, found up a hill and through a small wood. The Redgraves' Old English sheepdog came to greet me in the driveway, flopping on to her back and waiting for a tickle. This fleeting moment of fluffiness seemed a little incongruous. I had more expected a Rottweiler to chase me indoors.

Anne Redgrave, a former Olympic rower herself and now the British rowing team doctor, was there fussing over their third, and youngest, child. Steve led me into the kitchen and made some tea. 'Breakfast, Darjeeling or Earl Grey?' he asked, providing some sophistication lacking from the Leander weights room. Dressed casually, and in the comfort of his own home, he immediately came across as a far friendlier figure and the one I had known for all these years.

We talked of his health. Steve admitted that, for the first time in his life, he had seriously considered quitting his sport soon after his diabetes had been diagnosed. 'But you told me it wasn't a problem,' I said.

'I didn't think it was at first,' he answered. 'But my colitis came back at the same time. The doctors thought I might have Crohn's disease. The crew went down to Cape Town to train and I was coming consistently last in our cycling group. For the first time I was struggling to last the pace. I was going to tell Jürgen I'd had enough.'

I couldn't quite believe what I was hearing. Giving up was never an option in the Redgrave book. 'It's just that I started to shit blood,' he explained, guessing my thoughts.

We sipped our tea in silence for a moment or two, as he rocked his child to sleep in a pram. 'So what made you carry on?' I asked eventually.

'I couldn't give it up,' he replied, his face deadpan and emotionless. 'I've come through adversity before and I wasn't prepared to bow to it now. There's another gold medal to be won yet. By February I began to notice an improvement. Now I'm right back up to scratch.' He nodded his head in conviction. 'It's been worth the pain.'

I asked him where his combative, competitive nature stemmed from. He told me it was from failure. I spluttered into my tea. Failure? What did Steve Redgrave know about failure? The man is the most successful rower of all time. Failure was a concept that was surely alien to him?

'No, it isn't,' Redgrave insisted. 'I've had my times as a loser in the sport. I've competed now in 21 major events and only won 11 of them. That's all.'

That's all! I was about to scream at him when he continued. 'I was once eliminated from a race for not being fast enough. I was actually eliminated.'

'When was that?' I asked.

'In the early 1980s.'

A defeat some 16 or 17 years ago, when he was 20, still rankled?

'Oh yes, I've made sure to maintain that particular memory. It's helped to give me the mental hardness you need to keep on winning at this level. If I want to be an Olympic champion I've got to carry out all the required work. It's got to be done.'

I asked him if he knew when the 2000 Olympics coxless fours final was.

'Of course,' he replied. 'September 7th.' The date had been registered indelibly in his consciousness.

All this reminded me of the remaining 12K I still needed to cover on the ergo back in Henley. I had grown increasingly warm and comfortable on the Redgraves' living-room sofa and, quite frankly, the last thing I wanted to do right then was return to a further bout of weights-room punishment. This, so I realised, was exactly how the fours felt most mornings. I had been doing this for two days. Redgrave had 18 years under his belt.

As I left for Henley, Steve stood at the door and saw me off. 'Today is always the most important day,' he said. 'You can never get it back. What you do today is money in the bank. If you don't do it, then it's a day's loss of earnings. When the time comes for a repayment, it won't be there if you don't put in the work now.'

With those words still ringing in my ears, I returned to the Leander Club, changed and went to work on the ergo. One hour and 12K later I had deposited a couple of pounds into my bank account. I asked another rower to provide proof, if asked, of my distance. Three rows of symmetrical blisters had now appeared on both hands, the effect of gripping oars and the ergo for so long and with such force. I felt desperately fatigued, but also exhilarated. I had caught up with the boys again, and even though they handled the physical exertion with relative ease and I journeyed to the very depths of my willpower to match them, it felt well worth the effort.

In the portakabin that doubled up as a changing-room, the following morning I told the crew that I had stayed the distance. They seemed to approve. James pinned up a picture of their recent defeat in Munich from a rowing magazine. Underneath he placed another photo, this time of the top Australian foursome known in rowing circles as 'The Oarsome Foursome'. Twice the Olympic champions, in 1992 and 1996, they would be racing against the Leander crew, assuming both teams qualified, in the semi-finals of the Stewards Cup the following week. 'Won't do the motivation any harm,' James explained.

I led the way again during the morning jog, at least until Matthew started shouting. 'Come on, then,' he began. 'Show us how you beat the Kenyans.' A little later he added: 'You can't come first in this race. There's only one goody-two-shoes in this group.' He, Steve and Tim all pointed at a smiling James. I dropped back to join the others.

Jürgen suggested I joined him following the boys' progress up and down the river. Before we started I asked him what made Steve Redgrave so different from other rowers he had come across over the years. Jürgen gave this a little thought before answering. 'He's strong and he's skilful,' he said. 'But it's here that he has the edge.' Jürgen tapped his head. 'I was very concerned when Steve admitted he was a diabetic. It's a measure of the man that he's bounced back again.'

We grabbed hold of a couple of rickety old bikes and began to cycle along the towpath. For a man of 51, Jürgen is in remarkably good shape. I had difficulty keeping up with him as he hurtled through puddles and across cattle grates, around gates and up grassy verges. As if this was not hard enough, one also had to avoid fellow coaches cycling in the same careless manner, all of whom, still with their baseball caps and megaphones, were paying most of their attention to their crews and little to their fellow towpath riders.

As the fours completed the first 4K, Jürgen stopped a little short and waited for his crew to turn around. 'So,' he said, smiling at me. 'Now you are a triathlete.'

'I'm sorry?' I replied.

'Well, you ran this morning, you are now cycling and the other day you went for a long swim, no?'

I cycled on, determined to cover the exact distance the boys were rowing in their £6,000 purpose-built boat. I didn't think they would pick up on this, but I was wrong. Later on, over breakfast, Steve made a comment. 'We saw you on the bike turning round at the same point as us,' he said, before adding his verdict: 'Wanker.' This, I hasten to add, was said with a smile and greeted with a group laugh. They decided that whilst they rowed for 16K, my cycling constituted only 8K's effort. I owed them a further 8K. I noticed that Steve was busily injecting himself. 'Insulin,' he said, when he caught me gazing at him. 'I have to do it seven or eight times a day now to counter my diabetes. It's become part of my normal daily routine. I've got to be in good shape for our big race, haven't I?'

Matthew made a helpful suggestion. It was supposed to be a half day for the team – although they had packed in what any other sportsman would regard as a tough full day – but he would take me out in a double sculls boat that afternoon. 'You need the practice,' he explained. 'And that will cover the 8K you owe us.'

I returned to the dreaded ergo for the second half of the morning. My arms had noticeably thickened in the past couple of days and I was beginning to feel stronger. Another rowing establishment figure walked past as I was straining away. For some self-important reason, he felt it necessary to examine my action. Leaning over my gauge, he asked me if I had positioned it in that way. Without waiting for an answer, he jerked it upwards, resulting in my distance, which had registered 3K, plummeting back to nought. It may not mean much to a reader, but I found this a psychological blow. 'Sorry about that,' he said, without too much apology in his voice, and waddled on.

The boys left for home at lunchtime, including Matthew, who promised he would return within an hour. This gave me time to examine the Leander Club. I'd been there breaking my back for three days, without ever finding time to wander around one of the great old traditions of English rowing. The club was founded in 1818 in a ramshackle Lambeth boathouse before moving to its more salubrious surroundings on the Thames at Henley. It now boasts the most prestigious rowing club in the country, with its big-name oarsmen and its history of dominating the Henley Regatta. Along the wooden-panelled walls can be found portraits and old black-and-white photographs of past club presidents, interspersed with oars and more photos of Leander winning crews. Rows and rows of engraved wooden panels are also there, each sporting the names of winning crews, Olympic medallists or former club officials. The name Redgrave enjoys a great number of carvings. On one side of the bar sits a collection of blazered old colonels and their like, enjoying lunch whilst overlooking the river. Across the small corridor the current oarsmen are housed, in their sweaty all-in-ones and with their jugs of squash. They are just a few feet away from each other, the blazers and the all-in-ones, but in reality a world apart.

The clubhouse was particularly alive that week. The pre-Henley Regatta excitement was beginning to build, as were the various marquees alongside the river. The first Regatta was staged back in 1839, on a single afternoon, after a public meeting in the Town Hall decided to establish it as 'a source of amusement and gratification to the neighbourhood, and to the public in general'. It has been held ever since, except during the two world wars. Now, of course, it is one of the highlights of the English summer social season, as well as a must for the corporate hospitality brigade. This used to annoy Redgrave, who felt not only that nobody came to watch the rowing but also that the Henley Regatta and the University Boat Race created the upper-class image that seems to have stuck like a barnacle to his beloved sport.

I wandered back down to the Leander jetty just as Pinsent returned. We lifted a double sculls boat out of its position in the clubhouse and strode down to the water's edge. This time the boat felt a great deal firmer. It's amazing how much a double Olympic gold medallist can help you to keep your balance, allowing you to concentrate on your technique.

We sculled down the official one-mile-550-yard Regatta course, a distance that normally takes around seven minutes to complete if the weather conditions are good. Looking back over the straight mile we had just completed, I could see the Town Bridge and a collection of heads bobbing up and down above the river, but not any boats. 'That's due to the earth's curve,' Matthew explained.

It was that afternoon's sculling that brought back my confidence. There were even short spells when I sculled without error, helping to create a reasonably smooth pattern with my illustrious partner. As we cleared Temple Island, a head wind suddenly blasted into our backs and the water became choppy. Later on, when a number of motor launches went by, we dealt with more waves. After an hour on the water, we paddled back to the Leander jetty. 'Do you think there's any chance that Steve and I could beat you?' I asked Matthew. He took half a second to answer. 'No,' he said. 'There's no way.'

'What's Steve going to be like in the boat?' I ventured.

'He'll expect you to do your best, and he won't want to see too many mistakes. He probably accepts you're not going to win, but he'll still want a good performance.'

My sculling had undoubtedly improved thanks to Matthew's coaching that afternoon, but as I headed off back home I wondered if it was even close to being good enough in Redgrave's book. Somehow, I doubted it.

I had a bad night. My sprained pec made lying on either my front or my back difficult and now both shoulders, thanks to my excessive rowing, were painful. It left me with few positional options. My hands and fingers had become so gnarled and blistered that they now made the evil Queen's palms in *Snow White* look positively smooth. 'You can tell you've made it when you can ladder a girl's tights just by stroking them,' was how James Cracknell had put it. Fresh calluses had developed on the site of old blisters and when my alarm woke me from a fitful sleep a mixture of blood and hot water had stained my sheet.

I had to be at Henley for 6.30 the following morning. Steve and Matthew were playing in a celebrity golf tournament later that day at the Oxfordshire Golf Club in Thame and had to be away by 11. I had agreed to be Steve's caddie. As Jürgen went through his usual morning briefing, Steve and Matthew were in a playful mood. Finding a rugby ball, they practised drop kicks in the boathouse, much to Jürgen's annoyance. Occasionally a wayward kick would result in the ball colliding against one of the boats. Eventually Jürgen had had enough. He confiscated the ball and ceremoniously dumped it in a dustbin. Moments later, whilst Jürgen continued to talk, Steve sidled his way round to the bin and retrieved the ball. 'Two days to go,' he announced to Jürgen, before looking at me. 'Then it's the big one.'

I followed Jürgen along the towpath again on a borrowed old bike. I knew this would count for half the distance covered by the boys in the boat, but Tim had agreed to take me out for another sculling session at the end of training. I would then catch Steve up and join him on whatever hole he had reached at the Oxfordshire. When the crew returned to the clubhouse, however, Tim suddenly realised that while his healing hands could handle rowing, sculling would be too difficult. The last thing he or the crew needed was an injury a few days before Henley. So while the crew enjoyed their break, I set to work catching up on the ergo. Within moments of finishing, the coxless fours went back out on to the water. I had to complete a further and final 16K in the weights room. By the end of this, my hands were completely shot away, my shoulders kept making clicking noises and my backside had become extremely sore. On further inspection in the changing-room, I discovered the reason why. Two large blisters had developed on each buttock.

On my way to the car I telephoned Sarah, my physio, and made an appointment for the following week. 'How long do you want?' she asked me.

'How long have you got?' I replied. 'I need a complete body

overhaul. If I were a car, this would be my MOT.' I described my long list of rugby- and rowing-related ailments.

There was a long, thoughtful pause on the other end of the line. 'I'm sure we can help you with your back, legs and shoulders,' she said. 'But I'm not going anywhere near your buttocks.'

That afternoon, when he was not chatting to the three members of the public who had all given money to charity to join him on a round of golf at the Oxfordshire, Steve and I talked more. He said that he was proud to have been born working class and hoped that he was helping, in some way, to rid his sport of the plummy image it possessed. 'I know people think it's all about former public schoolboys,' he said. 'Well, I'm not, am I? And besides, it doesn't make a jot of difference what your background is. Not when you're in that weights room, or out on the river.'

I could subscribe to that view. An upper-class, public-school background may suggest a life made easy. I saw no evidence of this in the weights room. You need to possess a tremendous mental strength to withstand the rigours of rowing. Background does not come into it.

I wasn't sorry when Steve finally sunk his putt on the eighteenth green. It had been a long, tiring day and I tried, unsuccessfully, to add a further 5K to my weekly training after dragging a trolley-full of his clubs around all afternoon. Steve would have none of it. 'Doesn't count,' he said. 'Our rule is that training begins and ends at Leander. Go home and get a good rest tomorrow on your day off. You're going to need it. Sunday's the day of the race and I'll be expecting maximum effort.'

As my car carried my aching, throbbing, blistered body home that Friday evening, I wondered whether I had *any* effort, let alone maximum effort, left inside me. I would soon be finding out.

The boys were well into their training by the time I appeared at the Leander Club on the Sunday morning. My own training had officially ended and I had, for the past 36 hours, been in pre-race mode. I warmed up by jogging along the group's 800-metre course and then covering 3,000 metres on an ergo. Sporting my Great Britain all-in-one, now washed after its Thames soaking, and a pair of wrap-around sunglasses, I hoped I looked the part, even if I did not feel it.

Steve, Matthew and Tim emerged from the clubhouse rubbing their hands in anticipation. Matthew and Tim would be rowing, Steve and I would scull, thus having the advantage. James wished me good luck and dashed off home. We agreed to stick to 22 strokes a minute, which was supposed to counteract the physical imbalance between the two crews. Jürgen appointed himself as race referee and official timekeeper. Producing a coin from his pocket, he asked me, as captain of Steve's team, to call. I shouted tails, and won. First blood to us.

Jürgen then asked me which side of the river I wanted, Bucks (Buckinghamshire) or Berks (Berkshire). I didn't have a clue, so I plumped for Berks, cracking a weak joke about Steve and me looking like a couple of berks in the boat. Steve leaned over and whispered: 'That was the wrong choice. Bucks gives you a slight advantage.' Now he tells me.

We sculled down the river to the official Regatta start, using the time to practise our strokes. This was the first occasion that Steve and I had actually been in the same boat. He decided to place me at stroke, in front of him. 'You're in charge,' he said, by way of explanation. 'I'll follow you.' I remembered Peter Haining's assumption that Steve would stroke, and cursed.

I could feel his breath on my neck and his critical eyes boring a hole into my back all the way down to the starting point. We lined ourselves up as Matthew and Tim drew level and waited for Jürgen's signal. I asked Steve what time he felt we could record. 'We'll be lucky to beat 12 minutes,' came back the pessimistic reply.

It was a warm, mid-summer's morning, but the river seemed at its choppiest. 'No fast times today, then,' Steve added. People seemed to be lining the towpaths out of interest. A number of them had heard about this unlikely race and wanted to see whether the combination of Steve Redgrave and a total novice could beat the combined might of Pinsent and Foster. 'See you've got a new partner,' one or two would shout out at Steve, with smirks breaking out all over their faces.

This attitude had increasingly annoyed me. It had started on day one, with Mr Thames dipstick, and carried on throughout the week. Most of the guys within Leander itself appreciated my efforts, but a number of middle-aged soaks took it upon themselves to make sarcastic comments or pull know-all faces at my expense. 'At least I'm bloody well doing it,' I would mutter under my breath.

Now, however, came the moment of reckoning. I crouched forward, ready to complete my first stroke, and looked across at Jürgen. 'Attention,' he shouted from the towpath. I gripped my oars tightly. 'Set.' I made sure my wrists were in the correct position and blew out a deep breath. Now I could really feel the butterflies, the moths and a whole range of other flying insects floating around my stomach. 'Go!'

I produced my first stroke and was surprised to feel the response from behind. Steve's power became immediately evident, as if someone had turned on a motor, and we started to move. In the corner of my left eye I could see Matthew and Tim beside us. It was a vision that lasted no more than ten seconds. In that time they managed to pull away. Steve began to bark out orders. 'Keep it steady, nice and easy,' he would say. 'Remember, nice and relaxed. Take your time and you will scull smoothly.'

I had resigned myself to losing the race even before it had begun. All I was bothered about was completing the course in reasonable time and in acceptable style. We reached the quarter-mile stage. 'Calm down, calm down,' said the voice from behind. 'You're stroking too fast.' To my right I could see Jürgen pedalling along the towpath, watching us closely and, occasionally, glancing down at his stopwatch.

'Come on, now,' Steve said. 'Let's put a bit more strength into those strokes. Let's do our best.' I began to do my Monica Seles impersonations, as we glided and I grunted up the river. 'We're at the halfway stage,' added the voice from behind. The head wind beyond Temple Island hit us again and the water continued to batter the boat's hull.

Despite all this I was actually beginning to enjoy myself. It was hard work, of course, and sweat was steadily developing on my forehead and arms, but there I was, on one of the most famous stretches of river in the world, sculling with arguably the greatest oarsman in the history of rowing. I realised that within a couple of minutes the experience would be gone forever, and so I relished the adventure for as long as I could. Just for a moment I felt as if Steve Redgrave and I had become a team.

'Come on, a big push now for the final few yards,' Steve said as we sped past the finishing post and Matthew and Tim, who gave the appearance of having waited so long for us to join them that they were about to open up a picnic hamper.

Our sculling braked to a light paddle. 'Three cheers for the winners,' Steve shouted as I leant forward in the boat and clutched my painful left pec. 'Hooray,' we both yelled across the river towards Matthew and Tim. 'Hooray, hooray.'

A watery reply bounced back. 'Three cheers for the losers. Hooray, hooray, hooray.'

Jürgen stood by the jetty clearly looking as if he had enjoyed himself. 'Time for the winners,' he shouted, '9 minutes, 52 seconds. Time for the losers, 11 minutes, 21 seconds.'

It was undoubtedly the slowest time Steve Redgrave had ever recorded in a race at Henley but I, for one, was pleased. We had beaten his gloomy forecast of 12 minutes and I had sculled the whole course without once catching a crab. I wasn't expecting Steve to leave the coxless fours and team up with me for the Sydney Olympics, but I felt, remembering my earlier negative thoughts, that it could have ended in a far more embarrassing fashion. As far as I was concerned, we had not finished last, but second.

We all sat on the edge of the jetty and I asked each of the crew, plus their coach, how they felt I had performed over the week. Jürgen went first. 'I have respect for anyone who completes the course,' he said. 'You have worked hard and did well considering the lack of experience you have.'

'I'll take that,' I said. Then it was Tim's turn. 'A very gutsy performance in the weights room and on the ergometer,' he announced. 'It's a different story in a boat, though, isn't it?'

I nodded my head, like a schoolboy agreeing with a teacher's point. I looked at Matthew, who pulled a face and laughed. 'You did well to last the week,' he began. 'We were all surprised you managed it. You didn't scull too badly today. At least it was reasonably smooth and you didn't catch a crab.'

There was one final and potentially damning verdict left. 'Steve?' I asked, failing to hide my anxiety. He cleared his throat as if he was about to start a long speech. 'When you told me you wanted to spend a week with us with no dispensations, I had real doubts. You've done very well to keep up with us. That's credit to you and we'll give you that. But you've also discovered how hard rowing is now, haven't you? You can't just turn up and think you can row, and you definitely can't expect to scull immediately. It takes many years of hard practice. So you did okay today. It could have been a lot worse. But it could have been a lot better as well. I wouldn't give up your day job, not if I were you.'

With that we all stood up and shook hands. It was the end of my week and I, for one, was glad it was over. The ordeal had come to an end. Or at least I thought it had. There was, however, one final twist.

Matthew leant over and reached out for my sunglasses. 'Let's have a look at your shades,' he said. Totally unsuspecting, I passed them over. Suddenly Steve jumped in front of me and, with a hefty shove, threw me into the river. My body was submerged for a second before I floated back to the surface, gasping for air and from the cold and thrashing my arms about in the river.

Up above me the boys, not for the first time that week, were laughing. 'Sorry about that,' Steve said. 'It's a rowing tradition. It's a sign that you've been accepted.' And with that he and his crew went off to find a football. Within a few seconds half the Leander Club's oarsmen had initiated a small game in the boatyard.

Meanwhile, a shivering, sodden, newly accepted sculler attempted to haul himself back on to land. He managed to heave his upper torso clear of the murky water before becoming stuck on the wooden jetty, his body hanging over the edge like the bus in the final scene of *The Italian Job*.

It rather summed up the week.

THE AUSTRALIAN TEST AND
ONE-DAY-INTERNATIONAL SQUAD

You Pommy Bastard . . .

It took a number of weeks for my body to recover from the traumas of Henley. In the immediate aftermath I spent the days either sleeping or slumped on a sofa with a large, warm duvet wrapped around my battered body. During the first half of 1998 I had rediscovered the fitness and energy of my late teens and early twenties. After the double whammy of rugby in Johannesburg and rowing with Redgrave, though, I more resembled a wizened old man.

Sarah, my physio, had her work cut out this time. I only had to open the door to her practice and she knew, without looking, that it was me. 'It's the creaking of your joints and the cracking of your shoulders,' she would explain. 'It's just that you've discovered muscles you never thought you had and then expected them to be able to match people like Steve Redgrave. He's been doing it for 20 years. You expect the same in a week!' She would shake her head at me, as if I was a naughty schoolboy with a cut knee and a tear in my trousers. Meanwhile Amanda, the masseuse, would knead her fingers into the dough of my shoulder blades and back, trying to unravel the Spaghetti Junction of knots that had developed over the past couple of weeks.

Slowly the joints began to calm down, the pain in the shoulders eased sufficiently to allow me to lie on my side in bed and I began to exercise again, first with a jog, then with a burst on the bike and finally with a session on the ergometer. I had vowed after Henley never to sit in front of one of those damn machines again but, standing in the garage amid the garden tools and old newspapers, it possessed a strange lure that, one evening, enticed me back.

The return to fitness was less intense than before, partly because everyone in the physiotherapy practice had told me to stop killing myself, but also because my next sporting fantasy would be taking me to Australia to play cricket with the Test and one-day-international squad. This, I knew, would require a great deal of technique and skill, some guts and the ability to take a great deal of stick from a group of potential Pom-bashers, but not the same levels of fitness as for the Springboks and the Great Britain coxless fours.

After the rigours of rowing, I was looking forward to Australia with some anticipation and expectation. Unlike rowing, I had played a lot of cricket in my time and, despite the mixed experiences of the past few months, my natural competitiveness convinced me that there was a possibility I could hold my own in such lofty company. Never mind the fact that I would be mixing it with the likes of Shane Warne, Steve Waugh and Glenn McGrath, my completely unrealistic assessment was, as ever, that I fancied my chances.

Convincing the Australians that they should allow me into their camp proved to be an amazingly simple exercise. I contacted Patrick Keane, the Australian Cricket Board's Media Manager in Melbourne, and put the idea to him. In June I received a return fax, under the headline 'Your Walter Mitty Lifestyle'. Patrick proceeded to write: 'I am pleased to be able to tell you that the ACB's Board of Directors was most excited by your project and delighted that the Australian cricket team was chosen to be one of your subjects. The Directors voted unanimously to allow you to join the team during its training camp in Brisbane from September 3–7 this year, prior to the Commonwealth Games.'

That was that. Maybe the other individuals and teams involved in my project had impressed them, maybe they planned unspeakable acts of Pommy humiliation, or maybe they figured I couldn't be much worse than any other English cricketer they had played against in recent years. But for whatever reason, the door had been opened to me once again and I started to imagine, as I lay in bed at night, swatting Michael Kasprowicz for four, smashing Damien Fleming for six and then bowling Mark Waugh with one of my unplayable straight ones.

After all, I used to open the batting (and keep wicket) for my school first team and, as the 1983 edition of the *Wisden Almanack* will confirm, topped the batting averages in the summer of 1982 with a little over 47, thanks mainly to a series of not-outs. I also played regularly in village cricket, in both Wiltshire and Lincolnshire, until leaving university. After this, like the rest of my sporting career, it all rather went to pot. As much as I would have liked to have kept up my cricketing commitments, life got in the way.

I had played just a handful of matches in the last ten years, but the one that stands out is a game that is possibly the strangest fixture in the world. In my capacity as a sports writer, I managed to wrangle an appearance for England, no less, against that major force in world cricket, Switzerland. Where was this important international match played? Lord's? The Oval? Well, no. Actually, the two teams met on a frozen lake in St Moritz, some 7,000 feet above sea level, where a mat was laid on a cricket field of ice sprinkled with a smattering of snow and watered by the lake's 'groundsman' to make the ice that much harder. The 'England' team consisted of a ragtag collection of bankers and businessmen, but also Test players Allan Lamb, Nick Cook and Paul Downton, and me.

Batting at number three, I survived one over before being clean bowled for nought by an annoyingly accurate Swiss fast bowler, but I saved face later with my own crafty bowling. I say 'crafty' because when I toss down my medium pacers, batsmen assume that I have a collection of inswingers, outswingers, faster and slower balls in my armoury. This is a wrong assumption. My balls do absolutely nothing except trundle down close to the stumps. My first ever ball for England therefore slipped out of my hand and headed straight for the batsman's head. In emphatic style, he swung round and whacked the ball long, high and straight down the throat of one of our fielders on the boundary. Out! In true Ian Botham style, I had taken an international wicket with a rank bad ball. I ended my spell with two wickets for no runs from three overs, leaving Nick Cook, who had won Test matches with his spin bowling, spluttering with incredulity at the other end.

All this took place some time ago, however, and I realised that I could not rely on what limited talent remained to get by in Australia. No, I needed a couple of games under my belt, at least, as well as some up-to-date gear. My early 1980s collection, which had fast been gathering dust up in the loft, was now woefully lacking. Cream tracksuit-style trousers had replaced my white slacks, souped-up trainers with spikes were now the order of the day, not my white, leather efforts that more resembled golfing shoes, and proper cricket underwear, with a relevant pouch for the box protector, were far more *de rigueur* than my tatty old jockstrap. The last time I had bought the latter I was 14 and, when asked for my size, replied six inches. Twenty years on I understood that sports-shop assistants had probably heard that joke before.

I purchased all these clothes from a back-street specialist cricket shop in south-east London whose owner, John Copus, was friends with Ian Healy, the Australian wicketkeeper. On his suggestion, I chose some Kookaburra gear, plus a green, baggy cap, so that I could look like an Aussie cricketer even if I did not play like one. Then I contacted Bickley Park, one of the top Kent League club sides, and arranged a net with them one evening.

A friend loaned me his Newberry bat, gloves and pads, the same equipment I had used a couple of years before in what was supposed to be a gentle match between parents at my daughter's school but became so competitive it made an Ashes series seem unimportant. I was pleasantly surprised to discover that I could still play a few strokes and keep the good balls out when it was my turn to bat in the nets. My bowling, too, seemed relatively accurate, but a couple of days later, having bowled non-stop for over an hour, my right shoulder returned to the agony of those post-Redgrave days and nights.

A week later I was invited to play for Bromley Common Cricket Club against Hamsey Green in a local friendly. The day began well for me. Opening the innings, I moved quickly on to 19 and struck four boundaries in the process, before I lost my off stump to a ball that moved off the seam. I don't know who looked more surprised, the bowler or me. I asked him later if he had meant to make the ball swing. 'No way,' he replied. 'I couldn't believe it either.' I was not too concerned. I reckoned 19 was a decent start for someone who had not played any form of cricket for two years.

My fortunes dipped further. Taking my turn as umpire, I gave my own captain out for lbw, a decision, judging by the long, disgruntled stare he gave me, that was neither agreed with nor accepted. Then, fielding at extra cover, I dropped a firmly struck cover drive that came at me at an awkward height but was still a chance I should have gleefully accepted. Luckily, the same batsman, who was beginning to slog virtually every ball, skied a shot towards me a couple of overs later. The ball, spinning furiously, seemed to hang in the air forever, but eventually it fell down into my relieved hands. The game was all but lost when the captain tossed the ball to me and asked me to turn my arm. I managed to grab a couple of wickets to complete what was ultimately a satisfactory first outing, but came to the conclusion that, on this performance, the Aussies would hardly be quaking in their boots.

The next day I received another of Patrick Keane's increasingly entertaining communiqués. In this he outlined some of the Brisbane camp's itinerary. Australia would be training on day two, followed by three one-day matches, against the Australian Academy, New South Wales and New Zealand, on three successive days. He ended the message with this sobering thought: 'Just remember that Australian fast bowlers have a long history of never dying wondering if there is bounce in the pitch.'

The following week, just a few days before departing for Brisbane, I stepped up a class and played for Suttonians in the East Kent League. The match was away against Sherwood CC, whose own ground faced the rather intimidating and featureless walls of Chatham's Borstal prison. Old Suttonians, named because their home is at Maidstone's Sutton Valence School, were led by Ritchie Richardson, the former West Indian captain. Still only 35, Richardson, one of the most gifted batsmen in the world during the late 1980s and early 1990s and a man who had only retired from Test cricket the year before, had been clouting the ball to all parts of various Kentish boundaries all summer as he had become, wherever he played, the star attraction. Old Suttonians also boasted Amitava Banerjee, a young opening batsman and first-change fast bowler who played for Bengal and was on the verge of making the Indian Test squad, as well as Robert Joseph, a 16-year-old fast bowler who had already played for Antigua.

'We're batting,' Richardson announced after winning the toss. 'And you're going to open for us.' My already dented confidence quickly evaporated once I saw the bouncy wicket, heard that I'd be facing Kent's Under-19 opening fast bowler and was then asked to join in a prayer in the team dressing-room. After surviving a hostile initial over, including a first ball that I might have nicked if I had been a better-quality batsman and a third ball that nearly decapitated me, it was time to go on the offensive on the basis that, sooner rather than later, I would be out. With Banerjee and Richardson to follow in the batting order, there was no point in hanging around.

A half-volley on the off stump was sliced inches over backward point's diving hand for four, followed by a cover drive boundary which, had it been straight at cover rather than between him and extra cover, would have been a simple catch. Richardson, as the temporary umpire, had a bird's eye view of all of this. 'Feeling better now?' he asked, surveying my face. He added knowingly: 'It's good to be nervous.'

A couple of overs later I managed to dig out an inswinging ball for four through the slips and then pulled a short ball for another boundary. Richardson gave me the thumbs up and muttered: 'That last shot was played like a West Indian.' Somehow I had raced to 21 and couldn't believe my luck, having envisaged a humiliating duck. Just when the dream of a half century began to form, however, I was bowled attempting to hit a fast, low delivery out of the ground.

Although Banerjee was run out cheaply, Richardson stroked, caressed and sometimes thumped the ball to all points of the field. Once, after a straight six, the other Suttonians players rushed round to the car park to make sure none of their cars had been hit. In no time he had reached an unbeaten 79 and declared the innings. Over sandwiches, chocolate cake and tea, I asked the man for his verdict.

'Not bad, considering how little you've played recently,' he said. 'You were too nervous, especially against the quick bowler. I could see you wanted to get up to the far end and face the other guy. And I thought your strokes were a bit on the chancy side. Quite a few flew in the air, didn't they? Still, you did okay and you gave us a good start.'

More than pleased with that, I then asked Richardson for advice about playing with and against the Australians. 'When it comes to batting,' he said, wiping a crumb of cake off his bottom lip and taking a large gulp from his tea cup, 'you've got to be positive. I don't care if it's Glenn McGrath, if he drops it short on the middle or leg stump, pull him or hook him. If he drops it short on the off stump, cut him. Go for your shots, man, just like you did today. If he bowls it up and straight, then play defensively. And if he bowls a beautiful outswinger, then hope you don't edge the ball. As for bowling, what can you do? Inswing? Outswing?'

I told him I wasn't sure I did anything except send the ball down the wicket at a pedestrian pace. He frowned. 'Steve Waugh's the most stubborn batsman in world cricket. He's the hardest man to get out, that's for sure. But even he's susceptible to a little turn. So try and practise some swing in your bowling. The same goes for the rest of them. They're all fine players, but they're also human. You've always got a chance in cricket.'

After a further couple of cup cakes and a second helping of tea, Richardson led me and his men out to do battle in the field. Thanks largely to Robert Joseph's searing pace, we scuttled Sherwood out cheaply and won by 99 runs. It was nice to be part of a winning side and even better to have made a few runs. Still, as I drove home that night, I analysed Richardson's advice. If Glenn McGrath, arguably currently the world's finest fast bowler, drops a short one, cut or hook him. Well, that may be so if you are, as in Richardson's case, one of the greatest ever batsmen in the history of West Indian cricket. But what if the batsman is me?

On the morning of my departure I contacted Patrick Keane at the ACB one final time, just to make sure everything was organised and the Australians were expecting me. 'Oh yes, don't worry about that, Ian,' Patrick replied over the telephone. 'We're all looking forward to seeing you. Especially our fast bowlers. They'll be queuing up to have a pop at you in the nets, that's for sure.'

That afternoon the England cricket team, having recently beaten South Africa 2–1 in the home Test series, somehow managed to lose in a one-off Test to Sri Lanka. I resigned myself to merciless stick over the coming week. Before leaving for Heathrow Airport, I just had enough time to take my children to a Bank Holiday funfair in the same park where I had been running for the past nine months. After the waltzer and the Ferris wheel, we came across a coconut shy. I thought about having a throw and then changed my mind. After all, in a couple of days' time, down under in Queensland, I would be the coconut.

The journey down to Brisbane seemed to go on forever. Even though British Airways had kindly upgraded me into club class (incidentally, people still snore and keep you awake in club class), it was still a strange and not particularly enjoyable experience. Up there in the skies, in an aluminium tube, over a day of my life was lost, whilst down below the world continued its existence. Every so often I would take my cherished cricket bat down from the overhead compartment and out of its cover, check to see that everyone else was asleep and practise a few cover drives in the aisle. I only hope nobody was watching.

I was the first of the pre-Commonwealth Games training-camp group to arrive at the Quay West Hotel, which, at 6 a.m., was hardly surprising. The rest of the squad would all be converging from their various states later in the day. It gave me time to grab a few hours' sleep before reappearing after lunch just as some of the boys were arriving.

After introducing myself to Patrick Keane, Stephen Bernard, the Australian team manager, and Geoff Marsh, the team coach, I then began to work my way through the players. Steve Waugh, the Test vice-captain, one-day captain and one of the very best batsmen in the world, remembered me from the summer of 1997, when I had interviewed him over breakfast at the Westbury Hotel in London during the Ashes series. Proud of his own book-writing efforts that have seen his various Test-match and series diaries sell heavily in Australia, and with a book of his own photographs soon to be published as well, he showed immediate interest in what I was trying to do – but still could not resist the odd psychological jibe or two. 'We'll have to try and break your jaw when you bat,' he said. 'Just think, it would be good for the book, wouldn't it?'

Around 200 bats had been placed on a number of tables in the team room. Michael Kasprowicz, the big, friendly fast bowler, and Ian Healy, the bubbly wicketkeeper, were both moaning at the chore of having to sign all 200 of them. 'We're going to get wrist and back injuries before we even play,' the two Brisbane-based players grumbled, arguing that the tables were at exactly the wrong height for a grown man to sign bats. 'Just look at that signature,' Kasprowicz said, gesticulating to me to come over and pointing towards a bat. 'It looks like a spider's just crawled all over it. My earlier efforts are much better, but that's because my hand didn't feel as if it was about to drop off.'

Glenn McGrath ambled over and shook my hand. McGrath is one of the fiercest competitors on the field, a man unwilling to take any prisoners and a match-winner who destroyed the English batting attack in the summer of 1997. Off the field, however, he is a quiet, pleasant person, who likes to escape to his farm in the depths of the New South Wales outback. 'My nearest neighbour's 15 kilometres away,' he explained. 'And the nearest town is 160 kilometres further. It's just how I like it.' He wished me good luck for the week and smiled. 'Look forward to bowling at you, mate.' His look suggested there was no debate about that.

A sports writer from the *Brisbane Courier-Mail* had got wind of the additional member of the Australian cricket camp and promptly interviewed me about all the other sports I had played. By the time this had finished, I was a minute late for the first requirement of the camp, a racial vilification lecture initiated by the ACB in an attempt to lead the way in world cricket against potential racism. My tardiness prompted an immediate threat of a fine, but it never materialised.

Steve Bernard and Geoff Marsh were sitting at the head table and, after welcoming all the players to the camp, Steve asked me to stand up and explain my presence. The players, consisting of those picked for the Commonwealth Games, plus those who would be added to make up the Test-series party to Pakistan immediately afterwards, all swivelled round on their chairs and studied a rather nervous-looking redhead as he began his speech. When I explained that after Australia I was planning to box in America, they all burst out laughing.

Then the lecture began. Although the players welcomed the move from the board to be seen to be doing something about vilification in sport, they also expressed concern that by doing so they could be sending out the message that the Australians, already well known for their hard playing style and occasional sledging, needed to be corrected. Although the ensuing two hours had a serious overtone, they also provoked a number of laughs. For example, at one point the lecturer asked the players if they felt the following sentence represented racial vilification: 'Bloody Poms always whinge.' Most of them turned round and looked at me, forcing their guest to point out that this was not only a huge generalisation but also a sentence that would only seem offensive to the most sensitive of Englishmen. Another time the players were asked if they could come up with a list of well-used phrases which, in hindsight, might well contravene the ACB's Racial and Religious Vilification Code. Ian Healy chipped in: 'What about "You Pommy Bastard"?'

Over dinner I was introduced to the whole back-up team. A few years ago a cricket squad consisted of 11 players, a 12th man and a coach. Not any more. And certainly not when it comes to the country that has, since the late 1980s, taken over the mantle from the West Indies as the strongest Test team in the world. So the squad in Brisbane also included Trefor James, the team doctor, David Misson, the fitness and training coach, Mike Walsh, the cricket analyst (whose job was to video play and assess players), Lorna Garden, the team nutritionist, Trish Medwell, who organised the team clothing for the forthcoming foreign trips, Sandy Duncan, the team psychologist, and Errol Alcott, the physiotherapist, otherwise known as 'Hooter'.

Why 'Hooter', for goodness sake? The story goes that when Erroll first joined the team in the late 1980s, he was unaware of all the rudiments of the game of cricket. A fan of rugby league, he apparently said, towards the end of a day's play, 'When's the hooter going to sound?' The name has stuck ever since.

As I ate my pasta-based dinner, designed for the team by Lorna Garden, I discovered that everyone in the squad had a nickname and it was best if I learned them on the basis that nobody was ever referred to by their Christian name. The team captain, Mark Taylor, was known as 'Tubby', due to his girth. Steve Waugh was 'Tug', or 'Tugga'. 'Why's that?' I asked Patrick Keane. 'As in tug of war,' he explained.

Mark Waugh, his younger twin brother by a matter of four minutes, was therefore nicknamed 'Junior', whilst Glenn McGrath was christened 'Pigeon', a reflection on his thin, bandy legs. Some of the nicknames were uninspiring: Michael Bevan was 'Bevo', Adam Gilchrist was 'Gilly', Damien Martyn was 'Marto' and Shane Warne was 'Warney'. Others took a little more explaining.

For example, off-spinner Gavin Robertson was called 'The Riddler', on the basis that he bore a physical resemblance to the outrageous baddie in the *Batman* films. Fast bowler Damien Fleming, although known as 'Flem', also responded to the name 'Ace', after his favourite movie character, Ace Ventura. Michael Kasprowicz was 'Krabby', because when he first emerged on to the scene few could pronounce his Polish-originated surname, often saying 'Krabsovitch' instead. Ian Healy was either 'Heals' or 'Sav', as in 'Savlon antiseptic heals'. And Ricky Ponting, the baby-faced Tasmanian batsman, was 'Punter', based on his knowledge of all things connected to horse racing and trotting and his love of betting.

Even the management team were referred to by their nicknames. Steve Bernard was known as 'Brute', after an American wrestling star of the 1970s called Brute Bernard, whilst Geoff Marsh, a Test opening batsman during the 1980s, answered to the name 'Swamp' or 'Swampy'.

Whilst Steve Waugh, Damien Martyn and Damien Fleming (otherwise known as Tug, Marto and Ace) underwent a drugs test after dinner, the rest of us listened to an ACB drugs policy lecture delivered by Trefor James and an Australian Sports Drugs Agency official. This was important because cricket was, for the first time, being played in the Commonwealth Games in Malaysia the following week and it was crucial for the squad to understand which drugs were banned on the official Commonwealth Games list. There was always the danger that a player taking an innocent cold cure could end up being sent home in disgrace.

Although by the end of the evening I was shattered, following my flight from London and the completion of a whole day in Brisbane, I joined a few of the boys for a beer. Mark Waugh was enduring a fair amount of friendly abuse for a television commercial he had featured in in which he advertised anti-dandruff shampoo. 'Got dandruff? Not anymore,' some of the boys said to him, amid chuckles. Junior had apparently turned down the opportunity to advertise a cure for constipation. 'I would never have heard the last of it,' he explained.

He was particularly interested in my time in Rio de Janeiro playing football with Flamengo and began a friendly debate with the others over who were the best team in the June and July World Cup in France. Michael Slater, or 'Slats', the Test opening batsman, explained to me his ridiculous schedule over the next few days. He had spent the summer playing for the English county Derbyshire and had helped his team to the final of the NatWest Trophy at Lord's, due to be played in three days' time. The ACB had insisted that he should attend at least part of the Brisbane camp, so this meant that he had flown from England a couple of days before me and would be flying back on the Thursday night to arrive in London the following evening. The next morning he could well be striding out to the middle of Lord's to open the batting in the biggest domestic final in English cricket. 'I'll be on auto-pilot,' he said with a rueful grin on his face. 'I'll be so tired I'll probably forget to bring my bat when I walk to the wicket. The adrenaline should see me through, though.'

The adrenaline had just about run out in my tank by 10.30 that night. 'You'd better get some sleep,' Steve ('Brute') Bernard advised, as I yawned and made my way to the lifts. 'You'll be in the nets tomorrow, so try and be at your sharpest.' I must have been tired, because not even the fearful prospect of Glenn McGrath, Michael Kasprowicz, Damien Fleming et al. kept me from falling into a deep and desperate slumber as soon as my head hit the pillow.

Breakfast early in the morning was quickly followed by a two-hour team psychology workshop, initiated by Sandy Duncan, who had been working with Geoff ('Swamp') Marsh at Western Australia for a number of years, and then led by Ian ('Heals') Healy and Tom ('Moods') Moody, the batsman who for many years now has played for Worcestershire. The Australian international cricket squads were about to embark on ten months of virtual non-stop cricket, featuring 12 Test matches and a further 41 one-day internationals. After the Commonwealth Games, the Test squad would travel immediately to Pakistan for a three-Test series, and then on to Bangladesh for three one-day internationals. Then they would return home for the five-Test Ashes series against England, before travelling to the West Indies for another five-Test series. As if all this was not enough, they finally had the small matter of the cricket World Cup in England in May and June of 1999.

Swamp had already delivered his own speech, in which he outlined how far the Australians had progressed but how there were still goals out there to achieve. 'I want us to be the most competitive and consistent team in the world,' he said. 'I wanted to introduce new appointments, such as our first full-time manager in Steve Bernard, plus a strong back-up team, which I believe we now have. And, of course, I want to win just about every match we play.'

So, despite the fact that earlier in 1998 Australia had wrapped up their eighth consecutive Test-series win, having defended the Ashes for a record fifth successive time the year before, they were far from satisfied. The next ten months were seen to be crucial, and the point about the early-morning exercise in the team room at the Quay West Hotel was, to quote Heals, 'to create a mission statement concerning our planning, preparation and playing during this period of time'.

It turned out to be a fascinating insight into the way in which the best cricket team in the world prepared themselves. Heals and Moods split us up into four groups. Michael Slater, Mark Waugh, Stuart

('Magilla') MacGill (named after Magilla the Gorilla, an Australian cartoon character) and Michael Bevan joined me to discuss 'Preparation and Training'. Other groups concentrated on 'General Themes for the Australian Cricket Team' (in other words, respect, enjoyment, attitude), 'The Aussie Way to Play the Game' (how to approach batting, bowling and fielding), and 'Rules for the Team' (punctuality, headphones and other seemingly minor matters which, nevertheless, are important to the whole framework of the team).

Magilla was given a large sheet of plain white paper and a felt-tip pen and proceeded to write down all our thoughts. We split up 'Preparation and Training' into three sections: mental, physical and cricket. Under the banner of mental, Slats, Junior, Bevo, Magilla and, occasionally, even I chipped in with suggestions. Having previously co-written a book on sports psychology, I felt it was an area in which I could make a contribution, and the players were more than happy to hear my views. We talked about visualisation, intensity and concentration, as well as goal-setting. The ability to be patient was highlighted, together with a positive attitude (i.e. before a Test match watch a video of yourself scoring a hundred rather than getting a duck), confidence and a relaxed state of mind. The final point in this section was underlined: strive for excellence, but not perfection.

Moving on to the 'physical' section, we all agreed that it was imperative to be in as good a shape as possible. Stronger, quicker, faster, became the message here, and by being this the Aussie player would also become mentally more agile. It was important not only to gain the right condition but to maintain it and to make a commitment to recovery when required. Each of the players had an individual and collective responsibility to do this, and to be sensible. A passing Ian Healy chipped in, at this point, that it was important to gain the right balance. Whilst being professional about your physical state, it was also in the team's interests to have, on occasions, a beer or two in the name of maintaining team spirit.

All nodded their heads in agreement at this, before focusing on training which, so Slats pointed out, should be under stressful and therefore realistic conditions. When you are batting in the nets, for example, if you are out three times then your stint is over, whether you like it or not. That way there is little danger of the batsman not taking it seriously. 'Train as you play,' proved to be the crucial sentence Magilla wrote down, with intensity, enthusiasm and non-stop hustling. I mentioned to the boys the Kenyan athletes' attitude: 'Train hard, win easy,' I told them, was their motto. 'Can't argue with that,' Junior agreed.

Finally, we moved on to the 'cricket' section of our discussion. Work on weaknesses and improve our strengths seemed to be the order of the day here. Make a commitment to video research for fault finding and confidence boosting, and work on specifics, such as a bowler's delivery stride. Magilla, for example, was going to ask the batsmen that afternoon in the nets to try and hit him out of the ground. By doing so, not only would he be placed under pressure, it would also create a similar experience to bowling in the final ten overs of a one-day international match. Train with a purpose, searching for quality, not quantity, and commit to becoming the best fielding side in the world.

I found the workshop wholly impressive. The players seemed to throw themselves into the idea, speaking with real passion and purpose and recognising it to be an important process that they should all undergo. I would never have guessed, with training to follow, that a psychology workshop would overrun its designated period of time, but it did this morning, such was the enthusiasm on show. As we all gathered our gear and made our way to a series of minibuses, Sandy Duncan and Swamp were visibly delighted with the morning's work.

After a 15-minute drive through the streets of Brisbane, a smart, clean and modern city that, like Perth, still has a small enough feel about it to make it welcoming and intimate, we arrived at the Queensland Cricket Association's ground and facilities. The Waugh brothers had both spent some of the journey assessing my bat. 'It's a nice-looking stick,' Tug announced, holding it up and studying it like a rare ornament at an antiques convention. I told him that when I found the middle of the bat the ball shot to the boundary. I tried to make this sound like a common occurrence, although I'm not sure anyone was too convinced. At the QCA complex we changed into shorts and T-shirts and ran out on to the field. Dave Misson was in charge of the fitness session. He was interested to hear about my exploits in Kenya and knew all about the Irish priest turned running coach, Brother Colm, and his star athletic pupils at St Patrick's High School.

As we stretched our calves and hamstrings, back, hips and arms, as well as undergoing weighing and flexibility sessions, all the players were talking about the dreaded 'beep test'. What's the beep test, I asked. 'You'll soon find out,' said Darren 'Boof' Lehmann, his nickname referring to his large belly that seemed to make no difference to his prowess as a batsman for Australia and, at least for the summer of 1998, Yorkshire.

And so I did. We all lined up as Dave Misson placed a ghetto blaster on the grass. A computerised tape began to play in which every few seconds a 'beep' could be heard. We all had to run 30 yards or so before the sound of the next beep. At the end of each stage, the beeps would begin to grow closer and closer together, forcing us to have to reach B from A at a faster pace. Initially it was easy going and we could all afford to jog slowly. 'This bit's fine,' Boof explained as we jogged along together. By stage four, however, life was beginning to quicken up. 'Can't talk any more,' Boof explained, beginning to pant. 'I've gotta get my head down.'

I gathered that the acceptable stage to reach was ten, something I think all but one of us reached. Mark ('Tubby') Taylor reckoned that, as I had successfully completed a 3,000 metres steeplechase at high altitude in Kenya, I would be favourite to win the whole beep test. I pointed out that not only was I the oldest man in the squad, giving away some 12 years in a few cases, but also much had happened since Kenya, including my week of purgatory at Henley, and that, as a result, I was not as fit now as I was in Kapsabet. Besides, in Kenya I could keep to a steady jog. Here, in Brisbane, we were all required to speed up as the sound of the beeps became more frequent.

One by one the players began to drop out, gasping for air and, in some cases, collapsing to the ground. I, too, found it hard going and soon became the last of the remaining bunch to reach the cones marking out where we should turn and run. After beating six or seven of the squad, I ran out of puff at stage 11.4 and joined the others clutching their stomachs. The rest soon followed, save for Slats and a young newcomer to the squad, Brad Young, who has a big future in the game as a spin bowler and late-order batsman. The rest of us cheered the two on as they raced up and down until, eventually, Slats shook his head and gave up.

Lunch was quickly devoured in a nearby pavilion and on my way back to the ground I was introduced to the Australian selectors, former Test players Andrew Hilditch, Trevor Hohns and Allan Border, who pulverised most bowling attacks from the late 1970s to the early 1990s. The new ground we were training on that day, and where Australia would be playing the Australian Academy the following day in a 50-overs match, was named the Allan Border Oval in recognition of the Queenslander's record in Test cricket. Not only did Border score thousands of runs at the highest level, as his country's captain he can also justifiably lay claim to being the man responsible for turning Australia into the world-beaters of the past ten years. He had heard of my exploits and wished me luck. 'Don't worry, Ian,' he said as he grinned at his fellow selectors. 'Everything's ready for your batting session this afternoon. We've even got the ambulances on standby.'

I thanked him for his kind and caring words and made my way over to a section of the ground where fielding practice was taking place. Swamp, angling his bat, sent a series of balls heading towards me and a number of other players lined up in a cordon of slip fielders. I managed to hold more than I dropped, although occasionally I made a meal of my efforts. It prompted Tug, who was always available for a dry comment, to say: 'Nice catch, now you've just got to try and stop the posing.'

We reassembled into a tight circle to take a series of low and high catches from close range. After I dropped two consecutive chances, Swamp said: 'It's a ball, not a hand grenade, Ian.' The truth was that my left ring finger was beginning to hurt again. It had barely recovered from the injuries it had sustained catching those hundreds of punts and conversions in Pretoria's Loftus Versfeld stadium when Henry Honiball, Percy Montgomery and Franco Smith practised their kicking the day before the second Test match against Ireland. Now the hard leather cricket ball had inflamed this old injury. I decided not to say anything. On the first day of training, I was not going to allow myself to be accused of being a whinging Pom.

After a while, Swamp invited me to join the rest of the bowlers in the nets. Sharing net one with the likes of Damien ('Ace') Fleming, Brendon ('BJ') Julian, Colin ('Funky') Millar and Gavin ('The Riddler') Robertson, I proceeded to bowl my deadpan deliveries to Boof, Brad Young, Warney, Krabby and Pigeon. Shane Warne, the leg-spinner and useful late-order batsman, was recuperating from a major operation on his right shoulder following an injury which had threatened his career. Happily, from an Australian viewpoint, he was well on the road to recovery and on this day, although still some way off being able to bowl, he was more than able, and willing, to bat.

Occasionally he would step down the wicket and slog my straight medium pacer straight and high over my head. On other occasions he would be forced to play a defensive stroke, and just once he edged the ball behind for what would have been a straightforward catch to the wicketkeeper. 'Now that's a good one,' he shouted back to me down the net. 'Nice bowling.'

Nice bowling! To be complimented by a man who, at that time, had already claimed 313 Test victims at the age of just 28 from only 67 Tests, who looked well on course to beating the all-time record of 434 wickets held by India's Kapil Dev and who, as the English can testify, has won Test matches and even Test series with his often unplayable spin bowling was one of those special, unforgettable moments I had been lucky enough to have experienced several of over the past few months.

Krabby decided to try and slog almost every ball I sent down towards him. A number of them flew in the air for possible boundaries, but I made a point of telling him that, unbeknown to him, I had just placed a fielder in the exact spot he had just hit the ball and he had been suckered into playing such a shot by my clever piece of bowling. For example, when he hooked one of my short balls, I told him he had just been caught on the square-leg boundary. When he smashed the ball over my head, I celebrated the fact that long-on had just taken the catch. By my reckoning he had been out at least five times. 'You're just like all the other batsmen in this team,' he said with a smile. 'Whenever you boys get a chance to bowl in the nets, you always make out you've bagged five wickets.'

Finally, it was Pigeon's turn to don the pads. Now Glenn McGrath is the first person to admit that he is not the world's best batsman. With his astonishing haul of wickets and his intelligent and ferocious style of bowling, the man is under no pressure to score runs as well. But, as any bowler will tell you, batting practice in the nets is the chance for a bowler to reveal his prowess as a batsman, and Pigeon is no different from any other in this department.

Tubby and Warney came over to me as I prepared to bowl my first ball at arguably the world's greatest fast bowler. 'Here's your best chance to take an Aussie wicket,' Tubby said, somewhat disparagingly, about his team-mate. 'If you don't get him, you won't get anyone.' Warney had some further advice. 'If you beat him, or go past his bat, march down the wicket, stare at him and give him some abuse,' he suggested, with an evil grin on his face.

Yeah, right, Shane, and whilst I'm at it, why don't I call one of the most frightening and ruthless bowlers in Test cricket a bloody convict as well? Instead, to much amusement amongst the other bowlers, I made a point of shouting out 'Nice shot, Glenn' when he played one of my off-stump deliveries out with a firm drive.

I was interrupted in my run-up by Swamp's chilling request. 'Ian, pad up please.' This was the moment I had been looking forward to all day, probably all my cricketing life, but as I jogged back to a tent where all our equipment lay, my heart was pounding. After putting on the usual gear of pads, thigh pad, jockstrap, box and gloves, I asked the players, who had curiously gathered like vultures hovering over a kill, whether I needed anything else. A few began to laugh. 'It's more of a Pommy thing, really,' Slats said. 'But you'd better have one of these.' He handed me an arm guard, which was placed on my left forearm, covering the area from my elbow to my wrist. 'Get hit without this and we're talking about a broken arm,' Slats added.

Fine. Anything else? Boof suggested I should also wear an inside thigh pad for my right leg. 'If you take a ball there you'll really know about it,' he said, lending me his. Krabby had just finished his batting stint in the nets and was furiously rubbing his thigh. 'I took a ball right here,' he said, pointing perilously close to his groin and grimacing. The boys found another thigh pad to attach to my rib cage which, incidentally, was still not fully recovered from the sprained left pec administered by Adrian Garvey's head in the Springboks front row. Finally, Boof lent me his helmet, complete with a metal grill to protect my mouth, teeth and jaw. The helmet became stuck as I placed it over my head, so that I was looking out through the bars of the grill. 'You're supposed to be looking through the gap between the grill and the helmet,' Ian Healy said, as he slammed the palm of his hand down on the helmet to shift it into its proper place. I was just about ready, although I was covered in so much protective gear I more resembled a Knight of the Round Table than a cricketer.

I picked up my bat and started to walk purposefully out towards the net when I noticed that the face of my Newberry was suddenly covered in black, scrawled writing. It turned out that some of the players had written messages on it behind my back, in the knowledge that I would, at some time, be batting that afternoon. Steve Waugh had signed his name, adding: 'Play well.' So, too, had his brother, Mark. Shane Warne wrote out his autograph, whilst Tom Moody said: 'Play well!!' Ian Healy and Michael Slater also included their names.

It was a nice touch from the boys, who already seemed to accept me even though I had waltzed into their camp just the day before as a Pommy writer. But they were not to know that the bat did not actually belong to me. When I returned home, I thought, I had some explaining to do.

Still, as I made my way into the nets, this was the least of my concerns. I noticed how a throng of press reporters and camera crews suddenly converged on to net number two in the hope, no doubt, that something newsworthy was about to happen. I assumed that all were sports writers and correspondents, although one or two obituary writers may well have joined the interested gathering.

The Australian squad seemed to be almost fighting over the chance to have a bowl at me. Outright batsmen joined the queue, and the supposedly slow bowlers were marking out what looked like suspiciously long run-ups. Slats set the theme of the ensuing 20-

minute batting session by running up to the bowling crease as fast as he could and sending down a bouncer that shot quickly, but harmlessly, past my left shoulder and over the leg stump. He burst out laughing during his follow-through and said: 'Sorry about that, Ian, but you'd better get used to this.'

He could not have been more right. Bowler after bowler sent down short-pitched deliveries, most of which I was able to either duck down or swerve my head away from. After a while Brendon Julian, the tall all-rounder whose good looks made him the Casanova of the team, shouted out: 'When are you going to hit one, you Pommy bastard?' I shouted back, perhaps not altogether wisely: 'When you boys manage to bowl a ball on target.'

Colin 'Funky' Millar proved to be the most accurate of the bowlers, although even he, gifted enough to be able to bowl both right-arm off-spin and medium pace for Tasmania, concentrated on the latter of his skills. He was the only bowler to claim my wicket outright, when in driving a pitched-up ball an inside edge sent the ball on to pads and then into the stumps. I nicked a couple of other deliveries as well, but told the celebrating bowlers that both chances had been put down by the slips.

Stuart MacGill did not attempt to disguise his bowling at all. 'I've got to tell you,' he said, 'I'm going to pin one on you.' Luckily he, as a right-arm leg-spinner picked for the Pakistan Test tour in Shane Warne's absence, is no Glenn McGrath, and I had time to either duck or connect with his bouncers. Swamp called time and I emerged from the nets relieved and relatively unscathed, except for a throbbing finger courtesy of a ball from Funky that had bounced sharply and smashed into my gloves.

The boys seemed pleased with my efforts. 'You didn't get hit?' asked Boof. 'Not even on your inside thigh?' Slats was even complimentary. 'You've got good eyesight and awareness,' he said. 'You never took your eye off the ball, which is crucial when you're dealing with bouncers.' He should know. As the exciting opening Test batsman with Tubby Taylor, he has scored nearly 3,000 runs at an average of over 45, which, on anyone's terms, makes him one of the best batsmen in world cricket.

I felt a mixture of emotions as I proceeded to unstrap my assortment of protective clothing and equipment. I had enjoyed every second of the net session, in terms of both the challenge the Australians presented and the very act of batting and bowling to such stars. I believed I had conducted myself well. But I also felt a little low. This, so I was led to believe, was the best it was going to get. Although

I had persuaded the management to let me be 12th man for the three one-day matches Australia would be playing over the course of the next three days, which was, in itself, a great honour, I would be unable to actually participate. Australia were taking these games very seriously as part of their preparations for the Commonwealth Games and Pakistan, and, in any case, they would be unable, under the terms of their contract, to allow me on to the field of play.

On the way back to the Quay West Hotel I sat next to Shane Warne in the minibus. Arguably the biggest sports star in Australia, and certainly the Australian cricketer feared most by the rest of the world, Warney had already been out of cricket for five months following his shoulder operation. 'It's certainly helped me not to take what I do for granted,' he admitted, taking a long drag from one of the many cigarettes he seemed to smoke each day. He and Boof appeared to be the chief smokers in the team, and although I was a little surprised to see such top sportsmen smoke, it clearly had little effect on their performances. Warney continued, 'When you've been out of the game as I've been, and prevented from doing what I love most, then you come to realise how special it is to play cricket for your country. When I return, I expect to be a better player, and person, for my experiences.'

His return was imminent, incidentally, and although medical opinion reckoned it could take a year for Warney to make a complete recovery, the man himself was set for a comeback some time during the Ashes series against England between November and January. He could well have played county cricket in England, but for his injury. 'I had three good offers, the best being £400,000 for four months' work,' he said with a resigned shrug. 'That would have been nice. You know, there's nothing wrong with your players over in England. It's just your system and your attitude. You play too much, most of the standard is average at best and it just doesn't seem to matter as much to you guys.'

It was difficult to disagree with him over this. I asked him what it was like to be such a huge celebrity. 'I tell you, Australia's the best place in the world to be famous,' he replied. 'You don't get hassled, and even when, occasionally, you do, it's only for five minutes. Australians are prepared to give people like me some space. Mind you, it helps that I've remained so down to earth. Friends tell me I haven't changed much, which I take as a great compliment. My biggest problem is impatience, though. You see it in my batting. I reckon I could be a recognised all-rounder if it wasn't for the fact that I just can't seem to be able to hang around at the crease. But I'm like that with everything I do. When I'm talking to my manager, I always want something to happen immediately, which isn't always easy.'

Is there ever a time when he'd rather be someone else? 'No, not really,' he said, shaking his head and staring out of the window as we sped through the streets of Brisbane. 'Well, only sometimes. The other night, for example, I was driving in my Ferrari when someone pulled up alongside me. He was clearly calling me a cocksucker and then cut me up when the traffic lights changed and half forced me off the road.' He held his hands out and gave another shrug of his delicate shoulders. 'You get nutters wherever you go, don't you?'

On arriving at the hotel, Dave Misson took charge of a warming-down session for all the squad. The boys were trying to think up a suitable nickname for Dave, who was a newcomer to the set-up. 'Link', as in 'Missing Link', was volunteered. I suggested 'Impossible', as in 'Mission Impossible', but the general consensus was that this was too long. 'Patrol', as in 'Mission Patrol', soon became the favourite. Dave's warm-down constituted a spell in the cold swimming pool, followed by further periods of time spent in a warm spa and then the hot sweat of the sauna. We would then return to the pool and repeat the whole process.

In the heat of the sauna, Tubby and Swamp explained the Aussie way to play cricket to me. 'It's all about hustling the opposition, being prepared to fight and never, ever, giving up,' Swamp said. 'There's not much difference in ability between most of the Test teams, so you've got to gain the edge with your approach to the game and your attitude.'

Tubby, who had survived a bad run of form and calls for his resignation the previous year, chipped in about the English deficiencies. 'Your problem is that you're not prepared to go all out for a win. I remember the last time you came over here to play us. Some of your players, when interviewed, were talking about a draw being a good result. I couldn't believe what I was hearing. You've become too scared of losing, so if an opposition batter hits the ball into space, you immediately take a fielder out of an attacking position to try and prevent more runs being scored against you. You've got to be prepared to go for it sometimes.' Some of the other players, noticeably those who played in English county cricket, nodded their heads in agreement.

There was just enough time that night to enjoy another Lorna Garden-created nutritious meal and listen to a couple of speeches on contracts and security in Pakistan before it was time to retire. Hooter placed a bag of ice on my throbbing, ligament-damaged left foot, thus joining the list of the world's physiotherapists who have had the dubious pleasure of attending to my needs. Slats was heading off to the airport for his 26-hour dash back to Lord's to play in the NatWest final, Warney would be travelling back home to Melbourne in the morning and Tubby and Magilla were going to join their New South Wales team-mates. Tomorrow I would be 12th man for Australia. I was desperate to get some kind of game, but even being 12th man, I figured as I dozed off, was a position that most Australians would give their arm, maybe even their drinking arm, for.

As soon as I emerged at breakfast, a newspaper was thrust into my hands and the stick from the boys began. To my astonishment, the best part of a page of the *Brisbane Courier-Mail* had been devoted to me and my experiences. A large, unflattering photograph of me bowling in the nets with my tongue sticking out sat next to an equally large article. The joke amongst the team was that an article on Shane Warne could be found placed next to mine but filled only a third of the space. 'You've only been here a couple of days and already you're three times bigger than Warney,' Tug said.

My first duty as 12th man, so Steve ('Brute') Bernard announced, was to drive him and some of the boys to the Allan Border Oval. I can't remember the last time I drove a minibus, let alone one in a strange Australian city, but I managed to deliver everyone to the appropriate place. Dave Misson initiated a quick fitness and stretching session before the 9.15 start against the Australian Academy. It was when a rugby ball was produced that the fun and games began. Running at angles, we had to pass the ball to each other, producing more comments about getting me, as a Springbok, to show the boys how to do it. Each time it was my turn I tried to create something different, from a reverse pass to one from behind my back, a chip with my boot or a one-handed pass. They were greeted with cheers from the rest of the lads, who also added Australian Rules passing of the ball, in which you thump the ball with your fist to your colleague, to the general repertoire.

Swamp took over the warm-up, providing first slip catching and then, by clouting the ball high into the sky, a series of difficult running catches. In all the rush I had forgotten to change from my trainers to studded boots and as a result I skidded and slid on the morning dew around the outfield like a first-time ice skater. I managed to catch a couple of Swamp's big hits but also slipped and fell on my backside, provoking much mirth and merriment. Ricky 'Punter' Ponting led the way in running and catching, but in making a full-length dive in an effort to catch his final chance he landed on the bouncing ball and spent the rest of the day clutching an ice pack to his bruised chest.

Then it was down to action. Australia elected to field first against a team of young, enthusiastic and extremely talented players who will help shape the national team in the first decade of the twenty-first century. Coached by Rod Marsh, the former wicketkeeper who, still sporting his trademark moustache, could be found watching the proceedings with interest, these young men were the product of Australia's determination to discover and then nurture its sporting talent. This process, underlined by the Academy and, of course, the Australian Institute of Sport, has reaped major dividends in sporting arenas around the world.

I set to work tearing strips from white towels for the bowlers to use to wipe their sweaty foreheads and hands, as well as the greasy ball. Although this was a pretty menial task, I felt rather important as I stepped over the clutter in the dressing-room to hand out these individual towels. After the opening spell of overs I provided energy drinks and water to Krabby and Ace, before then coming on to the field with drinks and bananas for everyone. Boof and Adam ('Gilly') Gilchrist, the wicketkeeper, eagerly ate the fruit like a couple of hungry chimpanzees.

Shortly afterwards, a reporter and cameraman from ABC television turned up to interview me. They had seen the piece in the newspaper and wanted to follow the story up. It resulted in an embarrassing sequence of events. Just as Tug, as Australia's captain, required some assistance from the 12th man, the 12th man was seen standing by a sight screen being interviewed by ABC. Gavin ('The Riddler') Robertson saw the funny side of it and went over to Tug with a made-up message. 'Twelfthy says that you're just going to have to wait until he's finished with his media commitments,' he told him. 'Oh no!' I said to him, when The Riddler owned up to his prank later. 'What did he say?'

'Oh, Tug was all right about it,' The Riddler replied. 'But I reckon you're in for a big fine for neglecting your 12th man duties.'

At lunch I ran backwards and forwards from the pavilion to the food area gathering bananas and bread rolls for Gilly, who remained in the dressing-room preparing to open the batting for Australia. Like all wicketkeepers, he had his own idiosyncracies, and whilst the rest of the team enjoyed pasta and pizza in the pavilion, he made himself a banana sandwich. 'Best food you can have,' he exclaimed, looking down at the roll he had just made. 'It's got everything you need.' His wife is a nutritionist, so Gilly felt he knew what he was talking about.

It all went wrong for Australia after lunch. Chasing a modest target of 198, they were bowled out for 168 by a team clearly pumped up for a game which represented their big chance to shine and claim scalps they could later dine out on. Tug was philosophical afterwards. 'We haven't played for ages, we're clearly ring-rusty and it bears no reflection on how we will do when it matters,' he said, but he still did not look too happy about the day's events.

Pigeon was hardly ecstatic either. He had only just returned from a long injury lay-off and had now suffered a groin strain after just five overs of bowling against the Academy. It meant that he had to withdraw from a once-in-a-lifetime chance to compete in the Commonwealth Games. 'It's better to make sure I'm fit for the Test series in Pakistan and against England,' he said. 'But I'm still disappointed.'

Moments before the last Australian wicket had fallen, I had heard a strange 'ker-thud' sound from behind the pavilion. Curious to discover what, or who, was making the noise, I came across Ian Healy, who was throwing a golf ball against a concrete wall and then catching it, using just his wicketkeeper's inner gloves. He looked like the Steve McQueen character, 'Hilts', in *The Great Escape*, who always threw his baseball against the wall when sent down for a week's punishment in the dreaded 'cooler'.

Heals was not part of the one-day team leaving for Kuala Lumpur but would be Australia's first-choice wicketkeeper for the following Test series against Pakistan. Having caught and stumped 353 Test batsmen, he stood just two behind the world record held by Rod Marsh and fully expected to become the leading wicketkeeper of all time out in Pakistan. Despite the fact he was not playing over the weekend, he was still in practice mode.

I asked him why he was adopting such training methods. 'I always do this,' he said, his face dripping with sweat. 'I like to visualise the batsman standing in front of me and then practise collecting the ball from above some imaginary stumps. I can simulate any bowler I like doing this and can practise leg stump, off stump, high and low takes.'

I was growing more intrigued by the minute. How could he simulate the Australian bowling attack? 'Look,' he said, beckoning me closer. 'I'll show you. This one's a Shane Warne.' He threw the golf ball at an angle, quite slowly, standing initially at an imaginary leg stump and then moving across to take the ball quite high up to his right. 'And this one's a Glenn McGrath.' Heals stepped back a couple of paces, threw the ball lower and harder, and caught the return. When the QCA complex was constructed a couple of years ago, he had actually asked for the wall and concrete paving to be created for himself and his fellow Queensland wicketkeepers.

'Do you wanna have a go?' the number-one wicketkeeper in the world asked the former wicketkeeper for Stamford School, Lincolnshire. I nodded my head eagerly, like a child just offered an ice cream, and proceeded to throw the ball against the wall before trying my hardest to look stylish in my takes in front of such illustrious company. 'This one's a Glenn McGrath,' I told a singularly unimpressed Heals, before dropping the ball.

After a brief drink in a sponsor's marquee that evening, we left for the hotel. The following morning would require us to leave early for a 90-minute drive northwards to the Sunshine Coast, where for the next two days Australia would be facing New South Wales and New Zealand. I was not to know it as I went to bed that night, of course, but that Saturday would prove to be a day to remember.

We arrived at the John Blanck Oval, Maroochydore, just after 8.15 a.m. Andy Bichel, a Queensland fast bowler, had joined the Commonwealth Games squad to replace Pigeon and was to get a game that day. Dave Misson took the usual morning stretching exercises and I enjoyed my brief cameo performance, this time with a soccer ball, as I attempted to show off my skills honed on Copacabana Beach and Flamengo's Fla Barra training ground, to the usual chorus of whoops and whistles from the rest of the team. I always enjoyed these early-morning sporting moments with the boys. I felt as if this was the only time when I could experience real sporting equality with them. My slip catching had definitely improved as well, so by the time the match began I was feeling rather pleased with myself.

As 'Twelfthy' I was responsible, once again, for providing drinks, bandages, new gloves, caps and all kinds of paraphernalia required by my team-mates. Australia chose to bat first, which gave me the chance to make a proposal to Steve Small, the New South Wales coach. As I had already discussed it with Tubby, who had come to watch, and Magilla, who was playing for NSW, I hoped Small might allow me a couple of overs in the field. At least this way I could say that I had played against Australia. Small, with his bushy moustache that made him look like a cross between Ian Chappell and Rod Marsh, gave me a quizzical look, asked me if I could play this game at all and then shrugged his shoulders. 'Don't see why not,' he said. 'But just for a couple of overs, right?'

I thanked him and made my debut for New South Wales after the 17-overs drinks interval. I'd like to say I pulled off a stunning catch, a run-out and a spectacular stop, but the truth is that I failed to touch the ball, save for when I was positioned at mid-off and was asked to throw the ball to the bowler. I added a little touch of my own sweat and saliva to the Kookaburra ball which, I argued later to the Australian batsmen, played its part in their cheap dismissals. Tug and Damien ('Marto') were batting at the time and Tug later revealed his concerns when I ran on to the field. 'I could see you were at mid-off, so I couldn't afford to hit the ball anywhere near you,' he said. 'It just wasn't worth me taking the risk.' Like I said, Tug had a nice line in dry wit.

Yet another camera crew from ABC turned up to film this piece of action and to talk more to me, prompting more abuse from the Australian team about 'Twelfthy becoming a media star'. The reporter insisted on conducting the interview right in front of those Australian team members waiting to bat, which resulted in a series of silly noises, gestures and, thankfully just once, the sound of a batsman breaking wind throughout the recording. Meanwhile, out on the cricket pitch, Brendon ('BJ') Julian saved the day for Australia by smashing 86 runs off just 74 balls to give them a respectable total of 211. He returned to the pavilion with a beaming smile all over his face, in some contrast to the others who, having just been dismissed, would sit quietly for a while and keep their thoughts to themselves. Their team-mates would keep their respectful distance and silence until the batsman concerned felt ready to talk.

Within an hour of Australia fielding, it became obvious that their target was too much for New South Wales. Tug must have been confident because when Ace left the field he called for 'Twelfthy' to replace him. Now I had been told by Brute Bernard that, as much as he would like to help me, I was not allowed to play for Australia. I made this point to the Australian players close by, but they kept gesticulating for me to come on. As I ran on to the pitch, I saw Brute emerging. He looked at me for a second, shrugged his shoulders and waved me on my way.

Tug placed me immediately at short leg, which is just about the most dangerous position to field in. If the bowler drops the ball short and the batsman connects with a hook or a pull, your life is very much in the hands of the sporting gods. I don't know whether Tug did this on purpose, just to test my mettle, but I managed to make a stop with the very first ball bowled after my arrival. This prompted the other fielders to make up a new name for me. 'This guy's a ball magnet,' Gilly said, standing behind the stumps with his big, leathery gloves placed on his hips and his oversized ears sticking out from beneath his cap.

The ball magnet fielded for the full, and official, Australian team for a couple of overs, stopping the ball once more and giving it a hard rub on his whites until a warm, red patch appeared on the fabric before returning it to the bowler. It would have been more had I, at the fall of NSW's eighth wicket, not made a suggestion to Tug. 'Look, would you have a problem if I came out as an extra batsman for NSW?' I asked him. 'They need all the help they can get.'

Tug agreed. 'You're on,' he said. 'If you can swing it with Steve Small. And we'll try our hardest to get you out.'

I ran off the field, to be replaced by a confused Ace, and put the idea to Small. At this stage, chasing 211, New South Wales were 76–8, and Small had resigned himself to defeat. 'You may as well,' he said. 'But if you can win us the game, it'll be a bloody miracle.'

I dashed into the Australian dressing-room, collected my gear and began to change in front of the rest of the squad who were not playing that day. I borrowed Ace's arm guard and helmet but had no time to find a chest protector before the tenth wicket fell and I was on my way out into the middle of the pitch. As I walked through the Australian players back in the pavilion and opened the gate on to the field, Pigeon had some comforting words for me. 'We'll get the doctors ready for you,' he said as he joined the others in grabbing their cameras. Boof, too, was equally sensitive. 'You do know they'll be trying to knock your head off, don't you?' he said.

The strange thing was, none of this seemed to bother me. I was licking my lips with anticipation at this extraordinary opportunity to play in an official match against the might of Australia. My arrival on the pitch, winding my arms in a circular fashion with my bat, just as Ian Botham used to do as he strode towards the wicket, seemed to cause great consternation, both with the Australian fielders who were unaware of Tug's decision and with the crowd. Some of the Australians in the field prepared themselves by rubbing their hands together, no doubt looking forward to the small piece of theatre about to be acted out.

Meanwhile, the tannoy announcer went berserk. 'We have a surprise for you all now,' he announced. 'All the way from England we have a Pommy writer who is prepared to take on the best of Australia.' His announcement was met by a noticeable commotion in the crowd and a few shouts. 'Knock his head off,' someone yelled. 'Get the Pom,' said another wag. I approached the last NSW batsman, who was giving me a rather quizzical stare, and gave him some advice. 'We'll just try and hang in here and see what happens,' I said. He nodded his head and seemed eager to get to the other end of the wicket, as if I was totally deranged.

I asked the umpire for a middle-stump guard, made a line with my studs between middle stump and my batting crease and had a good look around the field placings. There were huge gaps on the leg side and I hoped to get the chance to flick the ball off my legs into these areas. From the slips I heard someone say: 'Get ready to catch the ball off his helmet.' I twirled my bat round and round in the air, mainly because I'd seen Alec Stewart, the England captain, do exactly the same, and then settled down to face my first ever ball from an Australian fast bowler in a match situation.

Andy Bichel was the man I would face, a bowler keen to prove himself now that he had been selected for the Commonwealth Games squad as the replacement for Pigeon. He had already made a point of introducing himself to me earlier that day and seemed a nice guy. As he began his lengthy run-up towards me, however, having already taken three NSW scalps, his previously friendly expression had changed into something far more disturbing.

'This is it,' I was telling myself in those few seconds before impact, my heart thumping away and my stomach filled once again with the various kinds of flying insects I had experienced during all my other adventures. 'This is it. You've scored 21 in front of Ritchie Richardson, you batted well in the nets against these guys. You can play this game. You can do it.'

This was yet another moment during my ridiculous year where, in another far-flung corner of the planet, fantasy and reality merged. Part of my fantasy was just to be out there playing with and against these boys. The other part was to perform well. For all my nerves, I would not have swapped my position right then with anyone else in the world. The reality of the situation, however, took command. Bichel's first ball shot just wide of the off stump. I tried to play a defensive stroke, but the ball was in Gilly's hands before I had even finished my stroke. I had barely seen the ball but tried to appear unconcerned as I looked around, practised a few strokes and twirled my bat again.

The second ball was almost identical. I played a sort of semi-push at it, before withdrawing my bat to leave it alone. In hindsight I think I pulled away having already played, and missed, the ball, but I still tried to give off an air of complete nonchalance to the Australian fielders, now resembling a pack of baying hounds, who had circled menacingly around me. Bichel was bowling fast, very fast. In fact, even the Aussie fielders commented on how they had never seen him bowl as quickly before. 'He really let them fly,' Junior admitted later.

As I settled down to face my third ball, I noticed that everyone from the Australian camp not actually out there in the field had assembled outside the pavilion, including Swamp and Brute, to watch the proceedings. Bichel came steaming in and this time dropped the ball short on the middle and leg stump. I instinctively ducked before, in a split second that seemed to be suspended in time, I realised the ball was not going to rise up as much as I had predicted. It was all over in a blink of an eye, but I still recall preparing myself for impact as I lifted my left arm and my bat upwards in front of my face in a desperate attempt to fend off the ball.

The cracking sound of the ball smashing against my arm and shoulder must have been loud, because it produced a huge cheer from the crowd. Some of the Australian fielders rushed forward to see if I was injured, but I waved them away. In truth I was in pain, but I was damned if I was going to reveal this to the rest of the team. Andy Bichel apologised and as he trudged back to his mark with noticeable purpose I practised a couple of pull strokes, partly in preparation and partly for bravado. It was a vain attempt to say to the boys: 'Not only am I not hurt, nor fazed by the situation, but the next time he bowls one of those balls I'm going to crack it to the leg-side boundary.' Gilly and the slips, clearly not convinced, burst out laughing at this.

Bichel's fourth ball proved to be my last. He returned his attention to the off stump and sent down a fast, bouncy delivery. I tried to nudge the ball over the slips but instead sent it straight to Tom Moody. It was all over in a flash. I heard the dreaded sound of a slight nick and just had enough time to swivel my head round to watch the ball fly upwards at a furious pace towards Moods. The tallest man in the Australian team stuck his hands up in front of his face and made a sharp catch look ridiculously easy.

I stood there for a second and blinked. Was that it? Was I really out? I looked at the umpire in the hope that he might have given a no ball, but he was already on his way back to the pavilion for a cup of tea. The Australian players first celebrated their Pommy scalp and congratulated Moods, then came over to me to shake my hand. I was cursing my luck at this point. I realised that if it had been virtually anyone else in the Australian team fielding at second slip, I would have nicked a four over his head and could have been on my way. Instead I had, to use universal cricketing parlance, failed to trouble the scorers.

Being the unrealistic competitor that I am, I was genuinely disappointed by my performance, although I had enjoyed and was grateful for the few moments I had just experienced. Any club cricketer in the world, on reading this account of my innings, will reckon he would have fared better. Maybe, but I had never experienced such frightening pace from a bowler before and tried to console myself with the fact that I did well to get even a touch on Bichel's final delivery. To my amazement, the Australian team, to a man, came over to say a few words.

'Don't worry, mate, you didn't do any worse than me,' said Ricky ('Punter') Ponting, who, together with Moods, had earlier scored nought against NSW. Moods spoke of his relief in catching me out. 'I would have copped some stick if I'd dropped you,' he admitted. The Waugh twins both shook my hand. 'Fair dinkum,' Junior said. 'You did well. You've got balls, that's for sure.' Tug was smiling. 'Fair play to you,' he added. 'That was quick, by anyone's standards, and it was a bloody good ball to get you out.' Even Tubby walked on to the field to say his bit. 'I'm not sure if I would have fancied facing that,' he said.

Andy Bichel, who had returned to his nice former self, made a point of checking if my arm was hurting. 'You've got to get it iced up,' he kept insisting as he led me to Hooter in the treatment tent. Tug followed and delivered a small speech reminiscent of Steve Redgrave's at the end of my first, dreadful day at Henley.

'Now you can really say you know what it's like to play against us,' he said. 'You wanted it to be for real and you've got it.' Junior joined him. 'Better still, you got hit,' he said brightly. 'That's good for the book, isn't it?'

'Well, yes, I suppose so, Junior,' I said. 'But I hardly planned it that way. Besides, I know what I did wrong.'

'What's that, then?' the Waugh twins asked, as Andy Bichel looked up with interest.

'I'm always susceptible to the slow ball,' I replied. 'I played my stroke too soon because I thought the ball would be going faster than it was.'

The three Australians looked at each other for a second and then realised I was joking. 'Yeah, right,' said Tug, as he slapped me on the back and began to change.

After another hot/cold session administered by Dave Misson that evening, this time at the Novotel Twin Waters Resort in Mudjimba, we all enjoyed a quick game of water polo in the swimming pool. Andy Bichel appeared sporting a tight, muscular body. Boof followed, sticking his hairy belly out in contrast. 'Now that's much more like it,' Tug said, looking at Boof with mock approval. A number of children's bicycles were parked nearby, which gave the team the chance to laugh at the baby-faced Punter's expense. 'Hey, Punter,' a couple of them shouted out. 'I see you brought your bike with you.'

Although offered the services of a large bus, everyone piled into a minivan and made a rather cramped journey to the nearby Surf Bar in Mooloolaba. I was on an understandable high following the afternoon's exploits, but still do not know quite why I agreed to a drinking contest with one of the New South Wales players who had a party piece of downing a pint of lager in less than two seconds. The players referred to this as a 'sculling race'. If they had seen me sculling with Steve Redgrave at Henley, all subsequent bets would have been off.

Magilla and I concocted this plan where we would stage a best-of-five race, on the basis that whilst the guy from NSW could drink quickly, he was unable to hold down large volumes of alcohol for too long. He would be drinking pints of beer and I would be handling tall glasses of bourbon and Coke. I was not convinced that all this was a good idea, especially as I would be 12th man for Australia against New Zealand the following morning, but before I knew it Magilla had organised bets and most of the Australian and NSW sides were laying their dollars down on the table. Even Junior and Punter dragged themselves away from the TV screens covering the night's trotting races to watch the drama.

The plan, like that of any good bar-room hustler, was always to throw the first two drinks. My opponent downed his two pints in customary quick fashion, whilst I sipped mine at a leisurely pace. Some of the players who had placed money on me grew concerned at these events. Magilla, who was lapping up every moment of the action in his self-appointed role as chairman of proceedings, told them to be patient. 'This is a marathon, not a sprint,' he said. Sure enough, I hit back by winning the next two, as my opponent became clearly affected by the alcohol. Some of the NSW players, whose support for the Pom had wavered, gathered round to shake my hand and give me encouragement. 'Now you've got him,' the NSW team physio said. 'We always knew you would.'

Dave Misson administered a quick shoulder massage and asked how I felt. 'Dave,' I said, 'winning's a habit, and I'm on a roll.' I noticed Brute Bernard shaking his head at this remark as he helped himself to a Bundaberg rum. Junior took 20 bucks off me, convinced that his tip in the next trotting race would come home first. It didn't. Luckily, I placed an each-way bet and recovered 15 dollars thanks to my horse's third place. 'You only lost five bucks,' Junior argued. 'You've got to be pleased with that.'

I hardly had time to figure out Junior's logic when the merry throng of Australian and NSW players moved on to another bar to administer the final rites. Magilla reckoned that the longer we left it between drinks, the more the alcohol would take effect on my opponent. In fact, it had the opposite effect. The break in proceedings gave my opponent sufficient time to sober up enough to pip me by a split second in the fifth and last round. I was not convinced and wanted to see a slow-motion replay, but everyone insisted, even those who had backed me, that I had lost narrowly.

For the second time that day, players from both Australia and New South Wales shook my hand and congratulated me. I thought those who had lost money on their faith in the Pom would be annoyed, but far from it. 'You did bloody well, mate,' seemed to be the general consensus. Moods came over for a consoling chat. 'I kept telling them that if there's one thing the Poms can do, then it's drink,' he said. 'You know, you've earned a lot of respect from the players after what you've done today and tonight.'

I made a very late journey back to the Twin Waters Resort with Tug, who was being rested for the final day's match against New Zealand. We talked mainly about our children and fatherhood. He also spoke of his commitment to helping 200 malnourished and severely under-privileged children in Calcutta. 'I know it may be pissing in the wind,' he said. 'But the way I see it, if I can help even one of them out, then it's worth it.' I fail to recall anything else said during the taxi ride home, but in the morning Tug, with a knowing look, would make a curious point of saying how he remembered every word I had said.

Five hours later I woke feeling remarkably refreshed in readiness for the New Zealand match, where I would resume my 12th man duties. I knew I would not be fielding or batting that day, so I made the most of the pre-game warm-up session with Dave Misson, throwing myself around to catch the ball like a man possessed. Tug had a theory about all this, which he later revealed to me. 'You must have had a hangover,' he said.

'Why do you say that, Tug?' I asked.

'Because you were trying so hard in order to hide the fact,' he replied.

Apart from providing the usual drinks, I also managed to obtain some jelly beans and snake-shaped jelly lollies from the pavilion kitchen for the Aussie fielders, which seemed to go down very well. In fact, this was just about the only time I ever heard an argument between the boys. 'That green one's mine,' said one. 'I saw it first,' cried another. Within a few seconds a whole bowlful of the jellies had been consumed. It was as if a plague of locusts had just devoured a field of corn. As I walked back to the pavilion, half a jelly snake suddenly landed in my empty bowl. 'I can't believe it,' Moods cried out in obvious glee from a few yards away. 'I managed to get it in the bowl even though Ian had made it a moving target.' It was probably the best example of throwing witnessed all weekend.

Through probable boredom, the remaining members of the Australian squad not playing that day began to show interest in the manner in which I made my entrance on to the pitch. At first I would merely open the small gate, but after a while I would vault over the wooden slats on to the field. 'Do a Fosbury flop next time,' shouted Krabby. I obliged him with a scissors kick instead. Later Krabby went on for a couple of overs' fielding. When he ran back off again, having failed to touch the ball once, he came over to me and announced: 'Now that's how you field, Ian.'

Despite all these antics taking place back in the pavilion, New Zealand were bundled out for 151 and Australia, thanks to a half century from Gilly and a brutal, unbeaten 98 from Junior, won at a canter. At one point Junior beckoned Twelfthy on to the pitch. 'What is it?' I asked him, panting from my sprint out into the middle of the wicket. 'Tell the next batsman to get ready,' he said.

I ran back to the pavilion. 'We know,' the batsmen said, almost in unison. 'Junior's going to hit either a load of sixes, or he's going to get out. Either way, it's not going to last very long.' Sure enough, Junior proceeded to find both a thicket of trees and a grandstand full of exuberant supporters with his hefty hitting. 'I wanted to see the footy on the telly this afternoon,' he said later in explaining the speed in which he had knocked off the runs.

That night, our last in Brisbane, the players gleefully revealed that my drinks in the Surf Bar had been spiked behind my back. They reckoned I was drinking triple bourbons, something I found difficult to believe, but they explained that that's why everyone congratulated me afterwards. 'We thought we'd be carrying you home,' they said. 'We reckon you won an honourable victory, because you were knocking back three times as much alcohol as the other guy.' Tug found my claims of soberness amusing. 'It was a good effort,' he reported, as if I'd just scored a 50. 'But you did walk straight into a post once, and we had to stop on the way back to the hotel for you to have the longest piss in history by the roadside.'

It was a strange sequence of events. In Kenya it took eight, exhausting laps of a high-altitude track to win over the athletes and the locals. In Australia it took facing and then being hit by the country's best pace attack, before taking part in a mammoth drinking session. By surviving both I had somehow gained the respect of all my new-found, if temporary, colleagues. The barriers between us had been removed long before, of course, but my efforts on and off the pitch the previous day had seemed to result in total acceptance within the camp. The drinking episode was not particularly clever and it is not something I would advocate again, but it seemed to go down well with everyone present. 'I tell you what,' Brute said to me on that Sunday. 'It provided some bloody good entertainment.' Just like with the Springboks, I genuinely felt as if I was now one of the squad and not an outsider invited in and therefore endured for a few days.

The boys enjoyed their last night on the training camp, united as a team, a band of brothers. That goes a long, long way to explaining their success in world cricket. Whilst enjoying listening to a rock group performing in an Irish pub – the band, incidentally, were signed up by Brute to perform for the team two days before the Ashes series began back in Brisbane in November – Swamp told me how I should have hit Andy Bichel's ball hard. 'You were fishing at it,' he said. 'Just like a Pom.' He took a long drink from his pint of Caffrey's, looked around the pub and gave his players a paternal look. 'Cricket,' he added. 'It really is the best game in the world.' Later, he was spotted slapping his knees and jigging to the music, oblivious to the fact that some of his highly amused team-mates were watching him.

The Pom in question was there, bleary-eyed, at seven the following morning to see the boys off to the airport. Resplendent in their Commonwealth Games team uniforms, they threw their mass of equipment into the luggage hold and then piled on to a bus. I had just enough time to thank them all before they were on their way to Malaysia.

A few hours later my jumbo jet also left Brisbane for London. As I lay back in my reclining seat and closed my eyes, I began to daydream. I wasn't out for a duck against Australia. The ball flew over Tom Moody's outstretched hands and hit the advertising hoardings by the boundary before an Australian fielder barely had time to move. I pulled Andy Bichel's next ball to the square-leg boundary and followed that up with a straight drive for another four over the bowler's head. Before I knew it, I was lifting my bat high into the air in acknowledging my half century to a crowd who had fully appreciated the Pom's efforts.

There I was, some 39,000 feet up in the air, repeating what I had been doing for much of my life. This time, however, it was under my rules, where fantasy always overcomes reality.

ROY JONES JUNIOR

Whipped Ass in the Deep South

From practically the moment my plane touched down at London's Heathrow Airport after a painfully long flight back from Australia I began to think about something I had been purposefully pushing to the back of my mind for much of the year. I knew that boxing had to be one of my chosen adventures. It had always been my intention to experience perhaps the most genuine, one-to-one, man-against-man sport in existence. I knew there would be dangers. I knew there would be pain. But, like death itself, although certain to announce its unwelcome arrival at some point, it was not something to dwell upon, especially when there was so much else to concentrate the mind on first.

Now, however, as I collected my baggage and hailed a taxi, I realised that I had completed all my other intended sports. There was nothing left, except memories, to fill my thoughts. Ahead of me lay a number of weeks of extensive training, fear and concern from family and friends, and then a final, potentially brutal test in the United States.

I can barely recollect the last time I intentionally punched someone. It must have been at school. I recall vaguely a few fights in the primary-school playground, and a couple when I was around 12 years old in a school common room, but that was 23 years ago, for goodness sake. Once, playing rugby for my school first team against rivals based in Nottingham, I received a full-blooded thump on my nose from an opposing player in the pack. It made my nose bleed a little and gave me a black eye. I was furious and vowed retribution, but when the opportunity arose, as I came across my aggressor lying on the ground at the bottom of a pile of players, I didn't possess the guts or a violent-enough tendency to kick him. I was too nervous about the physical consequences. I also remember a number of teenage village-hall parties in the late 1970s disrupted by an invasion of uninvited local skinheads. They normally beat up a few of the boys, but whenever it came to my turn, I managed to talk my way out of it, either by cracking a few jokes or by trying to act as if I was one of them. Somehow, I couldn't see either method working against a current world boxing champion.

I knew all the arguments against boxing and, like a rapidly expanding number of people, even sports fans, found being able to justify the sport increasingly difficult. I had been present at the traumatic Chris Eubank/Michael Watson world-title fight in 1991 as a sports writer and had stared in unprofessional but wholly natural horror as Watson's dramatic demise was played out in front of an audience who, moments earlier, had been baying for blood. Later, as I paced the corridors of St Bartholomew's Hospital on reporting duty and heard the cries of anguish from the Watson family members, I tried to fathom how a sport can generate such passion and pain in equal measures. Watson lived, and has slowly rebuilt what he has left of his life. Others have not.

My wife had always been against my boxing. She could not see one reason for keeping the sport legal in a so-called civilised society, let alone see her husband and the father of her children exposing himself to such risks. We quarrelled long and hard over the issue. I explained that I saw it as the ultimate challenge to a participatory sports writer, arguing that I wanted to discover why men chose to fight in the first place and that it would most probably provide a dramatic finale to my year of sporting dreams. I was intrigued to know what it was really like to feel the nerves of a pre-fight boxer, to be hit, over and over again, and to withstand the pressure. I wanted to know whether I, in turn, could respond to such measured provocation in a calm and assured manner.

I also argued that, in sparring for a week in England and then undergoing one three-round fight in America, I would have to be incredibly unlucky to be injured severely. Most boxers' injuries derive from accumulated punishment suffered over a number of years. It would be more dangerous driving to the airport than actually fighting. Statistically I was right. But we both knew there was always a chance that something could happen.

To her credit she relented, but she never felt truly comfortable with the notion. Her peace of mind was hardly helped when the young British super-bantamweight Spencer Oliver had a life-threatening blood clot removed from his brain hours after being knocked out at the Royal Albert Hall in May 1998. Mercifully, he did not join the growing list of boxing fatalities. But Spencer Oliver will never fight again.

I continued to convince myself that Oliver was one of the few unlucky victims of boxing as I began to search for an opponent. There were not many candidates to fit my job specification. Who in boxing is undoubtedly the best in the world? At the time of selection, Evander Holyfield and Lennox Lewis were vying for that position in the heavyweight division. It would have been nonsensical to have fought either of them, a David and Goliath reconstruction without the use of a catapult. Oscar de la Hoya, at lightweight, was also, to borrow a phrase from Marlon Brando, a contender. I even made tentative enquiries but was told that his people would not be interested due to insurance uncertainties.

'Don't worry about me,' I told Deana Duboeuf, de la Hoya's manager. 'I'll take care of that.'

Her reply was not one I expected. 'It's not you our insurers are concerned about. It's Oscar. We wouldn't want anything to happen to him.'

The thought of me, at best a novice boxer, inflicting any kind of damage on one of the finest boxers in the world was farcical. Still, despite de la Hoya's undoubted credentials, he, too, at lightweight would not have been ideal. I really needed to face someone my own 175lbs size. It was not difficult to come up with that name.

Roy Jones junior was, according to most boxing pundits in 1998, not only the best light-heavyweight but also the best pound-for-pound boxer in the world. Moving systematically, ruthlessly and seemingly effortlessly up the weights from middleweight to super-middleweight and finally to light-heavyweight, Jones appeared to be unbeatable. His one loss in his 38-fight professional career came when he was judged to have whacked Montell Griffin when his opponent was on the floor and was subsequently disqualified. In the rematch a furious Jones removed Griffin in less than one round. Enough said.

He seemed, from afar, to be a fascinating character. Beaten and stretched to and beyond his mental and physical limits as a boy by his demanding father who doubled up as his trainer, Jones grew up in the Florida panhandle town of Pensacola knowing all about a boxer's pain. The world first took note of him at the Seoul Olympics, where, in the opinion of everyone present at the ringside, including myself, he won the middleweight gold medal. Instead, South Korea's Si-Hun Pak was awarded the title amid much amazement and controversy, and Jones had to make do with the silver. Little was I to know back then that, ten years later, I would be facing that very same American in the ring.

Finally ridding himself of his overbearing father's presence, Jones went on to be advised by two Pensacola lawyers, Stanley and Fred

Levin, infuriating the big-time promoters such as Don King and Bob Arum by refusing ever to make a major commitment to any of them. Jones recognised his value in the savage but lucrative world of boxing, and as he fought his way relentlessly up the divisions, so his personal fortune amassed. He owned a number of properties, cockerels that he bred to fight in Mexico, world championship-winning horses and a private jet. A notoriously difficult man to deal with, he remained, nevertheless, the boxer I felt compelled to meet outside and, especially, inside the ring. At 30 years old, his record stood at 37 wins and just that Griffin loss to his name. Only six of those 37 defeated lasted the distance.

My initial approach to his personal assistant, Linda Padgett, was met with enthusiasm. 'Roy's interested,' she told me. Then the waiting began. We should have met in May 1998. This was put back to July. In July I was told Roy would be playing basketball, his second sporting love, for the Jacksonville Barracudas. The fight would have to take place in August. 'He's not running from me, is he?' I joked with Linda. 'You reckon?' her deadpan voice replied.

Finally, just when I started to believe it would never happen, Roy announced that he would allow me to train with him and then fight in the middle of October. This would be midway through his preparations for the defence of his world light-heavyweight title against Canada's Otis Grant, clearly an intense period of time to spend with the champion. Boxing might well have been the fourth sport in my year of unlikely adventures. It turned out to be my last. As I was to discover later, this proved to be fitting. In September, meanwhile, I celebrated my 35th birthday. My initial reason for embarking on this year of sporting fantasy was the passing of my 34th birthday. Now, in professional sporting terms, and if you ignore the fact that the grandfathers of boxing, George Foreman and Larry Holmes, were still fighting, I was fast becoming a veteran.

On hearing the news that Jones and I would, as they say in boxing corners, 'get it on', I was filled with mixed emotions. A part of me was delighted that I had finally snared the man. Another part, a larger, more prominent segment altogether, felt immediately nervous. Did I have any inkling about the enormity of the task I had just quite consciously arranged? Yes, I had survived a week's physical training with the Springboks. It was true that I had even come through five days of hell at Henley. Yet the thought of fighting Roy Jones seemed to raise the challenge to an entirely different level. I had a little over three weeks to learn how to fight before facing the most aggressive and destructive boxer on the planet. I had no real idea whether I was up to it or not. Only one thing was certain. I would soon be finding out.

Subsequent events merely served to chip away at my fragile confidence. I took out a video one night of an Al Pacino film called *Devil's Advocate*. There is a scene in the movie where Pacino and his co-star, Keanu Reeves, attend a Roy Jones fight. Unaware of this until it burst on to our television screen, my wife and I sat down and watched Jones all but kill his hapless opponent in the few seconds made available. 'Is that the person you're going to fight?' my wife asked. 'Yes, but he won't be like that with me,' I replied, trying to be reassuring. She remained silent.

Within a couple of days a tape arrived from Australia. ABC television had screened a feature on my exploits for their prime-time current affairs show, *7.30 Report*, centred on my time spent playing cricket with the Australians. At the end of the film they showed Jones in action, once again committing what looked like a murder in the ring. Afterwards the ABC presenter, on viewing the film, added: 'Smart of Ian to leave boxing until last, isn't it?'

Slowly the messages began to arrive at my home. John Sugar, a friend of mine who works for Wise Buddah, one of the major radio production companies in Britain, sent me a fax of a photograph depicting one of Jones's opponents lying, face down, on the canvas. Sugar, borrowing the phrase from the National Lottery, scrawled over the picture: 'It Could Be You!'

Kevin Mitchell, the *Observer* newspaper's highly respected sports writer, also contacted me. He had mentioned to Jones's last opponent, the light-heavyweight Lou Del Valle, that I, a writer turned novice boxer, would be fighting Jones over three rounds in Pensacola. 'Lock him up,' Del Valle reacted. When asked how he felt when facing Jones, he added: 'Man, I was shittin' my pants.'

I telephoned my old friend Frank Bruno, who, I was pleased to see, was enjoying his recent retirement, his health and his wealth. I had always been made welcome at the Bruno household over the years and recognised how, for all the criticism levelled at the former world heavyweight champion's boxing talent and pantomime antics outside the ring, he had been smart enough not only to invest his earnings well but also to secure a lucrative post-boxing existence and sustain his enormous popularity. The same cannot be said for the majority of fighters, even successful champions.

I told Frank of my plans. After listening to his unmistakable bellowed laugh for a few seconds (my wife could also hear his low-pitched guffaws, and she was sitting on the other side of the room), I asked him for advice. Frank launched into a long soliloquy. 'Fighting any boxer after just three weeks' training would be tough, but against a man like Roy Jones . . .' A short silence followed, allowing both of us to take in the imagery. Then Frank was off again.

'I'll tell you, that man's the business. He's as hard as they come, he's cocky, he's quick, he's strong and the best there is. You've got to be very careful, you know. He may well agree to play ball with you, but if he's in training for a fight, he could be in any sort of mood. When a boxer gets into a ring, any opponent he faces, even you, is a threat. Believe me, he won't see you as a novice. He'll see you as someone he has to beat.

'And if you manage to catch him with a good punch – which I doubt – nobody can guarantee how the man will react, not even Roy Jones. Once you start fighting, anything can happen. He might just want to get it over and done with quickly. The best way of doing that is to knock you out inside the first minute. He might decide to play with you. Even if he keeps to his word and lets you live with him for three rounds, he'll find it difficult to judge exactly how much punishment you can take. I'm telling you, Ian, it won't be nice.'

Grateful to Frank for his sports psychology which, as you can imagine, worked wonders on my confidence, I then asked him for some tips. 'You will be wearing a headguard, won't you?' he asked, sounding like a concerned parent. 'I'll lend you mine, if you like. You'd better start running with hand weights, too. Boxing gloves may not seem heavy, but after three rounds of three minutes each, where you keep your hands permanently up, they'll feel like two-ton weights. You should be taught all this in the next few weeks, but you must keep bending your knees, you must keep moving and when you throw a jab you've got to keep your right hand up in defence.'

I thanked Frank for his time and concern. 'I hope you know what you're doing, Ian,' he added.

'I'm pretty driven about this, Frank,' I replied.

'Oh, I know that,' he said. 'You've got the balls of a donkey. No, make that an elephant. But it won't be enough. Not against Roy Jones.'

On Frank's advice I called on Reuben Shohet at his Lonsdale Sports branch in Soho's Beak Street. Over the past 20 years or so Reuben has kitted out most of Britain's top boxers. Now he had the dubious task of making me look like a fighter, even if I hardly acted like one. Returning from a stock room at the back of the shop, he dumped a pile of gear by my side and said: 'Try that lot on for size.' Apart from a pair of shiny black gloves, Reuben also provided a flashy pair of blue boots, with red stripes and a small Union Jack emblazoned on the sides, and a long, red pair of glossy shorts that, once I had squeezed them over my hips, produced a small roll of flab that tumbled like a waterfall over the elasticated rim. Throwing in a tracksuit as well, Reuben showed me to the door, wished me luck and added his own words of advice. 'Whatever else you do,' he said, 'don't get hit.'

Frank had suggested that George Francis, his old trainer who sat as corner man through all his professional fights, should teach me the rudiments of boxing. I knew and liked George well, but he was based up in north London, which proved difficult logistically. Reuben suggested I should contact the Peacock Gym in Canning Town, where the Bowers family had set up a sporting mission amid the desolation of one of London's most run-down areas. Frank Bruno was a patron of the place and an increasing number of top British and foreign boxers were beginning to use the boxing facilities available there, notably the Croatian heavyweight Zeljko Mavrovic, who gave Lennox Lewis such a testing time in the ring that same weekend. Just half an hour from my home, it seemed the ideal solution. I contacted Martin Bowers, who runs the establishment with his elder brother, Tony, and asked if he could train me. Martin, ever the enthusiast, immediately liked the idea.

'Let's get this straight,' he said. 'You're a writer and you've arranged to fight Roy Jones in a little over three weeks' time, yes?'

'That's right, Martin.'

'And you've never boxed before?'

'Nope.'

'What, never?'

'Never, Martin.'

There was a pause over the line before he gave his verdict. 'Well, you'd better get down here this afternoon, hadn't you?' he said. 'There's not much we can do in the time we've got, but if you work hard you should at least be able to defend yourself and show that you can throw a few punches. But the next fortnight won't be easy for you. If you beat Jones, not only will it be a miracle, but I'll become the greatest boxing coach in the world.'

And I would have caused the biggest upset in the history of boxing.

The Peacock Gym can be found close to where Magwitch jumped ship in *Great Expectations*. Canning Town, in the rough and uncompromising borough of Newham in the east end of London, is not the prettiest, nor the safest environment to live or work in. High-rise council blocks, concrete flyovers and underpasses adorn the area, great monolithic monstrosities with boarded-up or smashed windows and graffiti smeared uncaringly and often savagely across them. Here crime and unemployment are rife, whilst nationalistic posters are still in evidence, plastered across many of the crumbling walls nearby. Like the Bronx in New York, Canning Town and surrounding areas provide a natural habitat for boxers seeking an alternative to the meagre options on offer in life.

You are provided with an instant reminder of the dangers of boxing as you enter the Peacock. There, outside the main door, stands a bronze statue of Bradley Stone, the young bantamweight who died following a fight in 1995. He was just 23 years old. An inscription at the statue's feet reads: 'Bradley Stone, a brave young man who died in the pursuit of his dreams.'

Martin Bowers has no problems with the statue's presence. 'It serves two purposes,' he explained as he led me into the boxing area of the gym. 'It is a tribute to Bradley and his family. It tells you that he was pursuing his dreams, which was his right and which was more than most are able to do. But it is also a government health warning. Nobody who enters the ring in this gym is blind to the realities of the game.'

The Peacock was both similar to and different from other boxing gyms I had frequented. It was in much better shape than many, with its modern equipment and bright walls, but the smell of sweat and the sounds of the punch bag, speed ball and ringing bell after each three minutes on the clock positioned in the centre of two rings created a familiar and welcoming atmosphere. For all the violence of boxing, I had never yet known a boxing gym in which the key characters, from owners and trainers to the fighters in all shapes and sizes, were anything but friendly, respectful and fraternal. It was recognised that anyone who stepped inside those ropes immediately became a brother in the harsh trade of boxing. Everywhere you looked you could see 'Proud as a Peacock' signs on the walls, a message the Bowers family drummed into all gym members. The Peacock created a haven for anyone walking the depressed streets of Canning Town and for a while, at least, men, women and children could discover the rules of respect and togetherness as they boxed, played football for one of the numerous Peacock youth teams or hurled themselves around on the upstairs judo mats.

As I made my entrance, resplendent in my brand new swanky Lonsdale equipment, one or two of the guys working out shrilled mock wolf whistles. After a work-out on a walking treadmill and three rounds of star jumps, Martin taped up my hands and fingers with thick bandaging and elastic tape and led me to a wooden-floored area of the gym. My first boxing lesson was about to begin.

I always believed throwing a jab would be a pretty straightforward routine until Martin went through all the key points. As a right-handed man, I boxed using an orthodox pose, meaning that I jabbed with my left hand and threw my bigger punch, the hook, with my right. In throwing a jab I had to remember a number of important points: I should roll my fist round at the last moment before impact; I must keep my weight on the back foot, in order not to lose my balance and become an easier prey to hit and topple; my stance should be almost sideways on, leaving as little of my body to hit as possible; as I threw a left jab, my right fist should be up defending my right cheek, with my elbow tucked into the side of the body, pro-tecting my ribs, stomach and head; my left fist, meanwhile, should return to a position in front of my face immediately after punching my opponent, thus rendering a counter-attack harmless; keep the knees bent and never push your face forward in front of your knees because you would not only provide your opponent with an easy target, you would also be off-balance and therefore easier to knock down; when moving around the ring to the left, lead with your front foot, which should be your left; when moving to the right, lead with your back foot, which ought to be your right.

Remember when you first learned how to drive a car? What may well come naturally to you now was, at the time, almost impossible to co-ordinate. It is the same in boxing when you are first taught the noble art. A more recent comparison for me was learning to scull and hearing Peter Haining reminding me about the position of my thumbs, fingers, hands, elbows, knees and just about every other part of my body while I had to contend with a couple of oars and the small matter of a choppy River Thames. In concentrating on my jabbing, I succeeded in getting two or three of the key elements right but the others wrong. Focusing more on my errors, I then merely substituted previous mistakes with new ones from other areas. 'You only need to make one mistake, Ian, for it to be your last,' Martin would remind me. 'You can throw a good jab, but if you're on your front foot and leaning, your opponent will knock you flying.'

Known as 'The Ballbreaker' for the physical workload he demands of his fighters, Martin then led a half-hour work-out in which I, together with an Irish light-welterweight called Pat Larner, was subjected to a series of exercises concentrating mainly on the stomach, the one area I had conveniently neglected over all the past months of training. The sight of my sweaty T-shirt each afternoon in the Peacock was a common one. Larner completed the various sit-up and stretching exercises with little difficulty. I, in comparison, ended the proceedings early by clutching my stomach and feeling sick.

'You did okay,' Martin told me afterwards as I knocked back two pints of lime juice in quick succession. 'Don't think you looked stupid today, because you didn't. I've told the others what you've already done around the world and they respect you for that. They also credit you for having the balls to try out boxing. They looked like you when they started out, so don't feel too conspicuous.

'There's no way you'll possess the full artillery when you face Jones, so we'll concentrate on your jab, your cross-shot and your defence. No boxer likes having someone jabbing away in their face, not even Roy Jones. And we must get you moving around that ring. You really don't want to get caught by a Jones hook now, do you?'

That night a strange thing occurred. On three occasions I was in the process of falling into a deep sleep when a muscle spasm resulted in me punching the headboard of my bed. The second punch woke my wife up. It was all rather embarrassing having to explain to her that I was inadvertently reliving my training in my sleep. She expressed her concern that one of my punches might connect with her jaw. She had a point, so I moved my body right to the very edge of the bed and clung on like a shipwreck survivor to his lifebelt for the rest of the night. I mentioned this to some of the boxers the following afternoon down at the Peacock. 'Yeah, I do that as well,' admitted Tony Griffin, a super-middleweight who resembled a pit-bull terrier. 'Been doin' it for years.'

My second training session involved more of the usual warm-up period and taping up before I was required to shadow box in front of a large mirror. Beside me a young boxer shimmied and shook in the way in which a shadow boxer should. I looked rather clumsy and jolted, and once stepped so close to the mirror that I landed a jab on the glass. Jimmy Tibbs, just about Britain's most respected boxing trainer and a man who had sat in the corners of the likes of Nigel Benn, Michael Watson and Charlie Magri, walked past casting a quizzical look over in my direction. It had probably been some time since he had seen a boxer actually outwitted by his reflection. After three rounds of this I moved on to the punch bag, before finishing the two and a half hours with more of what Martin termed 'groundwork'. While we all performed our sit-ups, press-ups, burpees and star jumps, Martin would sing along to whatever music was blasting out of the tannoy system. 'Got to be seen to be enjoying your work,' he would insist cheerily.

Slowly I became part of the Peacock gang. On day one I resembled a new boy at school searching for his locker and asking strange faces where the history class might be. By the end of my first week I knew the routine. I would arrive by 2 p.m., tape up my own hands, warm up and then present myself for whatever exercise Martin required that day. His uncle George would work with me in the ring, allowing me to crash my jabs and cross-shots against his pads. His other uncle, Jackie, would cast a watchful eye over me from time to time. 'When Roy Jones first sees you he's going to think one of two things,' he said to me one day.

'What's that, Jackie?' I asked.

'He's going to think either you're a fine boxer, or you've never boxed before.' He looked at me and waited for my inevitable reaction.

'Why's that, Jackie?'

'Because you have an aquiline nose, my son. But you may not have it for too long.'

Martin had spent the last day of my first week working on my defence. The natural human reaction to facing someone about to punch you is to move your head backwards and away from the shot. The boxer, however, should move his head forward and behind his firm gloves which, if positioned correctly, should be providing a wall of defence which, at worst, softens the opponent's blows. I found this difficult to enact and was constantly reminded of what Roy Jones would be likely to do to me if my defence remained non-existent. It was a sobering thought.

As I left for home, Martin decided I should have a boxing nick-name. I rather fancied something along the lines of 'The Hurricane' or perhaps 'The Force'. Looking at my reddish hair and my red shorts, however, Martin had other ideas. 'You should concentrate on jabbing at Jones,' he said. 'So we'll call you "The Red Pecker".' The nominal connotations merely added to his amusement.

That night The Red Pecker went out for dinner with some friends. One, a lawyer in the City, began to make up some Ali-style raps which, he suggested, I should recite in front of Jones.

'I know of no man punier, than Roy Jones junior,
I may well be crap, but I'm the Ginger Snap.'

And so on. You can guess the quality of the rest of his prose. I decided I should keep such poetry away from Jones. I felt that respect, if not downright, toe-curling worshipping, might well serve me better, at least until after the fight.

This, however, was not how Nigel Benn saw it. I had contacted him the previous day to ask if he had any thoughts about my imminent match with Jones. Benn had been big enough during the height of his boxing powers to admit that he was only the second-best super-middleweight in the world, behind Jones. As a man who had succeeded where Benn had failed – namely to lure Jones into the ring – I wanted to talk tactics.

'Who gave you my number?' he barked down the phone. 'I don't like strangers ringing me at home.' I said we weren't exactly strangers and, besides, I was about to do something even he would respect.

'Wassat?' his curious voice replied.

'I'm going to fight Roy Jones junior, and I want your tips.'

A suitably impressed Benn told me to phone him the next day. 'You've got to go for him,' he told me 24 hours later. 'Give him everything you've got. Try and knock him out. He'll respect you for it. You've got the chance to fight the greatest boxer in the world and he'll want you to try your hardest.'

I made the mistake of querying this 'advice'. 'Well, Nigel, I was rather hoping Jones will be in first or second gear when he fights me,' I said. 'I mean, I don't want him to kill me, do I?'

Benn almost self-combusted down the line. 'If you'd said that to me at the beginning of this conversation, I would have slammed the phone down,' he shouted. 'Stop wasting my time.'

I nipped into the fray. 'No, no, what I meant, Nigel, was that I intend to do him some damage, but obviously he could also hurt me pretty badly. That's if I let him catch me, of course.'

My bravado calmed Benn down. 'Oh, he'll catch you, all right,' he said. 'He's so quick, you'll feel as if you're fighting six Roy Joneses. You're going to feel surrounded by the guy.'

What would his fight tactics have been? 'I would have gone for him from the start,' he replied. 'It would have been the best, perhaps the only, chance I would have had. His only weakness, maybe, is that his legs seem a little puny. But the man's awesome. He can knock you out at any time and in any fashion he wants.'

I thanked Benn for his time and dismissed his advice. Perhaps I could question Jones's sexuality and parentage as well whilst I'm in the process of attempting to knock his lights out? Perhaps not. I wanted to last the full three rounds, and the only way I could foresee this happening was by the world champion recognising my failings and doing enough, but no more, to ensure his dominance.

During the course of my second and last week at the Peacock I began to spar. All my training before had been theory. Having someone bigger, stronger and quite clearly better than you in the ring, who not only moved around but also punched you in the face, was most definitely practice. Martin plonked a headguard and waist protector on me, placed the green and gold mouthguard I used for training with the Springboks on my teeth, smeared some vaseline on my face, neck and ears to cushion the blows I would be receiving and sent me out into the middle of the ring to face Graham Townsend, a former Southern Area super-middleweight champion who looked, with his blond, spiky hair and deep, intense eyes, like an Eastern Bloc baddie from a James Bond movie.

Like any good boxer, however, Graham was aware of my limitations and let me go to work on him. A few of my punches landed and I was able to dodge a few of his. But the effect of being punched still caught me by surprise. Occasionally, if I felt I had hit Graham a little too hard, I would apologise. 'Sorry, Graham. You all right?' This caused great consternation outside the ring. 'Get on with it,' Jackie Bowers would shout out. 'It's not the *Nutcracker Suite*, you know.' In the third round Graham stepped up the tempo, just so that I could get to know how it felt to be under pressure. Most of his restrained punches cannoned off me without causing much harm, but a couple of uppercuts crashed into my left pec, thus reintroducing me to the injury sustained in Johannesburg courtesy of Adrian Garvey's burrowing head.

It seemed very strange to hit anybody not in anger and even the experience of being punched back failed to light my own fuse. Besides, I told myself as we fought, if I became angry, how would Graham react? Tony Bowers was watching all this with interest and amusement. When I asked him for his verdict, he replied: 'You got in the ring, my friend. Believe me, that's more than enough.'

I continued to spar with Graham each afternoon for that week. My defence and movement improved as each day passed and as Graham increased the pressure. On my final afternoon he unleashed one hook that, for the first time at the Peacock, made me lose my senses for a couple of seconds. 'That was a hard punch, Graham,' I said to him afterwards.

'Not really,' he replied.

Martin lent me a headguard and a rib protector for my trip to America. My head throbbed a little, my nose ached, my ribs were in pain every time I sneezed, yawned or laughed, and I had a bruised thumb.

'You'll be fine,' Martin insisted. 'You've done really well considering how little time you've had with us. You've got a good jab, you're moving better and you can take a punch. I take my hat off to you.'

As I bade my farewells and left the warmth of the Peacock Gym, Jackie shouted out one final piece of advice. 'Ian,' he said. 'Miss that plane.'

In the couple of days before leaving for Florida, I continued to receive faxes, e-mails and other messages, all with gentle digs at my forth-coming predicament. One was addressed to Ian 'The Bruiser' Stafford. Another merely referred to me as 'Rocky'. Even my wife, in a dramatic change of attitude, had started to hum the theme tune to Stallone's *Rocky* films whenever I entered the room. I made a last-minute telephone call to Linda Padgett to ensure that I was still expected.

'We've just had a hurricane over here, you know,' she explained. 'And half of Roy's offices have been destroyed. But you can still come and we'll arrange that fight for you.'

Great news! Not only was I about to face the greatest boxer in the world, but the man in question had just been blown over by Hurricane Georges. He's going to want to take it out on someone, I thought, as I packed my bags. And he won't care if that someone is a complete novice. Even at this late stage, Jones versus Stafford seemed like a ridiculous notion. The thought of it would almost have been funny, if it wasn't for the fact that I knew I was in for some pain. How much depended entirely on the mood of Roy Jones.

The Red Pecker ignored Jackie Bowers' advice and caught that plane to Pensacola, which, although in north-west Florida, is just about as Deep South as you can get. Known as 'Florida's First Place City', Pensacola was America's first settlement in 1559 and has been under the governments of five different countries. As a result it is also known as the 'City of Five Flags'. The hotel manager of the Days Inn was interested to know what business brought me to Pensacola. I explained my motives. He put his pen down for a moment, looked me in the eye and said: 'You're dead, man.'

That afternoon Linda rang to tell me to make my way down to the gym, just a five-minute stroll away. You pass the Jones offices *en route* from the Days Inn to the gym, a large, typically Southern-style wooden house, clearly damaged at the back by the recent hurricane. The surrounding streets were still littered with branches and debris.

The gym itself is also owned by Jones. Outside, a large white noticeboard reads: 'Square Ring Gym, Home of 4 X World Champion ROY JONES, JR.' The message goes on to list his world titles: 'IBF Middleweight, IBF Super-Middleweight, 2 X WBC Light-Heavy-weight.'

Inside, as soon as you walk through the door, the music hits you full in the face. A quick flick through the CDs piled up by the sound system revealed a preference for funk and rap, although the theme music from the *Rocky* films was also in the collection. Frank Cornacchione, a psychologist by trade known as 'Mr C' by the boxers, who trained and gave his words of advice at the gym from time to time, used to play his Phil Spector music whenever the opportunity arose. 'It really pisses the guys off,' he told me. Sure enough, when Frank tried to play The Ronettes, he was met by a chorus of disapproval. 'Turn that shit off, man!'

There were six sketches of boxers on the walls. Those deemed worthy of the Jones selection were Jack Dempsey, Rocky Marciano, Mike Tyson, George Foreman, Roberto Duran and, of course, Roy Jones himself. A large ring dominated the gym, surrounded by six punch bags hanging from the ceiling, four speed balls on the walls and a further speed ball standing upright from the floor.

A couple of old-timers would turn up religiously every afternoon to watch the assortment of boxers at work. One told me how he used to drink with Jack Dempsey and, later, with Ernest Hemingway. The other, universally known as 'Pin', or 'Pinhead', would talk of how he managed to beat the legendary Minnesota Fats at the pool table. 'Mobile, Alabama,' he would begin, every day. 'Fats couldn't believe his eyes.' I gave up telling him I'd heard him tell the same story the day before. Pinhead also had his view on Jones. 'That man's so quick he can punch a light switch and his fist will be back by his chin before the light comes on,' he would say, borrowing a similar comment said about Muhammad Ali.

Six or seven boxers would always be working out on any given afternoon. This was the Jones entourage, all good fighters themselves but in the shadow of the world light-heavyweight champion. One, Derek 'Smoke' Gainer, was desperate to fight Prince Naseem Hamed. 'I tell you, he won't fight me,' Smoke would say to me most days. 'He knows I'll beat him.' It was a well-worn view adopted by every boxer who had never fought Naz before. Those unlucky enough to face the man had all, up to that point, been subsequently defeated in bewildering fashion. Smoke, nevertheless, was confident and determined.

Watching all the proceedings were coach Alton Merkerson, known as 'Merk', and his assistant Mario O'Francis, who both tended to lean over the top rope whilst their young gladiators went to work. A former light-heavyweight boxer, amateur army coach and assistant coach to the 1988 US Olympic team, Merk would always, at some point during training, remove his round, owlish glasses and his black, Dutch Boy cap and step into the ring himself to conduct sparring or pads work. 'I like to lead by example,' he would explain. Later, after training, he'd cook a large bowl of spaghetti bolognese in the gym's kitchen for those boxers requiring carbohydrates, then play with his three large Rottweilers, Bear, Blue and Money, outside in the car park.

Mario, originally from the Bahamas, wanted to follow in Merk's footsteps and train his own world champions. In the meantime he was content to learn from Square Ring and from helping to train Roy Jones. 'You might stand a chance against me in the ring,' he told me when I explained my intentions. 'But not with Roy.'

This, from the evidence before me, was painfully obvious. On first arriving at the gym, I caught Jones in the last throes of afternoon training. There, inside the ring, he systematically worked his way through a series of his boxing entourage, from Smoke Gainer to Lemuel 'Main' Nelson, and then on to Mark Lanton and Billy 'The Kid' Lewis. Whilst his beaten-up partners came and went, Jones remained in the ring. He moved like a lightweight but had the strength of a heavyweight, which is why he was happy to spar with lesser weights for speed and equal and heavier weights for power. He was recorded during one fight to have thrown six punches inside a second. Another of his hapless opponents hit the canvas after taking four hooks in a second. I reckoned I could land, at best, two punches in a second and would then need to take a short rest.

As Jones trained, he would chant out the words of the rap artist blaring from the sound system. Occasionally he would glance over in my direction as he did this. It all served up an intimidating spectacle. 'Talk is cheap, motherfucker,' he would shout, accompanying the soundtrack from *Voodoo Gangsta Funk*. Then he would return to pummelling a bag, a speed ball or a sparring partner.

Eventually he clambered out of the ring, threw a towel over his shoulder and proceeded to shake hands with a line of hangers-on who had queued up, as if meeting a dignitary, to greet him. When he came to me we shook using just the fingers of our fight hand. This is a typical boxer's greeting, protecting the more bruised and swollen palms and knuckles. From close up the man, although the same height, seemed twice as big as me. We were both supposed to be light-heavyweights, but my muscles were Cheviot Hills compared to his Himalayas.

Without saying a word, he walked out of the gym, climbed into his car and sped away. 'Was that it?' I asked a watching Linda Padgett.

'Yes, Roy says he'll see you tomorrow,' she replied. 'He's quiet and humble, you know, and you can't overwhelm him.'

There wasn't much chance of that, I thought, as I trudged back to the Days Inn.

Coach Merk had given his permission for me to join his training group the following day. That morning, in preparation, I went for a short jog round Seville Square, a neat, tree-lined oasis in the middle of the city's Spanish quarter. Over tea and toast back at the hotel I fell into a conversation with a local who, very helpfully, told me how to snare a rattlesnake using a pair of tongs. You never know, such information could come in handy the next time I come across such a creature in London. It turned out he used to make a living catching reptiles for zoos.

'Was bitten by a black widow once,' he informed me. 'My body temperature reached 106 degrees and I had to be wrapped up in ice. Also been bitten by a rattlesnake, a water snake – now that's a whole lot worse – and a 'gator. I once saw a teenage girl have her leg bitten clean off by a blue shark down at Pensacola lifeguard section.'

I asked him if he fancied facing Roy Jones in the ring. 'Oh no,' he said, taking a last gulp from his coffee and making a hasty exit. 'Now that's just plain stupid.'

I decided to leave my Red Pecker outfit under wraps until the day I actually fought Jones. Instead, on arriving at the gym, I changed into a vest and shorts. Rather like the Springboks' dressing-room at the Loftus Versfeld stadium, messages of motivation were pinned to the walls. 'Champions never take the easy way out,' one read. 'To perform like a champion, you must practise like one,' said another.

Remembering the process at the Peacock Gym, I taped my own hands and warmed up, using the gym's treadmill before performing three rounds of star jumps. A skipping rope was available, but as the boxers at the Peacock had discovered, skipping was not one of my fortes. 'I must be the only boxer who can't skip,' I'd say to anyone who cared to listen, untangling the rope from my legs in the process.

As I began to shadow box in front of the mirrors, Jones arrived. There then followed, in hindsight, a laughable process, the best pound-for-pound boxer in the world, in training for another defence of his world title, working out alongside the Red Pecker. We shadow boxed together, before going to work on the punch bags. Others, like Billy Lewis and the 1992 Olympic heavyweight silver medallist David Izonritei, from Nigeria, followed suit. At the sound of the bell, denoting the end of three minutes, we would all slacken off and enact our own walkabout around the punch bags, occasionally exchanging glances as we paced around the room like caged circus tigers. After 60 seconds the bell would ring again and we would return to our work. Whilst the others let out roars as they let fly with uppercuts and hooks, Jones would simply make a hissing noise each time he hit the bag. I would see him in the corner of my eye and try and emulate him. When Jones shimmied, I copied. When Jones delivered a five-punch volley in the blink of an eye, I followed with my own, albeit slower five-punch medley. When he skipped around the punch bag, I too treated my leathery opponent with disdain. I don't quite know what I was attempting to prove. Could it be that I, a total novice, was trying to impress my opponent?

Once he moved on to the upright speed ball, where he was joined by Main and Smoke, Jones began to enjoy himself. A three- or four-punch move would be followed by more chanting of rap, the occasional whoop and holler thrown in for good measure. Then it was his turn to spar, moving through nine rounds of lightweights, welter-weights and heavyweights watched closely by Merk and Mario. Nigel Benn was right. Jones does have relatively puny legs, at least compared to the rest of his body. My legs had twice the girth of his, something I put down to my rugby and rowing experiences. But his hands moved like flashes of lightning, his fists, even in sparring, seeming to cause great concern in his opponents' expressions. Nothing convinced me that I stood any chance at all of living with this man in the ring.

Jones left without talking to me. Two days had passed, and the only contact made between us had been a quick shake of the fingers and a few cursory glances. 'Roy will do what you want, but in his own time,' Linda told me. 'Yeah,' said one of the other boxers. 'But you're gonna find that in this country there's eastern, central, western and Roy Jones time.'

As I sat in Merk's office, I wondered how I would best be able to negotiate with Jones. 'Listen, Roy,' I imagined saying. 'This is the plan. I'm going to try and punch your face with everything I've got, but I don't want you to hurt me back. You can hit me, sure, but not too hard. Okay?' Somehow, for all my boxing deficiencies, it did not seem a likely agreement.

Merk, having served up more of his pasta, wanted to show me his boxing poetry which he had proudly pinned on his wall. One poem was entitled 'The Trainer'. Merk had written a few poems in his time, but this was his own epic, his 'Under Milk Wood' or 'Ancient Mariner'.

Promoters, managers and spectators too,
Do you know what a trainer has to do?
I am a trainer who takes pride in all things,
Especially those things that are done in the ring.
I think of my boxers as though they are kids,
And also watch spectators planning their bids.
The pain they feel from each blow they receive,
Is the same pain I feel from my head to my knees.
As they take blows, maybe one, two or three,
The same blows they receive are punishing me.
As I twist in my chair, and shuffle my feet,
I witness some boxers that rise to the beat.
But those that can't hear the sound of my feet,
They simply fall down and suffer defeat.
Oh, this is a feeling they cannot explain,
Do you know how it feels to lose a big game?
I wish a spectator could feel what they feel,
And then you would know that the ring is for real.
A trainer's job is so hard to do,
I feel in my heart sometimes I am through.
But this game of boxing is brain food for me,
So I just keep on working and soon you will see.
I hope that my boxers will outdo them all,
But we know without God anyone can fall.
So I'll just keep on praying and hope for the best,
And, almighty God will surely do the rest.

'What d'ya think?' Merk asked me.

'Not bad, coach, not bad,' I replied.

Merk nodded. 'I like to write poetry,' he said. 'Sometimes I feel it's the best way of expressing myself.'

Main and Mark Lanton appeared in the office. I asked Mark, a former New York cop who now patrolled the quieter streets of Pensacola, what it was like to spar with Jones.

'It's a physical game of chess, man,' he explained. 'It's all technology to Roy. That guy's so good he can work out exactly what punch you intend to throw next. He watches every move you make, your balance, your hands, your eyes. So he's not only ready for you, he's coming back at you with a sledgehammer of a fist knowing exactly where to strike.'

'Does he hurt you in sparring, then?' I asked, somewhat surprised.

'Well, he's going easy on you, but you feel it.' He nodded his head and smiled, in the process showing a half set of teeth punctuated by large gaps. 'Yep, you feel it all right.'

I was supposed to be paying Jones a visit at one of his homes the following morning. Linda said she would collect me and take me there. It never happened. Not for the first time that week, Roy's plans changed, although nobody quite knew why or, indeed, what he was up to. Instead of strolling around the Jones estate, I took breakfast with Pensacola's snake-snaring, spider-bitten answer to Crocodile Dundee. I was beginning to enjoy his company. This time he volunteered stories about being attacked by black bears, a pack of wild dogs, a mountain lion, a stray wolf and a wild hog. Tomorrow, no doubt, he would move on to that time when he was set upon by a Bigfoot and an abominable snowman. 'Oh yes,' I expected him to say. 'You get them in Alabama and Florida too.'

I decided to take a walk to the Jones office. Linda's white BMW was parked outside. She beckoned me in and showed me round the house. Roy has a recording studio here, where he likes to record his own entrance music before each fight. He takes this very seriously and always uses his own voice to rap over the music. 'I'm like a mama duck with her babies,' Linda announced as she took yet another call on her mobile phone from one of the boxers. A former banker who was introduced to Jones by Billy Lewis, she found herself helping out the boxer in all matters until, one day, he asked her to work full-time for him. Her phone tripled up as a pager and a radio. Just then it beeped. 'That'll be Roy,' Linda said with a smile. 'Don't ask me why, but I always know when it's him.'

She was right. There then followed my first verbal exchange with the man, albeit using Linda as the go-between over her two-way radio. 'I'm looking forward to the spar,' I informed him, deciding to tone down our planned encounter from 'fight' to 'spar'.

'Yeah, so am I,' I heard his voice crackle over the airwaves. 'From what I saw of you training yesterday, I'd say you couldn't punch your way out of a wet paper bag.'

Clearly my fancy footwork and darting hands had failed to impress the world champion. 'Maybe,' I replied. 'But you won't fault me for trying.'

'He says you won't fault him for trying,' Linda duly repeated over the radio to her employer.

'Can he do anything else?' Jones enquired.

'Tell him I shoot pool,' I said to Linda, mindful of the fact that there was a pool table at the Jones gym.

Jones took the bait. 'Hey, I'm up for any challenge,' he said. 'We'll do it after training.'

'Warn him that I don't like to lose,' I added, beginning to step into dangerous territory.

Jones seemed to hear this because he was back with a retort almost as quick as one of his hooks. 'Neither did the other 37 guys who lost to me in the ring,' he said, laughing. 'I'm looking forward to meeting someone who reckons he's as talented as me.' With that the radio let out a last, loud crackle and he was gone.

'Well,' Linda said in a cheery Southern drawl. 'You're off and running.'

Jones went through his usual repertoire during training, while I continued, judging by his wet-paper-bag comment, to singularly fail to impress. Still, at least he had greeted me on arriving with a mutual touching of a clenched fist, another well-used boxer's acknowledgement. Afterwards, he beckoned me over. 'Wanna shoot some pool, then?' he asked.

And so we did. Watched by an interested crowd of trainers, boxers, hangers-on and Pinhead (do you know, he once beat Minnesota Fats?), I went on to win the first frame, sinking the black with a resounding pot that made the ball slam into the pocket. Jones, who was sitting eating Merk's spaghetti and watching proceedings at the table with great interest, waved his hand frenetically at me. 'Well, rack them up, man.'

I would have been happy to have left it at an away win for me, by one frame to nil, recorded in the very heart of Roy Jones territory. He, rather like the Springboks coach Nick Mallett at the table-tennis table, had other ideas. Jones duly won the second frame, sat down to finish his pasta and insisted on a third and final frame decider.

I could and really should have won. I only had to pot the black. Although the shot was by no means easy, it was one I expected to sink. Instead, the ball cannoned off the lips of the pocket and nestled neatly in front for Jones to end the formalities. A look of triumph developed all over his face. 'Man, I told you,' he said. 'I don't lose.'

I sat down next to him. 'You lost once, though, didn't you?' I said, referring to the Montell Griffin disqualification. 'How did that feel?'

'It gave me five months of torture,' he replied, suddenly opening himself up. 'Until I fought him again. I was doin' my job, but the referee wasn't doin' his. Griffin was dangerous and I wasn't going to just stand there and let him hit me. I don't so much mind having that figure 1 on my records, it's just the nature of the defeat that rankles.'

What did he make of his next opponent, Otis Grant?

'Oh, I'd say Grant's dangerous.'

'Why?'

'Because he's a good guy and I don't like giving anyone a beating if he's okay. I only get mad when they deserve it. That's why I let Mike McCallum last 12 rounds with me. I respected him for what he's done in boxing and he deserved a good pay day. I'll beat Grant and I won't let him stick around for too long. No doubt if I don't knock him out inside three rounds I'll be criticised, but that's not my problem.'

Did he enjoy this stage of his training, with a world-title fight just four weeks away?

'It's okay now,' he replied, pushing his finished plate of pasta aside. 'I like getting into shape. Day one's always tough, but after that it's cool. I like the camaraderie of a boxing gym. We're a bunch of guys together, working as a unit. I'm the captain of the ship here and when I drive then everybody's driven.

'But you know the best part for me?' He didn't give me time to ask. 'It's when I've figured my opponent out and then knock him out. It's like a home run. It's when I know I've done my homework, I've coaxed everything outta the guy and then I decide to end it. I get the same buzz when my chickens fight. Even when I win a game of pool like I've just done against you.'

He rose abruptly to leave. That night he was due to play basketball. I asked if I could come down to watch, maybe even shoot a few balls with him. 'I'll give Linda the details,' he said, before adding: 'I've watched you training. It didn't take long to figure you out.'

Linda phoned me at the Days Inn. 'Roy's playing at 5 p.m. at the Cobb Centre,' she said. 'You'd better get yourself down there.' As I waited outside the main entrance of the hotel for my taxi to arrive, the hotel manager walked past with an associate.

'See that guy standing there,' he said loudly to his friend without even glancing at me. 'Roy Jones is gonna kill him.'

The Cobb Centre is rather like any other small-town American leisure centre, except for one distinction. In one corner, high on the wall, a large electronic scoreboard was sited, bearing the name Roy Jones Jr. Jones had donated the scoreboard to the centre, a venue he seemed to be spending a great deal of his recent time at. 'At least three times a week,' he said when he finally arrived on his motorbike.

The basketball court was occupied by a group of children, but as soon as Jones and a group of players ventured on to the court, the teaching ended. 'Hey,' he shouted across at me as I sat on a bench watching the proceedings. 'I thought you wanted to shoot?' I leaped to attention and jogged on to the court. Around me everybody seemed to know everyone else. I stood, rather conspicuously, in the centre amid all the laughter and banter. Eventually someone threw me the ball. I managed to miss the basket completely with my one and only effort.

'You're captain of one of the sides,' Roy explained. 'You've got to pick a team of five and play against whoever wins the first game.' I sat down again on the bench as others volunteered to be on my side. Jones played in the first game, a friendly but competitive affair, revealing his skills on the court on more than occasion as he turned from defence to attack in one fleeting movement. Team personnel, at least on my side, seemed to be changing by the minute until, by the end of the first game, I discovered that I was now captaining Jones.

I gave a quick mock team talk and lumbered on to the court, the only white man in the whole leisure centre, looking to everyone else crowded on to the surrounding benches like a spare part. Then something odd happened. The match began and Jones threw me the ball. At a conservative guess I must have been standing a good 15 feet from the basket, and at an angle. Seeing no obvious pass to make, I took a shot and looked on in total amazement as the ball sailed through the basket, barely touching the netting. It would have been a three-pointer if it weren't for the fact that the rules were that the first team to score 12 baskets would win the match.

The spectators erupted with laughter. Even Jones smiled at the unlikely moment. A number of those watching enacted high fives with me after this, but if they believed more was to come, they were to be disappointed. After giving my team the lead, I became surplus to requirements. The game, just like the football match on Copacabana Beach, was played out around me. I became so confused by the issue that at the end, as both teams trooped off the court, I had to ask whether we had won or lost. 'We lost,' Jones replied, looking far from amused.

His mood brightened as we both sat down for a breather. I asked him if playing basketball helped his boxing. 'Can't see it doin' much wrong,' he replied nonchalantly. 'Keeps me fit and it helps me relax. I've always wanted to be a good, competitive basketball player. That's why I spend a lot of my time on the basketball court, either here or at one of my homes. You see, I haven't changed my personality to be a boxer. I've made boxing fit into my personality. I'm still the same old Roy and I still act the way I did as a kid.'

With that he hopped back on to his motorcycle, placed his large black helmet over his unblemished and unmarked face and rode off into the night. Back inside the Cobb Centre the head basketball coach, one James B. Washington, who also happened to be Roy's cousin, approached me.

'What about that first basket, man?' he said. 'You surprised us all with that effort. But what happened after that?'

'Well,' I answered. 'As captain I wanted to lead by example. So I scored the first basket with a three-pointer and expected my players to just carry it on from there. What can I say? I was let down.'

James, thankfully, saw the joke. 'Sure thing,' he said, as he punched my arm and offered me a lift home.

I came to the gym early on the Thursday, just one day away from the big fight. 'How ya feelin', champ?' Mario asked as I dumped my bag full of boots and equipment down on the floor.

'Good, good,' I replied. It felt good to be called 'champ'.

Mario's gaze began at my feet and slowly ventured upwards to my face. 'You're going to get your ass whipped tomorrow, boy,' he said as a verdict. 'He's going to knock you out.'

'Oh, come on,' I replied, trying to enter into the spirit of the occasion. 'Give me some positive vibes, man.'

Mario shook his head. 'I can't. I'm a bad man. But I'll tell you what I'll do. After Roy's finished today, you can have a couple of rounds with me in the ring on the pads.'

I accepted Mario's offer a little too desperately. Coach Merk was in his office, leaning back in his squeaky office chair that tended to sink down whenever anyone sat in it. I wanted to talk to him about his star boxer. And I wanted to know if I stood any kind of chance of surviving my imminent ordeal.

'You can hit him with everything you've got, it won't make no damn difference,' Merk insisted. 'I've never worked with a better boxer. Note I said "boxer". Roy's not a fighter. He can work out your next move like a grandmaster chess player. And he's big enough to still listen to what I have to say, accept it and even acknowledge if a certain move doesn't work for him.

'But what I like most about the man is his heart. Take the McCallum fight. Roy decided to make the man look good. He wanted McCallum to save face, hold his head up high and take a good pay packet. He showed the man some courtesy. I respected Roy for that.'

Maybe, but wasn't he concerned that McCallum would repay Jones with a knockout punch in the later rounds?

'Nah, Roy was always in control. It's like your brother. If you went in the ring with him and you knew you were a much better boxer, would you try and knock him out? Or would you go easy on him? Roy rises to the occasion. That's why he was so good against James Toney. But nobody's really tested him yet. No one's seen Roy Jones at his best.'

He looked at me and laughed. 'Maybe you'll be the guy, hey?'

Not on the evidence of that afternoon's training. Jones acknowledged my presence with a wink and a smile as he set to work on Billy Lewis. I returned to the punch bag, my T-shirt now dark with sweat. Reluctant to tire myself out too much 24 hours before I was due to meet the light-heavyweight champion of the world, I eased off towards the end and skipped around the ring, exchanging clenched fists with Roy's entourage.

I asked Merk if, for all his confidence in Jones, he was ever scared. 'For sure,' he replied. 'Every time. After every fight I sit in that dressing-room and pour myself a whiskey. I'm always relieved it's over, cos you never know.'

And afterwards? Doesn't he party?

Merk shook his head. 'I just want to go home and eat with my family,' he said. 'I'm still too nervous to do anything else.'

I raised the same issue with Jones once he had towelled himself down and changed. 'I don't get scared, but I do know that anything can happen in boxing,' he admitted. 'Every boxer has a chance with one punch. Look at what happened to Gerald McClellan after Nigel Benn got to him.

'That's why I don't take punches, and even when someone connects, I've moved sufficiently for it to only brush me. But I'm aware. I'm only a human being. There's always a chance. That's why I plan to be out of this in two years' time, healthy and wealthy.'

I understood that there were plans for Jones to move up to cruiserweight and then possibly even heavyweight. I was under the impression he was aiming for six world titles and sporting history.

Jones snorted. 'People keep goin' on about me fighting Evander Holyfield,' he said. 'That would be crazy. I'm a fuckin' blown-up middleweight. I'd rather keep on fighting at super-middleweight and light-heavyweight, making the same load of money and keepin' safe. I tell you, the first sign of decline and I'll finish.'

He sat down for a moment and placed his head in his hands. I took this as a sign that he would talk a little more. I wanted to know more about his past, particularly the harsh learning curve he underwent as a kid whilst his father, 'Big Roy', as everyone seemed to call him, strove to create the finest boxer on the planet. His wish came true. 'Little Roy', to many, was now the best in the business. But were the beatings Big Roy administered on his son worth it? I wanted to speak about this, but felt uneasy about broaching the subject. In the end, there was no need. Roy brought it up himself.

'Sometimes I wonder if I really had to go through what I did to get to where I am,' he said, exhaling a deep breath. 'I didn't realise it at the time, but my mental strength was being built. That's fine, and it was good to have a strong upbringing, but it was too strong.'

'Maybe your father meant well,' I suggested.

'Yeah, well it may have been meant in the right way, but it was still the wrong thing to do. Once I had the flu and he still made me fight six guys older and bigger than me, one after the other. It's made me able to take anything in life. Nothing puts me off. But it's also given me a weak heart. I can't go to any funerals because I always break down crying. And I'm suspicious of everyone. That's what my upbringing's done for me. When I start a family I'll know how to be a good father, because I know what a bad father's like.'

He rose to his feet. I reminded him of our engagement the following afternoon. 'Now look, Roy. You can hit me, you can even hurt me, but don't knock me out and try not to kill me, hey?'

Jones smiled. 'We'll have a good, fair fight,' he replied. 'I'm not sure what time I'll be at the gym tomorrow. But I'll be there. And afterwards I'll show you my house and my animals.'

I asked him what he had. "Bout a thousand chickens, maybe 25 dogs,' he answered. 'You'll see.'

I paid the Levin brothers a visit in their swish attorney's offices in the late afternoon. Fred was busy negotiating over the telephone for another boxer he advised. 'I tell you, boxing takes up over 50 per cent of my time now,' he said, cupping the telephone receiver with his hand mid-conversation. 'But it's worth it. My association with Roy Jones has been very good for business.'

Stanley, whose involvement with Little Roy was more personal, stemming back to the days when Big Roy coached his son, entered his elder brother's office and shook my hand. I told him that the fight was on the following day. 'Hey,' he shouted out to the secretary seated outside the door. 'Book Ian a private bed in the medical centre for tomorrow night, could you?'

The Levins looked at each other and laughed. I tried to laugh along with them. Fred talked of the early days of their association with the boxer. 'I don't quite know why we did it,' he said. 'It didn't make any business sense, and we were poised to lose a whole lotta money. It turned out all right, though. In fact, I'd say it was the best mistake of our careers.'

He left for home, where he was required to cook fish for a barbecue, but Stanley took it upon himself to show me his own office, which, once he opened up all his cupboards and drawers, turned out to be a Roy Jones museum. For the next two hours Stanley described every fight, every deal, almost every living moment of his association with the Jones family. 'When Roy left his daddy I had to go with him,' he said. 'And that's why, to this day, Big Roy has never spoken to me since.' Conflict, it seems, in the Deep South remains.

It had long been dark by the time I returned to the Days Inn. Chris Bott, a Miami-based photographer who had flown up to Pensacola to take pictures of my fight with Jones, had arrived, leaving a message suggesting we should eat at an Irish restaurant downtown. My nerves were just beginning to take effect. As I ate my crab cakes and chops with Chris, I felt like this was my last supper. My mental state was hardly improved on returning to the hotel. A fax was waiting for me in reception, sent by a friend of mine from the American publication *Sky* magazine. 'Dear Slugger,' it began. 'I hear Mr Jones is going to kick your butt.'

I went to bed and woke in a worse state. The night's sleep had been patchy, rather like in Peshawar before facing Jansher Khan. The morning went slower than in Kapsabet, waiting to make my appearance in the 3,000 metres steeplechase final. The major difference between previous experiences and this was that although I had been apprehensive before, I had not been scared. Now, after all the months of planning and all the weeks of training, I felt fear. Was all this really necessary? Nobody was making me fight Jones, after all. There was still plenty of time to pack my bags and go home.

This, of course, was not really an option. I tried to sleep a little more, channel-surfed across my television set and lounged around the hotel breakfast room, looking for my reptilian adventurer friend. He was not there that morning and I missed his company. A couple of hours of his stories would have filled my increasingly anxious time. Linda had not telephoned to confirm when Roy would be arriving at the gym, but I strolled down there anyway just after midday.

As I arrived at Square Ring, Mario thrust a disclaimer in front of my nose and handed me a pen. 'You'd better sign this, that's if you still wanna go ahead,' he said. The words on the sheet of paper made disturbing reading. 'In consideration of my participation in boxing matches with Roy Jones, Jr, scheduled for October 1998, in Pensacola, Florida, I hereby waive, release and discharge any and all claims for damages for death or personal injury which I may have, or which may subsequently accrue to me, as a result of my participation in such sparring,' it read. The words 'death or personal injury' were high-lighted, just in case the imminent dangers were not crystal clear. The disclaimer continued: 'I fully understand that serious injuries occasionally occur during boxing and sparring matches, and that participants in boxing occasionally sustain mortal or serious personal injuries as an inherent risk in participating in the sport.' As you can imagine, it was a stark but necessary reminder which I could have done without.

As I changed into my Red Pecker outfit and looked at myself in the mirror in Jones's dressing-room, paying particular attention to the sight of my nose on the reckoning that it might never be the same shape again, the situation suddenly did not seem so funny. I had just about had my fill now of the amusing messages I had been receiving over the past few weeks. My head kept telling me that Jones, surely, was not going to get his kicks out of committing any serious damage. But then I remembered Frank Bruno's words of caution. I thought about Mario and Merk's verdicts. I recalled Martin Bowers' cheeky grin suddenly changing to a serious expression as I left the Peacock Gym. 'You'll be fine,' he said. 'But you've got to take this 100 per cent seriously. If you don't, it could go badly wrong for you.'

I warmed up on the treadmill and then shadow boxed for a couple of rounds. Each time the main door swung open I turned round in nervous expectancy. The sweat began to develop on my forehead, my arms and all over my T-shirt. The minutes, and then the hours, began to pass. 'If he's not here in the next quarter of an hour, he's not coming,' Mario said as I paced up and down the gym like a prisoner in his cell. I had been scared of Jones turning up. Now I began to fear for his absence. Billy Lewis, Mark Lanton and David Izonritei came and went. Brian Smith, a congenial heavyweight who sparred with Lennox Lewis but had a fight record of seven losses out of eleven, stayed with me for a while.

'I've been fighting with an injured shoulder,' he explained, excusing his record.

'Then why don't you get it fixed?' I asked.

Smith shook his head. 'Gotta pay the bills, man.'

The afternoon passed by without a word from Jones, or even Linda Padgett. Brian Smith left for home, Mario locked up and Chris Bott, the photographer, and I trudged back to the hotel. I was due to leave for New York early on the Sunday morning. If Jones and I were ever to fight each other, it would have to be on that Saturday.

It was the waiting that proved the hardest to bear. On the Friday evening Linda finally contacted me. She didn't know where Roy was, but was sure everything would turn out just fine. I remained in a deep state of nervousness, anxious that Jones should keep to his commitment but concerned about what damage he might inflict on me in doing so.

After another restless night's sleep Linda contacted me again. It was looking good for Saturday afternoon. I spent another morning in Pensacola attempting to kill time. By lunchtime, events, once again, had changed. There was still no sign of nor sound from Roy. I was growing increasingly worried. After all the training and all my time in north-west Florida, surely the man was not going to dump me now?

At three o'clock in the afternoon I telephoned Linda. Roy had finally been tracked down. He had invited me up to his house for 5 p.m., and would then fight me at the gym three hours later. I felt like a condemned man on death row being granted a stay of execution. 'Good news, Mr Stafford,' the hangman said. 'Your execution this morning has been delayed. I'm now going to hang you tonight.'

I was supposed to be collected at 4 p.m. by Linda. When the time reached 4.45 I guessed, using my expert intuition, that there was yet another problem. My nerves were now mingled with a growing anger. I had no divine right to expect Roy Jones, four weeks away from a world-title defence and in the midst of preparation, to fight me. But a promise was a promise. I had travelled an awful long way for this showdown, had already put myself through a great deal of effort in training and now was subjected to this appalling wait. Jones and his entourage probably had no idea how frazzled I had become, but then again only Jones was stepping into the ring, and he faced someone he could eat up for breakfast.

It was ironic that, after all my travels and all my adventures, I should be subjected to this kind of treatment at the eleventh hour of my story, before what would be undoubtedly my biggest and most dangerous challenge. I had already tried to explain to Jones's people how, in South Africa, the Springboks were, in sporting terms, as big as you can get; how, in Brazil, the likes of Romario were considered near deity; that the Kenyan runners were the heroes of East Africa; and how the earth moved in Pakistan when Jansher Khan walked by. Were the Australian cricketers lesser people, or smaller in sporting stature, because they allowed me into their inner sanctum? Were Steve Redgrave and the British coxless fours revealing their weakness by enlarging their tight-knit group by one for a week? I don't think so. Far from it. In my eyes, having seen them at close quarters, I could understand how they had reached the very pinnacle of their sport.

But what could I do? Pack my bags, slam my door and leave town? That would have been self-defeating. Was there an alternative option? Maybe I could track the man down myself, challenge him there and then to a fight and get it over with? The notion, when considered further, appeared like a thoroughly professional manner in which to commit suicide. There was nothing I could do. Except wait.

I had not eaten all day since some tea and toast that morning. I never eat less than two hours before vigorous exercise and I expected to be called up at almost any time. As the morning turned into afternoon and then into the first darkness of evening, so my stomach rumbled and my mood deteriorated. At seven o'clock, a relieved Linda phoned again. 'Roy says he'll see you down the gym at ten.'

'Ten?' I repeated. 'What, tonight? Why does he want to fight at that time?'

'That's Roy,' she replied. 'He could fight you at four in the morning. He does what he likes.'

Then she said something that deeply disturbed me.

'I've gotta tell you, Ian, he's going to fight ya.'

I wasn't quite sure what she meant by this. 'Well, yes, I realise that, Linda,' I said. 'It depends what you mean by "fight".'

'Well, he's not just going to stand there and let you hit him, y'know. You've said you want to know what it's like to fight Roy Jones. Well, you're going to find out tonight.'

I'd just about heard enough by now. My cosy Friday afternoon spar had turned into what sounded like a midnight mugging. Chris and I drove into town for supper. Chris tucked into a three-course meal. I, of course, had the little matter of a fight with Roy Jones in a couple of hours' time, so had to make do with sipping orange juice and watching my photographer devouring his food. Every so often Chris would turn round and apologise. 'I feel a bit sorry for you, sitting there all hungry whilst I eat all this,' he said. 'Still, I've got to eat, haven't I?'

We arrived at the gym at ten. Billy Lewis turned up to unlock the facilities. Frank Cornacchione came shortly afterwards. I changed into my Red Pecker outfit once again and began to warm up on the treadmill. After 15 minutes of this, I shadow boxed a little and stretched. There was no sign of Jones.

Linda arrived at 10.30. Others from the Jones entourage traipsed in over the course of the next 30 minutes. The clock slowly moved inexorably towards midnight. Billy Lewis gave me some tips. 'You've gotta keep movin',' he said. 'And don't get too near him, either.'

I suggested that if I wrapped my arms round him in a corner and clung on, he couldn't do too much damage.

'Yes he could, man,' Billy replied, with great emphasis in his voice. 'He'll knock your head off your shoulders with an uppercut.' He then proceeded to show me an uppercut, letting out a 'ker-pow' noise in the process.

At midnight the others began to leave. 'I've got kids, and I need some sleep,' Billy said, almost apologetically. Only Mr C and a worried-looking Linda remained. I felt sick, sick with nerves, sick with anger and sick with utter desperation. I had to be at Pensacola Airport by 8 a.m., and here I was, now in the small hours of Sunday morning, still waiting for my appointment with pain.

At 12.30 a.m. Mario appeared, just back from a day's trip to Alabama with his amateur boxers. Jones arrived moments later, giving me a quick nod before changing. 'You're in luck,' Mario said. 'I'm here now, so I'll look after you.'

I didn't know what to say to my opponent. 'Where the fuck have you been for two days?' came to mind but, a few minutes before I was due to fight him, it did not seem entirely sensible. Instead, Mario taped up my hands whilst Roy warmed up on the speed ball a few feet away. The rat-a-tat-tat of the ball pummelled by his devilish fists only served to heighten my tension. 'Roy, I don't mind what you do, but try not to punch me too hard on the left-hand side of my ribcage,' I said. 'It's a damaged area and I'm telling you it will hurt like hell if you land a good one there.'

'Don't worry,' he replied. 'I'll be aiming for your face.'

As I absorbed his promise, the sound of Louis Armstrong's 'Wonderful World' was playing on the radio. This happens to be one of my favourite songs. As I clambered into the ring, however, and Frank ran across the gym to switch the radio off, I couldn't help but think how inappropriate that tune was at that given moment. Mario thrust a shot of icy water down my throat, fixed my gumshield and made sure my headguard was placed tightly over my head. Jones did not even bother with any protection at all, save for his own mouth-guard and heavily strapped fists. For a few seconds we stared at each other from our opposite corners, Jones looking about as perturbed as a lion facing a field mouse. The clock read 12.45 a.m. Then the bell tolled.

We touched gloves and circled each other for ten seconds or so. Jones looked straight into my eyes with his yellow gloves thrust out menacingly towards me, providing an impenetrable wall. I began to wonder who was going to throw the first punch. Should it be me? In those few seconds I examined the options. By becoming the aggressor would I reveal that I had the balls for this, or would it merely antagonise my opponent? The tension became unbearable, like two gunfighters itching to make the first draw of their pistols.

I let fly with an exploratory jab. Jones, not bothering to defend with his gloves, flicked his head to one side and almost watched as my left fist shot harmlessly by. Still he tracked me, edging closer and closer, keeping his hands forward but motionless. I was almost willing him to punch me, just to get the first taste of his brutality over and done with. I jabbed again, then twice more. The first two shots rebounded harmlessly off his gloves, the third, a split second after a feint, caught him in the face. His expression remained completely impassive.

Then he hit me. I barely saw the shot coming. But I felt it. Even in whatever gear Jones was in, be it second, first or neutral, the jab crashed through my upheld gloves and straight on to my nose. I thought I would be prepared for such a moment. After all, I had grown used to taking punches in the face from Graham Townsend, back at the Peacock Gym. But this was different. This felt like Graham's heaviest punch, the one that left me groping for my senses.

Jones hit me again, then for a third time with another lightning-quick jab. I stepped back to regain my posture, blinking in the shiny lights of the gym. He eased off. For a moment I felt relief. That was as bad as it will get, I told myself. 'Come on, Ian,' Mario shouted from the corner. 'Attack him.'

I moved forward gingerly, like a soldier in a minefield. Jones just stared back at me, holding his gloves high in front of his face. I landed a jab into his exposed stomach. Again there was no impact. His stomach felt as firm as a concrete wall. With a minute to go, Jones suddenly upped the tempo. Instead of easing his feet towards me, he seemed to canter out of his corner. Suddenly the ring became very small. And Jones began to strike.

I took three punches in quick succession. I'd like to be able to describe them to you, but have no idea where they initiated from. I lost my senses for a few seconds. Jones continued to punch away at his easy target, and although I stepped back and to my side as quickly as I possibly could, with my gloves held out in some kind of desperate defence, he seemed to be able to pick his way through at will. It was like the sea breaking through a barricade of sandbags.

The bell rang to end the first round. Jones came over to say well done. I told him, in between gasps for air, that we were fighting for three rounds. He looked a little surprised. Taking his guard out of his mouth, he said: 'I thought it was for one. That's why I worked on you in the last minute.'

Mario asked if I was sure about this. I nodded my head. 'We've always said three.'

The bell rang again and Jones moved menacingly forward. This time there were no early-round niceties. The light-heavyweight champion of the world started to punch. I would take a couple and then move round the ring, letting fly a few jabs in retaliation which either missed his swerving head or plopped harmlessly against his gloves. Occasionally I would connect with his head. His complete lack of emotion unnerved me even more.

Suddenly Jones unleashed a right hook. I saw it at the very last moment, but had no time to react. It was like waiting for a bomb to explode. I felt a sickening thud to the side of my head and my body threw itself to its side. My feet were no longer upright and I waited for the canvas to greet my body. Instead, the middle rope saved me. I clawed myself back up to my feet from my horizontal position, shook my head and advanced towards Jones.

As I glanced quickly around the edge of the ring, the faces of those watching the carnage disturbed me further. I expected the likes of Mario and Linda to be relaxed about this. They'd seen this all before. Surely they didn't expect anything too serious to happen? But their expressions told a different story. Mario looked concerned, Frank anxious, and Linda's jaw was close to touching the floor.

The bell rang. Mario asked me if I'd endured enough now. I repeated my earlier words. 'Three rounds,' I said, choking on the water as it cascaded over my guard and into my mouth. These were worrying times. There was no doubt about it, Jones was, by his standards, going easy on me. If he had wanted to knock me out, he would have done so. But I was still scared. For all the fitness I had developed during my year of sporting adventures, and for all the training at the Peacock Gym, my threat to Jones that night was evidently non-existent. I do not regard myself as a physically weak man. I never have done. Yet there, in the early hours of that Sunday morning in Pensacola, I felt completely exposed and utterly helpless.

Something else scared me too. It was my mood. I was perfectly aware of everything that was happening to me. Jones was giving me a beating and there wasn't much I could do about it except hope and pray he chose not to step up another gear. But I had grown bullish, almost confrontational by the time of the sound of the bell denoting the third and last round. I had become like any other fighter in the ring. This is why a boxer always needs a corner man, and a good corner man at that, to make the crucial, sometimes life-saving, decisions. You will rarely see a boxer voluntarily quit during a bout. Given his way, a boxer will fight until he is physically unable to lift his fists up, no matter what damage he might have incurred. I felt the same way. Even though I knew what Jones could do to me if it was his whim, I wanted to last that final round. I wanted to look Jones in the eye, I wanted to keep standing and I wanted him to see that, although I lacked all of his talent and physical strength, I was still trying my hardest. I wanted him to understand that although he may have been a better boxer than me, he was not a better man. That attitude scared me. Someone later called me brave. It had nothing to do with bravery. A supposedly intelligent person should know better. But I was in the ring, and in there, where the laws are different, boxing takes a firm grip on you.

My minute's rest was up. It felt more like ten seconds when the bell rang once more. I gave up trying to defend against Jones. There wasn't much point. Every time he threw a jab or a hook at me, his gloves shattered my defence and hit their intended target. I decided to throw caution to the wind and attack him. As I tapped him, so he connected with two blasts from his armoury. Still I went forward, trading punches with a man who I knew possessed fatal artillery.

My face began to feel wet. My eyes had begun to water at the start of the third round. Towards the end torrents of tears were flooding down my cheeks, sparked off by continual punching to the bridge of my nose. But there was something else on my face too. Blood began to appear on Jones's fists, a bright, scarlet red contrasting vividly with his yellow gloves. My throbbing nose began to feel blocked, my breathing became harder and my mouth began to fill with my own blood.

'Thirty seconds to go,' Mario shouted. 'Hang in there, Ian!'

A volley of Jones punches forced me to turn my back on him in one corner. Even as I fumbled with my senses, Jones would hit me again and again. 'Come on!' Mario yelled almost in my battered ear. I swivelled round and unleashed a hook and a jab on Jones, as he, simultaneously, returned my popgun fire with a couple more of his bazookas. My headguard felt loose, my nostrils were matted with blood and my sweat-drenched vest was now dappled with red spots. Jones built up to a frightening climax, landing seven consecutive punches on to my face without reply. I almost sprinted away from the corner and into space in the ring before we exchanged a couple more shots at each other. Those 30 seconds, with my head and my heart pounding, seemed like an eternity. When the bell finally rang for the last time I threw my hands upwards in mock victory before slumping back to my corner.

I leant against the ropes to support my battered body. Mario jumped into the ring and wiped the blood away from my face. Frank, too, leapt through the ropes and offered me his handkerchief. Roy ambled over and we hugged. Just for a second there was a look of respect on the man's face, the first time I had witnessed such a look all week.

'You've got the heart of a lion,' he said as Mario threw more water down my throat and over my head. 'Believe me, you've got a lot of courage and nerve to get out there and do what you've just done. The boxers in this gym know what it's like to face someone, man to man. So we know what kind of a person you are when you can fight three rounds with me.'

My pride momentarily eased my discomfort. 'Honestly, Roy, tell me how hard you tried against me. Give me a percentage figure.'

Jones ripped his gloves off his hands and began to take his taping off. 'Oh, five per cent,' he answered. 'Maybe three and a half.'

'Five per cent!' I screamed back incredulously, ignoring his lesser verdict. 'Hey, I know you were holding back on me, but what does that say about me if you were only at five per cent. You beat me up, man.'

Jones grinned. 'Yeah, but you did well. You've got to understand, however fit you may be playing your other sports, you're not in shape to take that kind of punishment. Nobody is, except a boxer. That's why a boxer should never get involved in a street fight with someone. Cos he could do serious damage.'

Mario cleaned me up a little more. 'Don't worry about it, Ian,' he said, with fatherly concern. 'I train Roy, so I know how he fights. Believe me, you can honestly say you've been in the ring with the man. You wanted it for real. Man, you got it.'

A far friendlier Jones asked me if I still wanted to come up to his house. I looked at the clock. The time was now 1.15 a.m. I told him I had a plane to catch in less than eight hours' time. 'That's all right,' he said. 'Be there at seven. I'll be up.' He gave me some dollars for the taxi ride, and the code to his electric security gates. 'Don't tell anyone the number, now,' he smiled. 'See you later.'

As I walked out into the black night with Chris Bott and Frank Cornacchione, the coldness of the autumn air hit the bridge of my sore, throbbing nose. 'I think you're crazy,' Chris said, looking at me as if I was an extremely disturbed masochist.

'I'm telling you, Roy worked on you tonight,' Frank added. 'Even against you, who posed no threat to him at all, I could see the ruthless boxer in him. He stood back, sure, but not completely. Don't forget, I've seen him fight many times. I reckon many of those punches were more like 50 per cent, I'm tellin' you. I was getting real worried for you. You'll become a legend in Pensacola for this.'

Chris drove the legend home. I packed my bags in my hotel room and tried to rest for a few hours, but when I placed my head down on the pillow I felt sick. This reaction concerned me and I spent the rest of the night sitting up and dozing in a chair. A taxi collected me at 6.30 and drove me up to the Jones house, eight acres of prime Florida real estate. As I walked up to his door, past his Rolls-Royce Corniche and his Land Cruiser with a number plate reading 'I love my attitude', half a dozen of his pit bull terriers began to growl. Chained to their kennels, they rose from their slumber and stared at me.

I rang the bell. From inside I could hear music and conversation from either the radio or the TV blasting out. I pressed the button again. There was no response. I walked around the house. For as far as the eye could see there were chickens either wandering around or sitting by their roosts. Further away, the waters of a lake rippled in the morning breeze. The pit bulls now began to strain at their leashes. The dogs stood provocatively, their growls turning to barks. I rang the bell once more, keeping my thumb firmly on the button for a number of seconds.

The taxi driver stood by his motor, watching all this from afar. A cockerel began his morning call. I sat down on the wooden porch outside the Jones front door. I felt sick, I felt tired and I felt dizzy. I pulled some congealed clots from my nose and again sensed the sour taste of blood in my mouth. I placed my head between my knees and waited for the faint feeling to pass.

The cockerel was soon joined by others. His crows were amplified by first ten, then maybe a hundred others. Before long it sounded like all thousand of Roy Jones's roosters had waded in, their heads pointing skywards as they made their haunting, harrowing sound. At that precise moment, in my precise physical and mental state, I could not have imagined a worse scene or sound on earth.

'Just take me to the airport,' I said to the taxi driver, who had edged forward in some concern. 'I'm okay. I just want to get out of here.'

And I did. Out of the Jones estate. Out of Pensacola. And out of boxing. I had survived all year playing sport with the best in the world. Maybe the other individuals and teams had helped to disguise the huge gulf in class between us. Maybe I had genuinely fared better in the other sports. Maybe, this time, I had taken one step too far.

All I knew, as I slumped in the taxi and headed towards the airport, was that here, in the Deep South of America, my 'ass' had been whipped by a man called Roy Jones junior. I was through with it all, my job had been completed and it was time to return to my own place and my own standing in the world.

It really was time to go home.

EPILOGUE

There were aspects of my boxing episode which bordered on rank irresponsibility. I faced the world's greatest fighter in the ring without any medical back-up whatsoever. I should have paid for a precautionary brain scan prior to the bout and I should have insisted on a doctor being present during the early hours of that vicious Sunday-morning beating.

Although I had never experienced concussion before, this was clearly what I was suffering from as I flew from Pensacola to Tampa and then on to New York later that day. Anyone concussed should have a full check-up and a good rest. In a flagrant breach of medical rules, I spent the next 48 hours in meetings with media figures dotted around the city. From time to time I would be forced to stop in my tracks and lean against a wall to regain my balance. 'Jones really kicked the shit out of you, didn't he?' commented Chris Hunt, *Sports Illustrated*'s Articles Editor, as I sat feebly beside him in the Time and Life Building, nodding my head with a wry smile. I continued to feel nauseous, my head and aching nose throbbed with pain and my forehead remained drenched in a cold, matted sweat. An overnight, and therefore sleepless, flight back to London hardly improved my condition.

After a couple of days back home where I felt unable to do almost anything except sleep, I paid my doctor a visit. His concern unnerved me, and after we had gone through the 'how many fingers am I holding up?' routine, he carried out a blood test, just to ensure a clot was not developing on my brain. The only clot he could find, so he concluded, was sitting before him. Even my wife commented on how slow my general demeanour was for that first week back in London. I took longer to grasp things and seemed devoid of any energy. She also reckoned my nose looked a little bent. This resulted in repeated check-ups on my face in the bathroom mirror.

During this period of inactivity, I dwelled on the humbling experience I had just lived through in Pensacola. There was no doubt in my mind that were I to be subjected to that kind of beating on a monthly basis, I would very rapidly fall seriously ill. Nobody can persuade me that boxing is not a dangerous sport. It is brutal and totally unforgiving. Nine minutes in the ring with Roy Jones junior revealed how powerless I was in the company of such devastating force, seemingly borne out of childhood adversity and expressed through his deadly fists. I tried everything within my own powers to quell the storm but the truth of the matter was that Jones could, at any given moment, have sent me spiralling out of consciousness with one sledgehammer punch. I suppose I should be eternally grateful that he chose not to do so.

Otis Grant, three weeks later, was not quite so lucky. When Jones caught him with an arm punch during his defence of his WBA and WBC world light-heavyweight title, the Canadian hit the canvas so hard that his legs jack-knived into the air as he ended up almost performing a somersault in the ring. Bemused, bewildered and finally demolished, Grant returned to the deck again a couple of rounds later, this time the result of a crunching lead-right punch that saw him first sag and then collapse like a deflated balloon. For Jones, who recorded his 38th win in 39 contests (or 39th win in 40 if you include our fight), it was business as usual. For Grant it was a subtle lesson that sometimes the odds against can be insurmountable. And for me, who watched the carnage on tape, it was a cruel reminder of a night and an experience I never want to face again.

Two months later, in January 1999, Jones knocked out Rick Frazier, a New York police officer, in the second round of his mandatory world light-heavyweight title defence in Pensacola. A statistical breakdown showed the one-sided nature of the contest, with Jones landing 39 of his 92 punches and Frazier succeeding with just four out of 29. Afterwards, Jones apologised to his home-town supporters who had paid good money to watch the rout. 'It wasn't very satisfying,' he said. 'I'm sorry the fight got stopped early.' Frazier, on the wrong end of such savagery, was probably delighted the execution took less than six minutes.

In the meantime, I was still suffering. Bouts of dizziness began to affect me in the weeks leading up to Christmas, especially when I tilted my head back when sitting or lying down, or to my right-hand side. Subsequent blood tests were taken, followed by head and neck X-rays. The theory was that I had a compression of my vertebral artery which, at times, cut off my blood supply. This was a result of minor whiplash suffered at the start of 1997 after a car crash, an injury exacerbated by receiving repeated blows from Jones.

It seems to me that the only person who can beat Jones is the man himself. He will possibly lose one day, when sheer boredom sets in, or he could well retire in the next year or so to his chickens and basketball court, frustrated that the world of boxing could not find anyone in his division able to sustain even a half-decent challenge. He may have already forgotten about me, but I can assure you that I am never likely to lose the memory of my late-night encounter with Roy Jones junior.

But what of the other characters I had been fortunate to meet and, indeed, play sport with during my nine months of travels? How had they fared since I left them for adventures new? Had they continued to justify the label I placed upon them as the very best exponents of their trade in the world, or had sport, as is often its wont, turned against them?

Back on the samba-beating streets and beaches of Rio de Janeiro, all had not gone quite to plan for Flamengo, nor, ultimately, for the Brazilian national team. In fact, almost from the day I left South America, life turned distinctly sour for my ball-juggling former colleagues. As I flew back to Europe, the players and management from Flamengo travelled north to Salvador to play lowly Vitória in the Brazilian Cup. A win seemed a formality for Paolo Autuori's all-star team, but instead they were thrashed 5–0, prompting the resignation of the coach. 'It is a shameful and unacceptable situation and I will always assume my responsibilities and mistakes,' Autuori said in explaining his surprise decision. Meanwhile, angry fans fired gunshots and threw a grenade at the club headquarters at Gavea, damaging windows in the same trophy room Frederico and I had strolled around just three days earlier. Others painted insulting slogans on the nearby walls.

A day later Autuori changed his mind after the players, led by Romario, persuaded him to stay. 'The problem was with the team, which went into the game tired and apathetic,' Romario said. Judging by their exploits during Carnival the previous week, this was probably a correct analysis. Yet life was to get considerably worse. A week later, Flamengo's dire season continued when they were beaten at home by the supposed no-hopers Bangu. Towards the end of the game, when the 2–1 defeat seemed likely, the players were chased off the pitch by their own fans. The game was held up for ten minutes when spectators scaled the perimeter fencing. One man wearing Flamengo's famous black and red ran on wielding a huge stick, which he threw at one of the players before being bundled away by police. Meanwhile, the rest of the players and coaches took cover in the tunnel. As I was told all this by my Brazilian contacts, I wondered if Autuori would be desperate enough to call me back to Rio. It was certainly true that he had become a bemused and befuddled team coach. Two defeats later he was fired, and he can now be found training one of his former Rio-based clubs, Botafoga.

Brazil lurched their way towards the World Cup in France not quite knowing what they would produce. One week before their first group match, against Scotland, Zagallo did the unthinkable and dropped Romario from the squad. The Flamengo captain was dumped in France after a scan revealed lasting damage to his right calf muscle. He pleaded for more time to recover from the injury but was instead sent home and replaced by Emerson Ferreira. 'We waited until the last possible moment and gave him our full backing,' Zagallo explained. 'It wasn't us who dropped Romario. It was the scan.'

The man who three months earlier had told me that only winning the World Cup would suffice was reduced to tears. 'This is very sad for me,' he said. 'This is a very difficult moment in my life. I'd just like to thank the national team for having given me the chance to become what I am.'

Ironically, Romario is believed to have suffered his injury while enjoying a day off on Copacabana beach playing foot-volleyball. A symbol of hope for the ghetto children of the infamous Rio *favela* of Vila de Penha, Romario de Souza Faria had been looking for France '98 to provide a glorious last hurrah. It didn't happen, and I, for one, was disappointed. The tournament was poorer for the loss of such an enigmatic talent. Romario was to recover to enjoy better times with Flamengo during the 1998–99 season. His return to goal-scoring form had the Brazilian media clamouring for his recall to the national team at the age of 33. In April 1999, Romario was once more selected for his country.

On a more comical note, justice officials stormed his trendy beachside bar in Rio after the World Cup and seized the toilet doors. The doors in question apparently featured caricatures of Zagallo, sitting on the toilet with his trousers around his ankles, and his technical assistant Zico, toilet roll in hand, looking forlorn. Zagallo failed to see the funny side of this and responded with a lawsuit.

By this time, Zagallo had already resigned after the 'failure' of losing in the World Cup final to the hosts, France. Despite only sporadically playing to their potential, Brazil had still seemed to be the best side in the tournament but were clearly affected by the bizarre pre-match fit experienced by their star striker Ronaldo, who was first omitted from the team's line-up and then reinstated with just an hour remaining before kick-off. This led to a bewilderingly inept performance by the Brazilians, allowing France to emerge as comfortable winners. The world's media and the conspiracy theorists went beserk over the Ronaldo controversy and I recalled the tiny dirt track of a football ground under one of the many concrete flyovers of Rio. São Cristovo must have seemed a lifetime away to the quiet, buck-toothed football star.

Junior Baiano, who also played in that now infamous World Cup final, had told me how he hoped to play for Flamengo for the rest of his career. Instead, within weeks of returning to Brazil he was transferred to the São Paulo-based Palmeiras and within a few games found himself once more under the spotlight. The big central defender celebrated his side's winning goal in their 3–2 victory away to Portugesa by deliberately running over to the rival supporters and abusing them with provocative gestures. He was later escorted out of the stadium by police, who protected him from fans who tried to attack him.

The Palmeiras coach, Felipe Scolari, defended his player, claiming Baiano had been subjected to derogatory chants from the Portugesa fans. 'Nobody is interested in this idea of turning the other cheek,' he said, revealing why he never made a career in the diplomatic service. 'If someone talks about my private life I'll give them a good punching. I like to sort things out my way. Anyway, you can fit Portugesa's supporters in a mini-van.'

Jamir, the friendly midfield player who liked to play in goal during shooting practice, never made it to England. Instead he now plays in the south of Brazil, having left Flamengo last summer. But Iranildo is still there, practising his free-kicks late after training with his bag of balls and absurd wall of metal men. He has acquired a new nickname, 'Chuchu', which is a soft Brazilian vegetable, denoting the fact that he is a short man who tends to be easily knocked over during a match. Clemer, the big, affable, wannabe-centre-forward goalkeeper, has also remained, no doubt still munching his cheese sandwiches before training and staging penalty competitions with anyone who fancies their chances and is prepared to lose a few dollars. And although Autuori may be long gone, his assistant coach, Paolo Sosa, remains a part of the Flamengo furniture. The man who took charge of my technical-skills test no doubt continues to derive enormous pleasure from hearing the noise of the ball hit the back of the net. The most beautiful sound in Brazil.

Finally, Frederico Pinheiro, the besotted Botafoga supporter and my driver and companion for most of the week, became a father in September 1998. To his delight he had a son, whom he named Carlos. And yes, baby Carlos was presented with a football by his proud father within days of his birth. One day, Frederico, your boy may play for Botafoga.

Across the world in Pakistan, life took a turn for the worse for Jansher Khan. Of course, it is arguable that losing four points to me on court was just about as bad as things can get, but Jansher's plans for a quick and remarkable recovery from his injuries never materialised. His knees were, indeed, operated on a fortnight after I failed to provoke a bead of sweat from his furrowed brow, and he spent the summer recuperating and training in readiness for his much-vaunted comeback tournament in Hong Kong that September.

He faced his compatriot and no doubt distant relative Farheem Khan in the first round of the Cathay Pacific Hong Kong Open but had to withdraw after just ten rallies with a groin strain. The injury proved to be persistent, although Jansher, mindful of the whispers in the sport that his time at the top had ended, did not help himself by continuously attempting to train after only a fortnight's rest and then breaking down again. An MRI scan in Cardiff in November 1998 revealed a tear in his groin and forced the former champion to sit it out until completely recovered.

Peter Nicol, too, had his disappointments. After his British Open success in 1998, he went on to the Commonwealth Games in Malaysia to win a gold medal for Scotland. Clearly his dominant performance against me the previous February had boosted his confidence, although he failed to mention this in his subsequent victory speeches. Yet in November 1998 he failed to complete the jigsaw, losing to the Canadian Jonathan Power in the final of what is proving for him to be an elusive World Open. During Jansher's enforced absence from the world scene, no one player has yet taken over the Pakistani's mantle, although Nicol is still best positioned to do so.

Life back in Peshawar continues, as ever, in its hectic, noisy, colourful, aromatic way. Mohibullah, Mehboob and Atlas – the world's strongest man – still keep a watchful eye over Jansher's progress, tea is sipped on the lawns of the Khan household and the hordes of young, poor but dreamy hopefuls continue to flock to the squash courts in Peshawar. Jansher's nephew Amjat won the Pakistani Open, thus maintaining the long tradition of this particular title being the personal property of the astonishing Khan family. There may well be a slight lull in the Khan domination of world squash after Jansher retires until the next batch of talent emerges. Maybe little Farhan, or the determined Imran, who both took such great delight in seeing off the 'British champion' that Sunday morning, could follow Jansher to the top. Or perhaps I had sat next to future world champions that day in Nawakille, when the children from the village, carrying their rifles and racquets, crowded round to look at this red-haired Westerner.

Jansher is determined that his own story remains unfinished. His self-belief remains unshakeable. 'When I am completely fit, I will be the best again,' he promises. 'And I will be completely fit.' Time, as always, will tell. But if it transpires that my match against him was the penultimate competitive challenge of his long and incredibly successful squash career, I will consider it a significant, if unlikely, personal honour, one that will rank alongside that strangely emotional afternoon at the Kapsabet stadium in western Kenya and, indeed, the following morning in the home of Kip Keino.

The Nyahururu-based runners have had a mixed year. Daniel Komen was married in November 1998, having taken both the Commonwealth Games and World Cup 5,000 metres gold medals. Most athletes might well settle for that, but not Komen. He was disappointed with his year, so Duncan Gaskell told me, and plans to do better.

Moses Kiptanui ruptured his Achilles tendon during the Goodwill Games in New York three months after I had bidden farewell to him. It was, by all accounts, an injury that could, and probably should, have ended his glittering career. The three-times former World steeplechase champion and Nyahururu camp leader had the bottom of his foot sewn up before it was placed in a plaster cast for eight weeks. The best prognosis given was that it would take a year for him to make a full recovery. Instead, within a matter of months, this proud and driven man was back training. Mindful of his injury, he is not pushing himself too hard and will probably miss the 1999 World Championships so that he can concentrate on the one race that has continually eluded him. Moses Kiptanui plans to be on the starting line of the 2000 Sydney Olympic Games 3,000 metres steeplechase final, and I, for one, would not bet against him.

Elsewhere at Nyahururu, Jimmy Beauttah continues to knead his baobab hands into unsuspecting Kenyans, and Joseph Chesire still sits up at night. Laban Rotich became both the Commonwealth and World Cup 1500 metres champion, while Godfrey Kiprotich, who drove me some of the way to Kapsabet before finding a taxi-driving friend, seems to be in demand these days as a pacemaker for the world's top marathons. William Tanui, whom I dined with on my last night in Nairobi, finished fourth in the 1500 metres at the World Indoor Championships, which was some feat considering that he is now in his late thirties.

Other Kenyans, some familiar names and others new faces fresh off the natural production line, won the various World Cross-Country Championships, the World Half-Marathon and other Commonwealth medals. In the Commonwealth 3,000 metres steeplechase final, Kenya enjoyed a clean sweep of the medals, with John Kosgei taking gold. The fact remains that at least three other Kenyans would have taken the next three places in that particular final, if only Kenya had been allowed to enter them.

Kip Keino remains a contented farmer, providing a refuge for some of his country's orphans, and a beacon of hope to all Kenyan athletes. The gourd he presented to me sits proudly on a shelf in my study. Every so often I take it down and hold it as if it is a delicate crown jewel. The gourd still contains old ashes, however, so whenever I tip it upside down the smattering of dirt on my clothes and the furious rubbing that follows normally shatters the moment.

Ibrahim Hussein continues his rising eminence in the world of Kenyan sports politics and staged another Kapsabet weekend meeting in April 1999. This time the 15,000-strong crowd had to make do with eight fine local athletes in the 3,000 metres steeplechase final, instead of seven Kenyans and one *mzungu* who, by omitting the barriers until the last lap, falling waist-high into the water jump and trailing two laps behind the other finalists, provided an unwitting cameo performance that is, so my Kenyan friends assure me, still referred to to this day.

At this point, with Flamengo's demise, Jansher's injury and the Kenyans' topsy-turvy fortunes, you may well be thinking that I proved to be an unlucky charm for the best sportsmen in the world. The thought crossed my mind, too, when I began to hear of some of the misfortunes that were befalling my new-found friends. I am therefore delighted and somewhat relieved to report that my other choices enjoyed considerable success to justify their selection in this eve-of-new-millennium record of sporting deity.

Six days after I left South Africa, the Springboks amassed an incredible 96 points against an admittedly reserve Welsh team at the Loftus Versfeld stadium in Pretoria. I sent them a congratulatory fax suggesting they should have declared at half-time. They went on to see off a depleted England team 18–0 in Cape Town, before making the rugby world really sit up and take notice by winning the Tri-Nations series without losing any of their four home and away games against

New Zealand and Australia. In doing so they became the unofficial world champions.

It was during the Tri-Nations that 'Bobby-mania' took off. Bobby Skinstad sat next to me on the subs bench during the second Test against Ireland. His talent was already obvious to all, but Nick Mallett, the astute coach, wanted to nurture his young star. Skinstad, naturally, just wanted to get on with it. I remember telling him one night, not without some envy, that everything stood before him. 'Maybe,' he said, a little gloomily. 'But I want to play today, not tomorrow.' Well, Skinstad was given his chance shortly afterwards and duly took it, producing an outrageous dummy to score the crucial try to beat Australia and secure the Tri-Nations trophy. South Africa went Skinstad crazy, especially the country's young females, and Bobby found himself the centre of attention.

When South Africa came to Britain in November 1998, Mallett and his men stood just four Tests away from breaking the world record for successive international victories. Almost all of the squad with whom I had trained the previous June had travelled, together with a few new faces. I was keen to meet up with them all again but realised that in sport life moves quickly on and I was probably history in their eyes. The 'Boks came through tough encounters against first Wales, then Scotland and finally Ireland, to draw level on 17 consecutive wins with the great All Black team of the late 1960s. Mark Andrews had by now completed his dream of winning 50 caps, and Skinstad had forced his way into the starting line-up at the expense of the friendly André Venter, giving Mallett what he described as 'one of the hardest selection decisions in my career'.

Three days before they were due to face England at Twickenham for the last match of their short but arduous tour, the boys called and invited me out for a private dinner with them in an African restaurant in west London. I was quietly pleased that they should still want to have my company, even more so when I discovered that I was the only non-member of the South Africa squad present that night. Gary Teichmann and his team colleagues were greatly amused by the photographs I showed them of my time in South Africa and subsequent weeks elsewhere. In particular, they took great delight in my account of my bout with Roy Jones junior. James Dalton, a keen fight fan, wanted a graphic description of every punch thrown, whilst Nick Mallett merely laughed and shook his head. 'You don't do things in half measures, do you?' he said. I think that was a compliment.

That Saturday the winning streak came to a grinding halt when England beat South Africa 13–7 in front of a passionate home crowd.

I was there to watch the spectacle and felt slightly traitorous for my delight at seeing an English side finally proving superior to a southern-hemisphere giant. I then consoled myself with the thought that the boys in green and gold would have expected me to have supported my own country. Their dignity in defeat was typical of a side that Mallett and his trusty cohorts had totally transformed in the space of a year. Come October 1999, when the World Cup would be staged in the British Isles and France, South Africa would undoubtedly be a major contender.

A few weeks later, into the New Year, Nick Mallett sent me a note which he said I could use if I ever wanted to persuade another sports team to allow me to play with them. This was a typical gesture from the man. He made a number of kind references and stated that, since South Africa had beaten Ireland in the second Test after a week's training with me, I clearly brought good luck to his team. He could be right there. After all, South Africa never lose a Test match if I've been training with them.

He ended his note by stating that, in his opinion, I was a very good table-tennis player. As I write this, the score between us remains 2–1 in my favour, but it would not surprise me in the slightest if, one day, Mallett appears at my door wishing to continue the series. After all, as he insisted in Johannesburg, the contest is only over when he takes the lead. Could be a long series then, Nick.

Meanwhile, back on the rivers of Europe, the Great British coxless fours reasserted themselves on the world stage. You may recall that in their last race before I joined the crew, they had, minus an injured Tim Foster, been beaten in Munich, an event so rare that the story made global headlines. A great deal was riding on their performance at the Henley Regatta, which makes their willingness to incorporate my dubious talents just days before even more surprising.

In the semi-finals of the prestigious Stewards Cup, on exactly the same stretch of water where Steve Redgrave and I had been beaten so soundly by Matthew Pinsent and Foster a few days before, the boys saw off the 'Oarsome Foursome' from Australia in emphatic style, a real statement of intent against the former double Olympic coxless fours champions. Pinsent celebrated the triumph five strokes from the finish post by making a series of gestures with his arm, an action later described as 'inappropriate' by the Regatta Chairman Mike Sweeney. Rowing correspondents in the British broadsheet newspapers also viewed Pinsent's reactions with disdain, one going as far as to say the race was 'spoiled by a crude series of one-arm gestures over the last five strokes'. Apart from making it sound as if Pinsent had just re-enacted a series of Nazi salutes, you would have thought the blazers at Henley would have understood and, indeed, shared his exuberance. Heaven knows how they would react if oarsmen start kissing and hugging each other like football players. In the final, the British fought off a challenge from the Danish world lightweight champions to win the Stewards Cup, Redgrave's 17th Henley title. Normal service had been resumed.

A fortnight later at Lucerne they did it again, this time beating the Romanians who had had the temerity to defeat the British in Munich. Australia were back in a distant third place. Redgrave duly became a world champion for a staggering eighth time in Cologne in September 1998 when the coxless fours he shares with Pinsent, James Cracknell and Foster dismissed the challenge from the French and Italian crews. Pinsent's sixth world title, itself a monumental achievement, was once more overshadowed by the old man of the crew, while Foster and Cracknell became world champions for a 'mere' second time.

Mission was therefore accomplished for the year, and another crucial step – for this is how they saw their success at Henley, Lucerne and Cologne – was taken towards their Olympic goal in Sydney. I saw Steve, Matt and James at a dinner that Christmas where they were, once again, the recipients of an award. They, too, found my experiences with Roy Jones entertaining. I could just imagine Jones hitting Redgrave in the ring. Steve would look the American straight in the eye during the 85th round, as blood poured down his face, and say: 'I'll never give up.'

Like so many other great athletes in the world today, the Great Britain coxless fours have one year to go before they have their chance to attain their personal goal. An Olympic gold medal would be a first for James Cracknell and for Tim Foster. Matthew Pinsent would have collected an amazing third Olympic title, and could then be considering achieving more with a new partner. As for the old man in the boat, the Sydney Olympics will, for sure, signify the end of a truly remarkable sporting career. In Atlanta he asked anyone to shoot him if he was ever seen near a boat again. In Sydney he may have a sniper in position after the final. To win an unprecedented fifth Olympic gold medal may have something to do with Redgrave's race with Father Time. My money's on the man who shoved me into the cold, dark Thames that Sunday morning.

And so to Australia, or rather Kuala Lumpur, where the Australian one-day squad reached the final of the Commonwealth Games' inaugural cricket competition before losing to South Africa. This, to captain Steve 'Tugga' Waugh, was a major disappointment, although he and the rest of the boys had thoroughly enjoyed the experience of the Commonwealth family. 'It was one of the best weeks of my life,' he reported cheerily. In the semi-final, incidentally, they had dismissed New Zealand for 58, a total Australia reached in just 65 balls. Unlike the previous Australia versus New Zealand one-day international, played up on Queensland's Sunshine Coast a week earlier, the services of a hung-over English 12th man were not required.

It is for their undoubted position as the world's greatest Test team that I chose Australia for this book, and over the course of the following few months they reaffirmed their status. In Pakistan, in what would prove to be Mark 'Tubby' Taylor's farewell tour, Australia won their first ever series amid a host of notable performances. Tugga and Michael 'Slats' Slater both scored centuries with consummate ease, although the batting, as well as the sportsman's, honours go to Tubby, who declared the Australian innings during the second Test while he was undefeated on 334, a remarkable gesture. He required only a further 42 runs to beat the world's highest Test innings of 375, held by the West Indies captain Brian Lara, but felt the extra time taken would have hampered his country's chances of winning the Test. In the event the match was drawn, but Taylor, after equalling the great Don Bradman's highest mark, harboured no regrets. 'It's the only way I can ever be compared to the Don,' he said, in typically modest fashion. He would later be named Australian of the Year, be featured in an hour-long special of *This Is Your Life* and even be the subject of an article in the *New York Times*.

Ian 'Heals' Healy, meanwhile, caught Wasim Akram during the second innings of the first Test to record his 356th victim, a new world record for wicketkeeping Test dismissals and more proof, if it was needed, that those hours throwing a golf ball against a brick wall pay off. And with Shane Warne still on the mend from his shoulder injury, a new leg-spinning star was born. The name Stuart MacGill meant little to most cricket fans around the world even as he helped to spin Australia to victory in Pakistan with a veritable haul of wickets. Oh, but it meant something to me all right. The English batsmen would discover, too, how lethal he can be with a ball in his hand, yet he is far more dangerous when he has an angelic look on his face and his arm around your shoulder, offering you a drink he has just prepared himself.

The Ashes series followed the well-rehearsed script of many before. England were saved from certain defeat by a flash storm in Brisbane but were beaten convincingly in both Perth and Adelaide, where Tugga and Slats again proved their worth as world-class batsmen and

Glenn 'Pigeon' McGrath, Damien 'Ace' Fleming and Magilla bowled the Poms out. It had been a bit of a running joke between myself and Ace in Australia about how bad his batting was. When he lent me his helmet to face the Australian pace attack playing for New South Wales, he informed me that I couldn't do any worse in it than him. Ace went on to knock a score of 70-odd against England. Australia lost the fourth Test in Melbourne but came back well to win the fifth Test and wrap up the Ashes 3–1.

Off the field, though, problems began to mount. First Mark 'Junior' Waugh and Shane 'Warney' Warne were embroiled in an unsavoury scandal after it emerged that both had taken cash from an illegal bookmaker in Sri Lanka five years before for providing seemingly unimportant information about weather and pitch conditions. Knowing Junior a little from my experience in Queensland, I would think his actions back in 1993 were nothing more than naïve. Anyone who regularly loses money – and once my money – on trotting is hardly likely to be at the centre of mass match-fixing or bribery.

Ricky 'Punter' Ponting, too, was in the wars after admitting he had a drink problem and would undergo counselling. The Tasmanian was knocked unconscious at a Sydney nightclub hours after playing in an Australia v. England limited-overs match and was promptly dropped by the Australian Cricket Board. I felt sorry for Punter. I liked the man who was kind enough to remind me that he, too, had scored a duck that day against New South Wales, and if I had known about this problem I might have thought twice about pouring numerous bourbons down my throat during the Surf Bar drinking contest. Happily, he has since bounced back and reclaimed his place in the Test side.

Tugga took over the responsibility of the captaincy for the tour to the West Indies and again excelled with the bat. For once, though, his exploits were overshadowed by Brian Lara, who came back from the dead to win two Tests for the Windies almost single-handedly. After Australia lost the memorable third Test to fall 2–1 down in the series, Tugga remarked that it had been the best Test match of his career. Always quick to congratulate and commiserate, he exemplified the spirit of the Australian side. They bounced back to draw the series 2–2 and remain the best Test team in the world.

Then it was back to the one-day game and the World Cup, played primarily in England. This competition represented the end of an arduous ten months on the road and, as it turned out, would provide the team with their greatest achievement. After a slow start, the mental strength of the Australians became the dominant force of the whole tournament. Set a challenge of winning all seven remaining matches in order to become world champions, Australia collectively delivered, although Steve Waugh's captaincy and dogged batting, particularly in the two games against South Africa, and a rejuvenated Shane Warne, who reminded a questioning world that his spin can still win big matches, emerged as the key designers of this success. No target set fazed the Aussies, and when they were required to defend a total, they did so with utter conviction, a point best underlined by the outrageous manner in which they won the semi-final against a South African team requiring one run off the final four balls to win. Even I, an unashamed admirer of the Australian team, had given up on them, but somehow they kept their poise enough to orchestrate a run-out and a victory by the narrowest of margins. After that, nothing was going to stop them winning the World Cup, least of all Pakistan, whose opposition in the final at Lord's was negligible. Tugga and the boys returned to the streets of Melbourne and Sydney to enjoy ticker-tape receptions, national deification and the sweet, sweet fruits of all their labours.

Steve 'Brute' Bernard, meanwhile, did a Nick Mallett and also sent me a letter which, he said, should be used to further my Indian summer of sport. In this equally kind reference, Brute referred to me as 'journalist, writer and possible lunatic'. This last point was meant to refer to my time, on and off the cricket field, in Australia. Yet it became even more appropriate six weeks later when I stepped into the ring to face Roy Jones junior.

Today I look back on all my sporting adventures with a certain degree of disbelief. The sun is shining over my leafy garden, life has returned to normality and it seems difficult to take in everything that happened during the course of one year. The sands of Copacabana and the courts of Peshawar, the dirt tracks of western Kenya and the intensity of the Springbok team bus, the pace attack of the Australians bearing down on a nervous Englishman and the dark and frightening Pensacola night – they all seem as if they belong in my dreams. Even Henley, much closer to home, appears unreal when I remind myself that I partnered Steve Redgrave in a race on the Regatta course.

I've tried to keep my fitness going. It's nothing special, you understand, but a couple of runs, maybe a swim, a stint or two on the exercise bike in front of the television and, just occasionally, a session on the dreaded ergometer that still sits amid the dust of the garage all help to keep me in reasonable shape. It would be a shame to lose all that fitness I had gained. The sportsmen who made my fantasies become reality for a week would expect nothing less.

The funny thing, though, about all this is that the whole notion of playing sport around the world with the best was supposed to end my nights of sporting fantasy in bed. It has not. I still while away my unconscious hours scoring goals, tries, runs and points. The only difference is that whilst before I would be winning the World Cup, the Olympics or the Ashes, now I am simply performing better in all the unlikely situations that I found myself in during the past year.

In Brazil, for example, I not only pass the ball to Romario in a training match but also run on to collect his return and hammer the ball high into the roof of the net to win the game for the Flamengo first team. Against Jansher Khan I hit peak form and soon have him running around the court trying and failing to return my deft drop shots and perfect lobs. The large crowd in Kapsabet sees the Englishman clear all the barriers before sprinting past the race leader in the home straight of the 3,000 metres steeplechase to win, while in South Africa I actually manage to get a game against Ireland, coming off the bench at Loftus Versfeld to receive a pass inside from Joost van der Westhuizen and dive over in the corner. Steve Redgrave and I prove too strong for Matthew Pinsent and Tim Foster in Henley, powering away in the last quarter of a mile to win by five metres, and Andy Bichel's bouncer, instead of hitting me on the shoulder, is despatched with a flick of my wrists over the long-leg boundary for six as I carve out an imperious half-century.

It is only when I turn to boxing that my powers of imagery fail me. As hard as I try, I just cannot conjure up a painless victory in the ring. Instead I see what actually happened. In my dreams, Roy Jones junior is pounding my face and my head is lurching from one side to the other. One day, either he is going to kill me or I am going to knock him out with a counter-punch of explosive force created by the desperate situation I find myself in.

To date, neither has happened. Instead, I tend to wake up and discover that the birds are singing and daylight is streaming through my bedroom curtains. My wife lies next to me and my children are arguing outside the door. For someone who has wanted to transform himself into the surreal world of his sporting dreams for so many years, this everyday scene always comes as an enormously welcome relief.

LIST OF INJURIES

Football: Continuation of ligament injury in left foot; osteo-condritis; sunburn; mosquito bites

Squash: Right calf-muscle tear; sprained right thumb

Athletics: Continuation of calf-muscle tear

Rugby: Sprained left pectoral muscle; sprained ligaments in left ring finger; new muscle tear in right calf; cut and bruised knees; sore, flaky ears

Rowing: Three rows of calluses on fingers and palms of both hands; large, sore blisters on both buttocks; sore, stiff shoulders and upper back

Cricket: Bruised shoulder and left wrist, where hit by Andy Bichel's fast bowling; sore head, following drinking on the Gold Coast!

Boxing: Return of sprained left pectoral muscle; cut nose, mouth and lips; concussion – dizziness, nausea, headaches; sprained left thumb; suspected trapped nerve in neck causing subsequent faintness